Lights!
Camera!
Kai Shi!

In depth Interviews with China's New Generation of Movie Directors

Lights!
Camera!
Kai Shi!

In depth Interviews with China's New Generation of Movie Directors

Shaoyi Sun & Li Xun

EastBridge
Norwalk

Signature Books

Copyright © 2008 by EastBridge

All rights reserved.
No part of this book may be reproduced in any form
without written permission from the publisher
EastBridge 64 Wall Street Norwalk CT 06850 USA

Chartered in the State of Connecticut, EastBridge is a nonprofit publishing
corporation under section 501(c)(3) of the United States tax code.

Cover and book design by Westernesse

The characters 开始 —*Kai Shi*—translate as "Action"
to complete the familiar three word movie director's
phrase used to start shooting a scene.

Library of Congress Cataloging-in-Publication Data

[pending]

Printed in the United States of America

Contents

Acknowledgements — VI

INTRODUCTION
Prelude: The Changing Context — VII
The Politics of Naming: The "Sixth Generation" and Beyond — IX
Censorship: The Last Obstacle to a Healthy Film Industry? — XIII
About This Book — XV

THE DIRECTORS — XVIII

CHAPTER ONE
BFA, CATA, and Beyond: The Road to Filmmaking — 3

CHAPTER TWO
Chinese Cinema after *Yellow Earth*:
Toward a Working Definition of the "Sixth Generation" — 41

CHAPTER THREE
"Dancing with the Shackles":
The (Un)Censored Voices of the "Sixth Generation" — 65

CHAPTER FOUR
Waves from the Margin: Cinema as a "Narcissistic" Mirror — 93

CHAPTER FIVE
On the Other Side of the Camera:
Male Directors and Representation of Woman — 113

CHAPTER SIX
Under the Shadow of Commercialization:
The Box Office and Individual Expression — 134

CHAPTER SEVEN
Films that Matter:
Dialogue between the "Sixth Generation" and World Cinema — 159

CHAPTER EIGHT
Chinese Cinema in the Context of Globalization:
Dilemmas and Opportunities — 176

CHAPTER NINE
Filmmaking in the New Millennium:
Post-Cinema, Postmodernism, and the Crisis of Originality — 206

THE INTERVIEWERS — 225

Index — 229
Endnotes — 237

Acknowledgements

This project was conceived at the turn of the century, when a group of then young Chinese filmmakers began to emerge from the shadow of the renowned "Fifth Generation" filmmakers of China and started to make a mark of their own in the international film community. With a few exceptions, most of the interviews took place in the summer of 2002 in Beijing, when the reform of the Chinese film industry was about to turn a new page. In the following years since then, we've maintained regular contacts with the interviewed filmmakers so as to make sure the information and ideas remain updated when the book comes out.

We are deeply grateful to a number of people who have made this book possible. Shi Chuan, nicknamed River Stone, of Shanghai University provided professional assistance to our interview with director Lou Ye. Sun Jie, Shaoyi Sun's niece, helped transcribe some of the recorded interviews. Fu Yanxin, our longtime friend back to college days, vacated his cozy apartment in Beijing for Shaoyi Sun's extended stay in the summer of 2002. We also benefited from the two symposiums convened in Beijing and Shanghai in 2002: the "Symposium on Young Chinese Filmmakers", organized by the China Film Art Research Center and the China Film Archive, and the "Symposium on the New Generation of Chinese Filmmakers", sponsored by the School of Film-TV, Shanghai University.

We are particularly grateful to our publisher, EastBridge, whose editorial staff have provided understanding, professional insights, and editorial aid which have proven invaluable to us. We are, of course, solely responsible for any errors in the book.

SYS & LX

INTRODUCTION

PRELUDE: THE CHANGING CONTEXT

In March 2002, Xu Jinglei, a 1997 graduate of the Acting Department of the Beijing Film Academy and best known in film circles for her consecutive roles as the city girl trapped in love triangles in *Dazzling* (d. Li Xin, 2001), *Spring Subway* (d. Zhang Yibai, 2001), and *I Love You* (d. Zhang Yuan, 2003), went to the National Film Bureau to register her directorial debut, *Me and My Dad*. To her great surprise, Xu learned that she no longer needed to secure a license from one of the forty-two state-owned studios to get her film made or released. Instead, as the legal representative of her own business, Beijing Yinian Cultural Development Company, she could apply to obtain a "Single Feature Permit", which would grant her the right to make and release the film on her own. According to the newly revised "Regulatory Rules of Film", which was issued by the State Administration of Radio, Film, and Television (SARFT), China's top overseeing body of all media industries, any private or state-owned enterprise, as long as it meets certain requirements, is allowed to make and release films on its own. In other words, anyone, at least in theory, can "legally" make films in today's China. "*Me and My Dad* is the first [approved] independent film in China", recalls Xu in her interview with the authors, "I had no idea at all about independent filmmaking in China. When I went to see the Film Bureau with the screenplay, I was told that according to the regulation just issued on the first day of February my company itself is qualified to make films.... To a large extent, I feel I should thank the Film Bureau...I didn't know the regulation until they advised me."[i]

The "Single Feature Permit" policy is not the only film-related reform that was implemented in the past several years. When China officially became a member of the World Trade Organization on the first day of 2002, the pressure to reform the moribund state-owned studio system and to fundamentally change the old model of film distribution and exhibition dramatically increased. Alerted by the sharp decline of theater attendance and the annual output of film in the late 1990s and sensing the imminent "threat" from Hollywood, Chinese film authorities and industry insiders came to realize that marketization or "liberalization" might be the only antidote to the grave situation Chinese cinema found itself in.[ii] To build a market-driven film industry and depoliticize the role of film in society has been the guiding principle behind the execution of a series of reform policies introduced since 2002, among which the "Single Feature Permit" plays only a minor role.

Introduction

From a broader point of view, prior to China's entry into the WTO, faced with the challenge posed by the global trend of media consolidation that has concentrated power in a handful of transnational corporations, the Chinese media industry reconsolidated its otherwise disparate media entities and formed six large film or media corporations (that resemble, for example, GE-owned NBC Universal or Rupert Murdoch's News Corporation), among which the China Film Group, the Xi'an Film Studio Corporation, and the Shanghai Media and Entertainment Group are the most prominent. The main objective of this consolidation, of course, is to prepare China to compete with multinational corporations once its film and media market opens up to the outside world (since 2006 China has allowed forty-fifty foreign films to be put into theatrical release yearly).

The major change in film exhibition was the formation of thirty-eight cinema circuits nationwide, which consist of 1,140 film theaters and 2,285 screens, most of them equipped with computerized box offices. The immediate advantages the cinema circuits have brought about are many. First, since some of the cinema circuits are transprovincial (at least eleven of the thirty-eight are in more than one province), they help break down the regional barriers that have plagued the Chinese film industry for more than half a century. Second, this newly formed system could reduce the middle layers between production, distribution, and exhibition. The production company can now directly sell its films to the market (thirty-eight cinema circuits) or let professional distributors handle the marketing campaign. Third, this system also stimulates fierce competition among the cinema circuits, particularly in cases when more than one cinema circuit exists in a single city or province. In its competition with the Grand Cinema Circuit in Shanghai, for example, the Shanghai United Cinema Circuit, which consists of more than fifty-six theaters, including both top-rated ones like Paradise Warner Cinema City and Kodak Cinema World and some third-class theaters in Shanghai and Jiangsu Province, became the largest cinema circuit in China. Its 2005 gross box office surpassed 246 million RMB, which accounted for approximately one-ninth of the nation's total box office returns in 2005. [iii]

In the area of film production and distribution, in addition to the introduction of the "Single Feature Permit" policy, the second half of 2004 saw the further lowering of the market access level, allowing companies, private or otherwise, with minimum registered assets of one million RMB to engage in film production and distribution. SARFT has also issued several rules that specifically encourage so-called "full co-productions". In recent years, China has signed co-production agreements with Canada and Italy, and similar treaties are expected to be signed with Australia, India, Bulgaria, the UK, and France. Allegedly "mutually beneficial", such treaties will allow co-produced films to be freely distributed in China without being affected by the quota system, thus giving foreign partners competitive advantages in the potentially lucrative Chinese market. On the China side, such "full co-productions" will certainly benefit the industry through co-financing and co-marketing, thus giving Chinese partners the opportunity to gain access to non-Chinese film markets. Under a similar framework, an agreement between mainland China and Hong Kong, the Closer Cultural Partnership Arrangement (CCPA), was reached, giving Hong Kong-based companies equal status to those of the mainland.

A sign of the changing times, even the notorious practice of censoring each script and final cut has been somewhat loosened. Up until the end of 2003, prior to production, every script had to be submitted for full approval from the Film Bureau in Beijing. Now, only a 1,000-word synopsis is required for this, although the final cut is still subject to censorship. In early 2004, Chinese censors lifted the ban on Wang Xiaoshuai's critically acclaimed feature *Beijing Bicycle*, making Wang one of the first young filmmakers to emerge from the "underground". "The film censors came to me and said we are ready to forget about your past. We want to reform Chinese cinema because, otherwise, we realize it would die", recalls Wang about a conversation he had with the film authorities, "From now on film will not just be propaganda, but film can also be a product. You can sell it and market it." Critics and scholars have noted that this "change of heart"—film recognized not merely as a propaganda tool of the Party but as a product that is ultimately driven by market forces—is of monumental importance to the restructuring of the Chinese film industry.

Another remarkable trend that is gaining momentum and deserving of our full attention is pan-Asian production and distribution, which has been facilitated by the loosening of governmental regulatory and censorship standards. Besides cooperation within the Greater China region, which is enhanced by cultural, historical, and linguistic bonds, cross-national flows of talent and financial resources within Asia have also transformed the landscape of Chinese filmmaking. From Zhang Yimou's *Riding Alone for Thousands of Miles*, which features the veteran Japanese actor Ken Takakura, to Stanley Tong's *The Myth*, which features a pan-Asian cast, including the Korean female star Kim Hee Sun, one senses the coming-of-age of the "Asian Wave", which can potentially rival the dominance of Hollywood on a global scale.

THE POLITICS OF NAMING: THE "SIXTH GENERATION" AND BEYOND

The practice of identifying Chinese filmmakers by generations has, to say the least, been controversial ever since the "Fifth Generation" label was attached

Introduction

to the "Class of 1978" of the Beijing Film Academy. If for any reason the group identity and the specific condition of Chinese society in the early 1980s made the practice of labeling the 1982 BFA graduates the "Fifth Generation" somewhat legitimate, to continue this practice by calling the "Class of 1985" of BFA the "Sixth Generation", as this book shows, speaks little to the changing nature of Chinese society and the Chinese film industry. When the label was circulated worldwide in the early and mid-1990s when the "Class of 1985" made their first films, however, it gained popularity for several reasons.

First, the label "Sixth Generation" is genealogically linked to the Beijing Film Academy. The year 1985 saw the first recruitment of students into all BFA majors (including directing, which had been frozen since 1978) since 1978, thus giving this group of film students (or the Class of 1985—*bawuji*—in Chinese) a rare sense of identity previously found only among the Fifth Generation filmmakers. The fact that they all graduated in 1989, a month after the June Fourth student movement, also added some historical significance to this particular group of film students. Prior to their graduation, the core members of the "Class of 1985", including Wang Xiaoshuai, Lu Xuechang and Lou Ye, convened in Beijing to discuss their future as filmmakers, and the transcript of the conversation was later edited and published as a manifesto-like article titled "The Post-*Yellow Earth* Phenomenon in Chinese Cinema: A Conversation on Chinese Cinema".[iv] Signed by students in all departments of the "Class of 1985", this article has been widely viewed as the most salient declaration of the coming of a new generation, or a "new wave", after Zhang Yimou and Chen Kaige.

Second, if differentiating themselves from the established "Fifth Generation" filmmakers reflects the anxiety of the "Class of 1985" and their eagerness to cast aside the overarching shadow of their alumni, then the international embrace of the "Sixth Generation" label is closely related to the universal belief that China was a "repressive" nation. Rather than being exclusively celebrated as film *auteurs*, therefore, the new film-school graduates have been embraced by Western critics, festival programmers, and art-house distributors as "outlaw" or "dissident" filmmakers, thus "meet[ing] the need of international circles in the desire for a new 'other' to succeed the Fifth Generation and a new vocabulary to define Chinese cinema".[v] This politicized reading of the "Sixth Generation" is by no means groundless, since the early works of the "Class of 1985" directors have been either banned or severely censored by the Chinese government. The fact that these works are continuously marketed in the West as a voice of dissent, however, indicates that the "Sixth Generation" label is not entirely based on the cinematic achievements of the young filmmakers.

Critical convenience also plays a role in the circulation of the label. It goes without saying that attaching a single label to a variety of filmmakers with diverse styles and backgrounds is a common practice in cinema studies. It simply fulfills our desire for an orderly world in which everything can be neatly stored in certain labeled categories. Critics and the press in the West, for example, saw the decline of the Hollywood studio system and the introduction of the film rating system as officially tolling the death knell of the Production Code and enthusiastically embraced what they dubbed the "New Hollywood", a label that refers to a new generation of film-school-educated directors working at the margin of the Hollywood studio system. Likewise, the "demise" of the "New Hollywood" in the 1980s also prompted critics and the press to label directors such as Quentin Tarantino and P.T. Anderson the "video-tape generation", meaning that they were the first generation of filmmakers to apply video tape technology to filmmaking. There is no doubt that this approach simplifies the complicated process of making pictures in Hollywood operative from the 1960s through the 1990s and thus tends to neglect the distinct style of individual filmmakers, but it also speaks to a certain truth about the otherwise difficult-to-categorize directors. In the case of the "Sixth Generation" label, this desire for critical convenience and neat categorization should also be taken into account. Since there is a "Fifth Generation", why can't we continue calling the newcomers the "Sixth Generation" or even the "Seventh Generation"?

Despite the above, generational categorization has proved to be increasingly shaky with the rapidly changing conditions of Chinese society in general and of the film environment in particular. The China of the turn of the century is quite different from the China of the early and mid-1980s. When the Fifth Generation filmmakers began to attract worldwide attention, they were probably the only young men or women who were allowed to make films, albeit tightly monitored by the state. It was relatively easy, therefore, to associate the label solely with the graduates of BFA. When the BFA graduates of the late 1980s and early 1990s started their film career, however, filmmaking was no longer a practice for a small group of privileged people. Some culturally and artistically important films, both "legal" and "underground", were made not by BFA graduates but by filmmakers with diverse background. Meng Qi (b. 1972), director of *What a Snowy Day,* for example, never received a higher education, let alone formal training in filmmaking. While many bright young people of the same age went to college, he joined the military police and served as a prison guard. It was only after several other odd jobs, including managing of a restaurant, that Meng started something (mostly in advertising) that would eventually lead him to directing. "I was born in 1966 and graduated from college in 1989", says

Introduction

Wang Guangli, a graduate of Shanghai's East Normal University and director of *Maiden Work, Go for Broke,* and *Karmic Mahjong,* "the same year as Zhang Yuan and Wang Xiaoshuai. Logically speaking, therefore, I am a classical member of the so-called Sixth Generation…but…first of all I am not a graduate of BFA…. Emotionally I have no objection to my being included in the group…but from a rational point of view, I don't think I belong to the so-called Sixth Generation….We have a different background."[vi] Wang Guangli's mixed feeling toward the "Sixth Generation" label reveals that easy labeling makes less and less sense in the filmmaking scene of today's China. Because of this, critics and scholars of Chinese cinema must look beyond BFA and find a more inclusive term in their criticism.

Perhaps the most important factor that has made the label "Sixth Generation" and the practice of identifying directors by generations less relevant lies in the changing situation of the core members of the "Sixth Generation" themselves. The rapid commercialization of the Chinese film industry and the gradual loosening of governmental regulatory and censorship standards have made the previously defiant young filmmakers less willing to bypass the censorship apparatus and depend entirely on foreign critical recognition if it means their films cannot be shown in domestic theaters. Zhang Yuan, a symbol of the "underground" Chinese cinema, was among the first to emerge. "Before *Seventeen Years,* basically any of my films could not be shown in China", says Zhang in the interview. "As far as Chinese audiences were concerned, I was an unknown director. They couldn't see my pictures."[vii] This frustration probably explains why Zhang has been making officially sanctioned films since 1999. Joining Zhang Yuan's camp, Wang Xiaoshuai, Jia Zhangke, and Lou Ye, the three BFA graduates of 1989 known for their unflinching stance toward censorship, have also been negotiating a space of their own within the censorship apparatus. While this "change of heart" does not necessarily mean they have made any significant concessions, it is certainly an indication that the core members of the "Sixth Generation" are moving to the center stage of Chinese cinema. The celebrated "aura" that has shined since the emergence of this "outlaw" or "underground" group of filmmakers is fading fast.

Given the fact that it appears quite problematic to keep using the "Sixth Generation" label to discuss these filmmakers, why does this book still adhere to the old practice? For one thing, allowing for some simplification, there does seem to be some common threads that string their works together.[viii] For another, if the practice of labeling or naming is sometimes unavoidable in creative endeavors, then the "Sixth Generation"—in light of the wide circulation of its films and compared to such other terms as the "Post-Fifth Generation" (*hou wudai*), the "New Generation" (*xinshengdai*), the

"Post-Cultural Revolution Generation" (*hou wenge yidai*), and the "Generation Born in the 1960s and 1970s"—is probably the only label that makes some sense in addressing the group identity and the complexity of these filmmakers, as long as it is used in a more inclusive and flexible way and with less emphasis on its "dissident" connotation. It must be also noted that "Sixth Generation" always appears in quotation marks in this book, indicating the interviewers' awareness of the problematic nature of the term and willingness to move beyond the practice of generational categorization in addressing the ever-evolving situation of Chinese cinema.

CENSORSHIP:
THE LAST OBSTACLE TO A HEALTHY FILM INDUSTRY?

Although it is still too early to predict the demise of the state-owned studios, the rising importance of private capital in Chinese cinema has already transformed the Chinese film industry from a socialist planned model to a semi-, if not completely, market driven business. If one views the Chinese film industry as an integral part of the Chinese economy and places it in the context of the dramatic growth of private business in other economic sectors of China, then it might not be so far-fetched to think of the possibility that in the foreseeable future the size and capital power of a few private entertainment companies may well take over the dominant position currently occupied by the state-owned film-production studios. Despite the fact that it remains unclear whether film distribution and exhibition will follow the trend of extensive privatization, suffice it to say that the old Chinese-style "studio system" established since the 1950s is on the verge of collapse.

But the dismantling of the state-controlled film industry does not necessarily mean the Chinese government would significantly loosen its grip on filmmaking. Despite the weakening role film plays in the everyday life of the Chinese people, it continues to be regarded by the government as an effective and powerful form of "education" (or propaganda). This seems to be in conflict with the recent acknowledgment by the Film Bureau that "film can also be a product". In reality, however, this conflicting view of film is a perfect reflection of the pendulum of Chinese politics. The pendulum can swing either to the right or to the left depending on the changing climate of domestic politics. This unpredictability is the very reason why we have to remain cautious despite the recent loosening of governmental censorship standards. As the door of film production, distribution, and even exhibition opens ever wider to private capital, institutionalized film censorship will probably become the only and last mechanism that enables the government to exercise its muscle over the increasingly freewheeling film industry.

Introduction

If film censorship continues, the clash between film production and film regulation will inevitably intensify, which in turn will further discourage private companies, already wary of the high risk involved in the film business, from investing in filmmaking. This is also the reason why film censorship is viewed by almost all the filmmakers interviewed for this book as the most serious obstacle to Chinese cinema becoming an important player on the world stage. "I sent all my films to the censorship committee [but none of them passed]. The experience of *Platform* was the saddest", recalls Jia Zhangke. "[…after the screenplay was submitted,] I waited, waited, and waited. [Without an answer,] I went to the Film Bureau several times. What disheartened me most was that I was completely in the dark about whom I was facing. Although there was a person responsible for my case, the word 'leader' [*lingdao*] constantly popped up. I didn't know who this 'leader' was, and I had no right to know.… Then, I was told that I could start shooting the following week, but one day I was suddenly summoned to the Beijing Film Studio, where I was informed I couldn't make the film, because one 'leader' said it was 'inappropriate'. …I felt extremely powerless."[ix] Tang Danian, director of *City Paradise* and scriptwriter of *Beijing Bastards* and *Beijing Bicycle*, is probably representative of the interviewed filmmakers when he speaks about his frustration with the censorship apparatus: "I feel the censorship system has almost strangled Chinese cinema.… As a whole, it has lost its vitality. It cannot match Korean cinema. If you go to Korea, you will immediately feel the audiences' passion for film as well as the thriving of the whole film industry there. Although film censorship in China will be slowly loosened in the end, it is still disastrous for individuals, because an individual's life is measured year-by-year. If the censorship system remains intact for another ten years, perhaps the most creative time in one's life will have already idled away."[x]

If the censorship system is really the "last man standing", then to bring it down requires not the act of trying to negotiate it, but the act of confronting it. Most of the directors interviewed in this book are willing to explore creative ways to push open the locked door of film censorship, or at least to constantly test the limit of tolerance of the censorship system. In this sense, despite the fact that many attempts to break the "iron house" are destined to fail, one remains hopeful that one day the whole censorship apparatus will be history. As Lou Ye, director of *Suzhou River*, eloquently puts it, "Ten years from today, if you look back, you will feel it's quite ridiculous that these films [*Suzhou River* and others] did not pass the censors. If the situation changes fast enough, sometime in the future film censorship will eventually be abolished. Or, it will become more scientific and democratic. If this is really the case, then I think these directors…are real heroes, because it is they who begin to really confront the censorship system. They will make the would-be directors, who might just begin their film career ten years from today, forget the word 'censorship'. This is the most valuable thing this group of directors has accomplished."[xi]

In fact, as indicated above, there have been encouraging signs of change with regard to the practice of censorship in recent years. In addition to the further loosening of standards, reports are also being circulated that SARFT is deliberating the possibility of adopting a MPAA-like film rating system. Although it's discouraging to hear that the implementation of this possible rating system won't automatically relegate film censorship to history, it is at least an encouraging sign that the Chinese film industry is moving forward. The most promising aspect of Chinese cinema lies in the fact that the two wings of a healthy cinema, the commercial and the independent/artistic, are gradually taking shape. On the one hand, smash box-office hits such as *Hero*, *House of Flying Daggers*, *A World without Thieves*, and *The Promise* are leading the way to the recovery of the domestic film market and to the worldwide success of Chinese cinema. On the other hand, small-budget productions, such as Wang Xiaoshuai's personal memento, *Shanghai Dreams*, and Jia Zhangke's *The World*, both of which could not get an official endorsement just a few years ago, are continuing to feed an eager niche market both inside and outside of China. To label such a development the "renaissance of Chinese cinema" would be an exaggeration, but it at least makes one exuberantly hopeful and optimistic for Chinese cinema.

ABOUT THIS BOOK

This book grew out of a series of interviews the authors conducted in 2002 and 2003. In the case of the directors who have made new films since 2003, additional questions, either via e-mail or through telephone conversations, were directed to them to inquire whether they had anything new to add to their interviews. The selection of the interviewees proved to be a difficult task, since there were many qualified candidates to choose from. We wrestled with a number of choices and decided to adopt the following criteria in the selection process: first, to reflect the state of Chinese cinema after the Fifth Generation as completely as possible, and to reinforce our belief that the "Sixth Generation" is by and large an open-ended term, we wanted to look beyond BFA to include filmmakers of diverse backgrounds born in the 1960s and '70s. Certainly, graduates of BFA's "Class of 1985", the core members of the "Sixth Generation", were our primary interest; second, to convey the message that these filmmakers are creating something "new" in Chinese cinema at the turn of the century, we intentionally picked twenty-one directors to interview; third, we knew we wanted to include some young and active female filmmakers on our list. Needless to say, we are not quite satisfied with the limited representation of women filmmakers in this book.

Introduction

Unlike most interviews, which are built around individual interviewees, the interviews in this book are structured around nine broad themes. Each theme includes two or three questions we originally posed to the featured directors. While this structure may interrupt the smooth flow of the narrative, which would give the reader a clear understanding of a particular director, it foregrounds the most pressing issues facing filmmakers and Chinese cinema today, at least in the opinion of the interviewers. We hope this issue-driven structure will not only help give the reader a better understanding of what's behind the works of these so-called "Sixth Generation" filmmakers, but help to enrich their knowledge and understanding of cinema in general as well.

* * *

All Chinese names in this book appear last name first, first name second. Chinese titles of books, articles, and journals are translated for the convenience of the English-speaking reader.

SYS & LX

The Directors

Guan Hu
Jia Zhangke
Jiang Wen
Jin Chen
Li Xin
Liu Binjian
Lou Ye
Lu Chuan
Lu Xuechang
Ma Liwen
Meng Qi
Shi Runjiu
Tang Danian
Wang Chao
Wang Guangli
Wang Quanan
Wang Xiaoshuai
Xu Jinglei
Zhang Ming
Zhang Yang
Zhang Yuan

GUAN HU
(1968-)

Guan

Born in 1968 in Beijing, Guan Hu spent one year at home after high school. In 1987, Guan was admitted to the film directing department of the Beijing Film Academy, and graduated from BFA in 1991 with a Bachelor of Arts degree. Guan began to work for the state-owned Beijing Film Studio immediately after BFA studies, and served as an assistant director for various film and TV projects. In 1994, Guan made his feature debut, *Dirt*, a film about disaffected youth in Beijing. Financed "independently" (non-studio money) and reluctantly approved by the censors, *Dirt* is considered to be one of the several important films that announced the emergence of a new generation of filmmakers in China.

Mature and attractively enigmatic, Guan Hu's *Eyes of a Beauty* delivers a subtly devastating critique of sex roles in contemporary China. The film won the NETPAC award (Network for the Promotion of Asian Cinema) at the 2002 Hawaii International Film Festival for its cross-cultural value and ambitious experimenting in cinematic language.

A filmmaker and scriptwriter active in China, Guan Hu is also an acclaimed TV drama director. His TV titles include *Black Hole* (Hei dong, 30 episodes, 2001) and *The Winter Solstice* (Dong zhi, 36 episodes, 2004).

Woman's Predicament in Guan Hu's
Eyes of a Beauty (2002)

GUAN HU FILMOGRAPHY:

Dirt (Tou fa luan le), 1994

Cello in a Cab (Lang man jie tou), 1997

Farewell 1948 (Wo de 1948), 1999

Eyes of a Beauty (Xi shi yan), 2002

JIA ZHANGKE
(1970-)

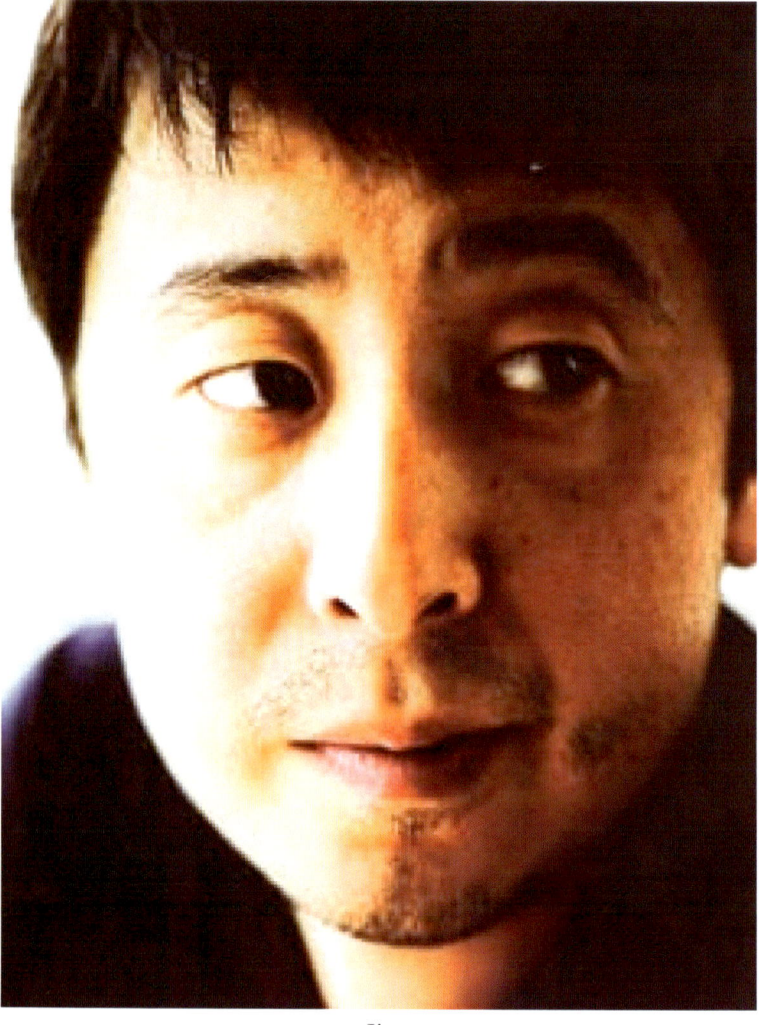

Jia

One of the most visible faces of his generation on the world stage, Jia Zhangke was born in 1970 in the small, remote town of Fengyang in Shanxi, a northern province of China known for its coal mines and historical link to the rise of the Chinese Communist Party. At the age of eighteen, Jia was a painting student at a fine arts school in Taiyuan, the capital of Shanxi. At the same time, he also developed an interest in fiction, writing his first published story "The Sun Hung on the Crotch" in 1991. In 1993, Jia was admitted to the Literature Department of the Beijing Film Academy to start his study in film theory. Two years later, while still a sophomore, he founded the "Youth Experimental Film Group of BFA", arguably the first independent film production organization in China.

He directed two feature videos with the group, and one of them, *Xiao Shan Going Home*, won the Gold Prize at the Hong Kong Independent Short Film & Video Awards. Immediately upon his graduation in 1997, Jia Zhangke made his first feature film, *Xiao Wu* (Pickpocket), which won him many international awards and established him as a leading voice of the so-called "underground" filmmakers.

The two hometown-based features following *Xiao Wu*, *Platform* and *Unknown Pleasure*, while hailed abroad, were also banned from public showing in China.

In late 2003, partly due to the relaxed policy of the Film Bureau, China's official film regulator/censor within the State Administration of Radio, Film, and Television, Jia Zhangke emerged from the "underground" and made the first officially approved film, *The World*, which turns away from Jia's hometown of Fengyang and focuses on Beijing city life as it is viewed through the eyes of a migrant worker. His *Still Life* won the Golden Lion Award at the 2006 Venice International Film Festival.

Aimlessness in a Chinese small town, Jia Zhangke's *Platform* (2000).

Jia Zhangke Filmography:

Xiao Wu (Pickpocket), 1997

Platform (Zhan tai), 2000

Unknown Pleasure (Ren xiao yao), 2002

The World (Shi jie), 2004

Still Life (San xia hao ren), 2006.

JIANG WEN
(1963-)

Jiang

Born in 1963 in Central China's Hebei Province, Jiang Wen was the son of a senior captain in the People's Liberation Army. He entered the Performing Arts Department of the Central Academy of Theater Art in 1980, and graduated with a Bachelor of Arts degree in 1984. That same year he started acting both on the stage and in films. Jiang's starring role in *Hibiscus Town* (1984, directed by Xie Jin) established his credentials as an actor, and the subsequent roles in Zhang Yimou's *Red Sorghum* (1987) and the TV drama *A Beijinger in New York* (1992) crowned him with the title "most talented male star of China". Jiang Wen also starred in many films by emerging directors, such as *The Missing Gun*, *Me and My Dad*, *Letter from an Unknown Woman*, and *Jasmine Women*.

After appearing in many television serials and films, in 1994 Jiang wrote and directed his first film, *In the Heat of the Sun*, adapted from a story by famed Chinese novelist Wang Shuo. The film won the best actor prize at Venice in 1994 for actor Xia Yu and garnered six Golden Horse awards in Taiwan.

Jiang's second feature, *Devils on the Doorstep*, is a black-and-white masterpiece about the Japanese occupation of a Chinese village in the 1930s. The Grand Prix award at the Cannes Film Festival won Jiang international recognition for his directing talent. The film was banned and never shown in China.

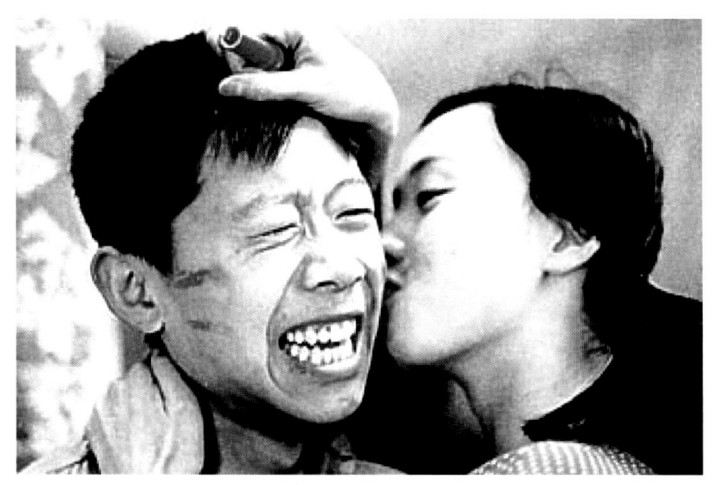

Adolescence during the Cultural Revolution,
Jiang Wen's *In the Heat of the Sun* (1994)

Jiang Wen Filmography (as Director):

In the Heat of the Sun (Yang guang can lan de ri zi), 1994

Devils on the Doorstep (Gui zi lai le), 1999

The Sun also Rises (Tai yang zhao chang sheng qi), 2007

Jin Chen
(1969-)

Jin

Born in 1969 in China's southern city of Hangzhou, Jin Chen worked for the Zhejiang TV Station after graduating from a professional school, where he developed an interest in editing. Jin visited Beijing in 1989 and witnessed the historical June Fourth student movement. In 1992, Jin was admitted to the Directing Department of the Central Academy of Theater Art. He graduated from CATA in 1996 with a Bachelor of Arts degree.

Two years later, a time when the Internet was still a novelty for the majority of the Chinese, Jin made his directorial debut *Love in the Internet Age*, which won him the New Director award at the Eighth Golden Rooster Awards Ceremony.

Nicknamed one of the "Three Musketeers of CATA" (the other two are Zhang Yang and Shi Runjiu), Jin Chen made his second feature *Chrysanthemum Tea* in 2000, which was marketed as a film that broke the sex "taboo" when it was officially released in China. Since then, Jin has been actively involved in various television projects. His TV drama credits include *Three Doors* (San chong men, 2002), adapted from a high school student's novel, and *Resurrection* (Fu huo, 2004).

Problems of Chinese sex life in Jin Chen's
Chrysanthemum Tea (2000)

Jin Chen Filmography:

Love in the Internet Age (Wang luo shi dai de ai qing), 1998

Chrysanthemum Tea (Ju hua cha), 2000

Crossing Over (Feng huang), 2007

LI XIN
(1969-)

Li

Born in 1969 in Shanghai, Li Xin grew up in a film-friendly family. Li's father is a veteran filmmaker of the state-owned Shanghai Film Studio, best known in China as a director of the "main melody films", a euphemism for the works that feature "great leaders" and "great themes" of the Communist revolution. In 1987, Li entered the Beijing Film Academy to study film directing. Immediately after his four years of study at BFA, Li returned to Shanghai in 1991 to become a Shanghai Film Studio director. In 1995, after several years of making television commercials, Li Xin made his feature debut *Your Black Hair and My Hand*, which, although distributed by the Shanghai Film Studio, was financed by private money. This debut film established Li as one of the most stylistically innovative filmmakers of his generation.

In 2001, Li Xin directed his second feature, *Dazzling*. Stylish and avant-garde, the film pays tribute to a fast changing metropolis that rivals New

York, London, Paris, and Tokyo. Three years later, in an effort to expand his scope of vision, Li Xin made the martial arts comedy *Master of Everything*, adapted from a newspaper report about how village farmers discovered the magic of the DV camera. The controversial film was selected to unveil the 2004 Shanghai International Film Festival.

Love lost and love regained
in twenty-first century Shanghai,
Li Xin's *Dazzling* (2001)

Li Xin Filmography:

Your Black Hair and My Hand (Tan qing shuo ai), 1995

Dazzling (Hua yan), 2001

Master of Everything (Zi yu zi le), 2004

Three City Hotshots (San wen nuan), 2006

The War on the Other Shore (Dui an de zhan zheng), 2007

LIU BINGJIAN
(1963-)

Liu

Born in 1963 in Anhui, Liu Bingjian worked briefly in a local government after graduating from high school. He was soon bored with the job and decided to go to Beijing to study film. In 1985, Liu was admitted to the Cinematography Department of the Beijing Film Academy. After graduating from BFA in 1989, Liu landed a job at CCTV, the largest TV station in China.

Bored again by the mechanical nature of the job, Liu decided to work as a freelance filmmaker in Beijing, a bold move few people would even consider in the early 1990s. In 1995, when some of his classmates began to make their first group of "underground" films, Liu Bingjian directed his feature debut, *The Stone Bed*, a film that won official approval but was largely ignored by both critics and audiences.

Liu's second feature, *Men and Women*, was independently financed and produced. The film casts a humorous look on homosexuality in the Chinese society and, largely for this reason, was banned by the Chinese authorities. His third feature, *Cry Woman*, though shown at a large number of international film festivals, was again prohibited from public showing in China. Black and humorous, *Cry Woman* is an indictment of China's post-socialist materialism. In 2004, Liu re-emerged from the "underground" and made his second officially approved feature, *Plastic Flowers*, a love triangle with a catastrophic ending revolving around a young widow named Chunhua who inherits her husband's plastic flower factory.

Tradition and materialism collide in
Liu Bingjian's *Cry Woman* (2001)

Liu Bingjian Filmography:

The Stone Bed (Yan chuang), 1995

Men and Women (Nan nan nu nu), 1999

Cry Woman (Ku qi de nu ren), 2001

Plastic Flowers (Chun hua kai), 2004

LOU YE
(1965-)

Lou

Born in 1965 in Shanghai, Lou Ye developed an interest in painting when he was a child. He studied painting in a Shanghai Animation Studio-sponsored vocational school and worked briefly on several animation films. In 1985, after a failed attempt to get into the Central Academy of Fine Arts, his first choice, Lou Ye entered the Beijing Film Academy to study directing. He was one of the most active students in BFA's "Class of 1985". Lou returned to Shanghai after graduating from BFA in 1989 and spent several years working as a producer and assistant director. In 1993, Lou made his feature debut, *Weekend Lover*, which won him the Rainer Werner Fassbinder Prize for Best Director at the 1996 Mannheim-Heidelberg Film Festival. Financed by non-studio money, the film established Lou as an emerging independent filmmaker in China.

Lou Ye is arguably the most stylistic of China's "Sixth Generation" directors. Although his second feature, *Don't Be Young*, was nominated for Best Cinematography and Best Sound at the 1995 Golden Rooster Award Ceremony of China, it was his 1999 feature, *Suzhou River*, that made Lou an internationally acclaimed art-house *auteur*. Banned from theatrical release in China, *Suzhou River* won many international awards, chief among them the VRPO Tiger Award at the Twenty-ninth Rotterdam International Film Festival. Lou's fourth feature, *Purple Butterfly*, shot with an official permit from the Film Bureau, is a personal and stylistic take on his hometown of Shanghai during the period of the Japanese occupation. *Summer Palace*, Lou's fifth film, premiered at the 2006 Cannes International Film Festival.

Fragile love in an eternal city,
Lou Ye's *Suzhou River* (1999)

Lou Ye Filmography:

Weekend Lover (Zhou mo qing ren), 1993

Don't Be Young (Wei qing shao nu), 1995

Suzhou River (Su zhou he), 1999

Purple Butterfly (Zi hu die), 2002

Summer Palace (Yi he yuan), 2006

Lu Chuan
(1971-)

Lu

Born in 1971 in Xinjiang Uyghur Autonomous Region, China's Muslim West, Lu Chuan moved to Beijing at age six with his writer father, Lu Tianming.

Unlike most young directors who go straight to the Beijing Film Academy to learn their trade, Lu entered the PLA International Relations University in Nanjing for his undergraduate studies, majoring in American literature. He graduated from that university in 1993 and worked as an English translator for several years. In 1995, Lu was admitted to the graduate program of the Beijing Film Academy, where he studied film directing and scriptwriting. After graduating with a master's degree in 1998, Lu joined the state-owned Beijing Film Studio and waited for three years to make his directorial debut, *The Missing Gun*. The film had a wide release in China and made Lu a household name. From his very first film, Lu has secured funding from Columbia Pictures Film Production Asia in Hong Kong, a Sony Pictures Entertainment's international motion pictures operation. His follow-up, *Kekexili: Mountain Patrol*, a docudrama about a band of vigilantes on the hunt for poachers who are killing the endangered Tibetan antelopes, was also partly financed by Columbia Asia. The film won Lu Chuan many international and domestic awards, including a special mention at the 2005 Berlin International Film Festival, a special jury prize at the 2004 Tokyo International Film Festival, and the Best Asian Film award at the 2006 Hong Kong Film Awards ceremony.

The struggle between humans and nature in Lu Chuan's *Kekexili: Mountain Patrol*.

Lu Chuan Filmography:

The Missing Gun (Xun qiang), 2001

Kekexili: Mountain Patrol (Ke ke xi li), 2004

home to recover from a kidney disease. It was not until 1997 that Lu debuted with *The Making of Steel*. Heavily criticized by the Chinese censors for its treatment of such touchy subjects as alcohol, drug addiction, and casual sex, the film underwent severe edits before it satisfied the authorities. Lu's second feature *A Lingering Face*, also about a young man's quest for identity and manhood, was once again heavily edited to meet the requirement of the government censors.

A core member of the "Sixth Generation" filmmakers, Lu Xuechang became known to the general public with the 2003 light comedy *Cala, My Dog!*, starring award-winning actor Ge You and produced by China's box-office "king" Feng Xiaogang. The film reaffirms Lu's humanistic concern for the socially disadvantaged groups of people in contemporary China. Lu's fourth feature, *The Contract*, which features a fugitive prostitute hired to pretend to be a young man's fiancée, opened in limited release in 2006.

Searching for the father figure in Lu Xuechang's *The Making of Steel*.

Lu Xuechang Filmography:

The Making of Steel (Zhang de cheng ren), 1997

A Lingering Face (Fei chang xia ri), 1999

Cala, My Dog! (Ka la shi tiao gou), 2003

The Contract (Zu qi), 2006

A Room for Two People (Liang ge ren de fang jian), 2007

Ma Liwen
(1971-)

Ma

Formerly known as Ma Xiaoying, Ma Liwen was born in 1971 in the eastern province of Jiangxi but grew up in Harbin, a major city in China's northeast. She went to Beijing in 1993 and managed to enroll in a thee-year certificate program in film and television directing at the Central Academy of Theater Art. She worked as an assitant director for several film and television projects after graduating from CATA in 1996. Ma decidded to make Chinese woman writer Zhang Jie's semi-autobiography *Gone Is the One Who Held Me the Dearest in the World* into a film immediately after she finished reading it in 1996, but it would take her another four years to make it a reality. Ma's debut feature, named after the semi-autobiography, surprised many at the 2002 Changchun Film Festival, winning the Best Chinese Feature, Best Director, and Best Supporting Actress awards.

While film direction in China is still dominated by men as in the rest of the world, Ma Liwen is among the few female directors in China who continues to shake up the male-dominated profession. Her second low-budget feature, *You and Me*, a film largely based on her own experience as a CATA student living with her old landlady in a courtyard complex, picked up the Best Actress award at the 2005 Tokoyo International Film Festival, and Ma herself was crowned as the Best Director at China's prestigious Golden Rooster Award ceremony of 2005, an unusual award that made an unprepared Ma speechless, in tears.

Emotional bond developed
in Ma Liwen's *You and Me*.

Ma Liwen Filmography:

Gone Is the One Who Held Me the Dearest in the World
(Shi jie shang zui teng wo de na ge ren qu le), 2001

You and Me (Wo men liang), 2005

I'm Liu Yuejin (Wo jiao liu yue jin), 2007

Meng Qi
(1972-)

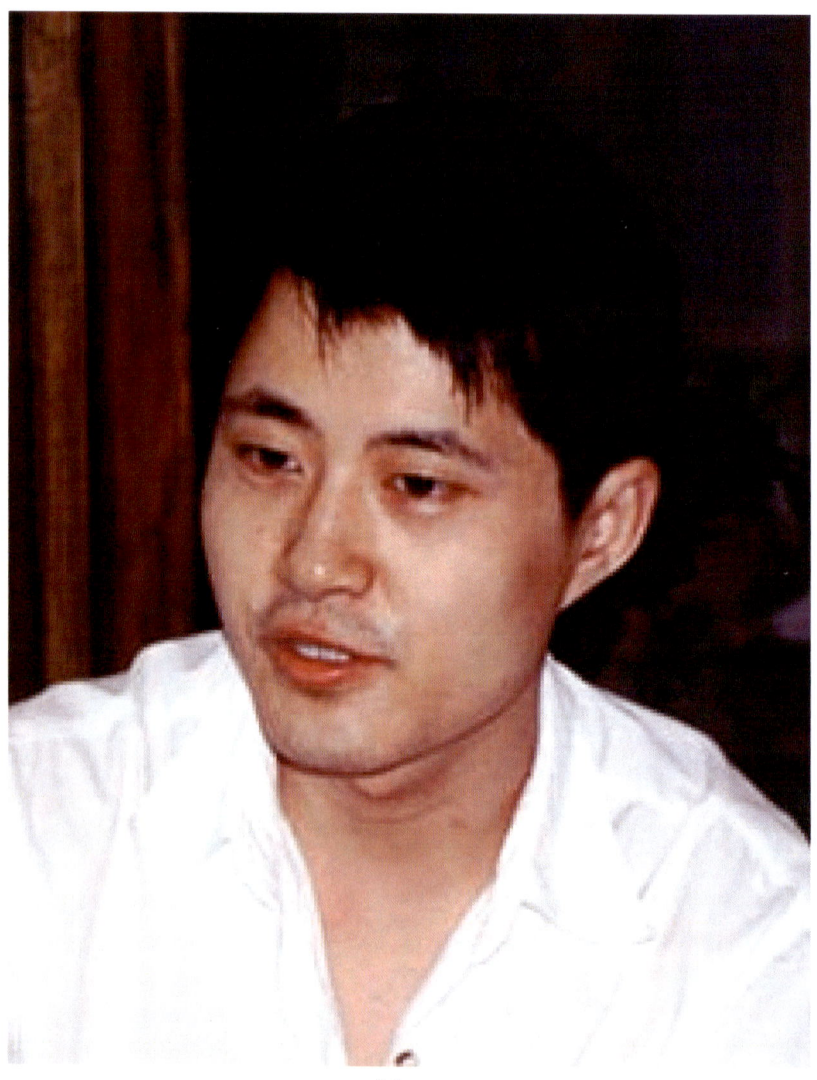

Meng

Born in 1972 in Zhengzhou, capital city of Henan, in central China, Meng Qi became a legend in the last days of 2001 when his feature *What a Snowy Day* debuted in Shanghai. Meng joined the Chinese army after high school, and got involved in restaurant business after being demobilized. In 1998, with no connection to either BFA or CATA and no practical experience in filmmaking, Meng decided to adapt Chinese writer Liang Xiaosheng's novella *The Dead Tired Man* into a film. He sold his restaurant business and brought his lifelong friend Ding Zhanhong, a hotel manager with no knowledge of celluloid film, on board to make their first film. They took their script to many potential investors and finally managed to secure initial funding from a stock trader. With no intention to make it an "underground" film, Meng submitted the script to the government censors. As it turned out, it would take Meng more than a year to satisfy the censors.

Warmth in a cold and snowy day
in Meng Qi's *What a Snowy Day*.

The legend of Meng as a filmmaker continued to grow after *What a Snowy Day* was finished. Without a distri-butor, Meng and Ding took the film's two copies, the only two they could afford, to Shanghai and talked two theater managers into screening the film. To make the screenings known to the public, Meng and Ding put up posters themselves in Shanghai's busy shopping malls and business centers. In a sense, Meng's filmmaking experience resembles the life of the soy bean factory cadre in *What a Snowy Day*, bitter yet never short of sweetness.

MENG QI FILMOGRAPHY:

What a Snowy Day (Wo zui zhong yi de xue tian), 2001

SHI RUNJIU
(1969-)

Shi

Born in Shanghai in 1969, Shi Runjiu commuted between Shanghai and Beijing regularly to see his Beijing-based parents. Shi spent his childhood with his Shanghai grandmother and eventually moved to Beijing to live with his parents. In 1988, Shi took the college entrance examination and qualified to enter either the Central Academy of Theater Art or the Beijing Film Academy. Between the two, he picked CATA's directing program. At CATA, along with stage directing, Shi also developed an interest in filmmaking. Upon graduation in 1992, therefore, Shi Runjiu began to direct some of China's best-known underground music videos. He concurrently produced a series of four documentaries and served as a pre-production assistant director on *To Live* (directed by Zhang Yimou) and as an assistant director on other film and TV projects.

The sky's no limit
in Shi Runjiu's *A Beautiful New World*.

In 1998, with the financing from New York-founded but Beijing-based Imar Film, Shi made his feature debut, *A Beautiful New World*, a light comedy about a small town nobody who, after winning a Shanghai apartment through a lottery, comes to the new wonderland to realize his Shanghai dream. Allegedly China's first "road film", Shi's second feature, *All the Way*, set in wild and beautiful Guangxi Province, tells the story of a girl, her gangster boyfriend, and an ordinary truck driver caught up in a head-spinning escapade in the aftermath of a spectacular robbery. The film shows Shi's special talent in characterization and his marked interest in making genre films.

Shi Runjiu Filmography:

A Beautiful New World (Mei li xin shi jie), 1998

All the Way (Zou dao di), 2001

Tang Danian
(1968-)

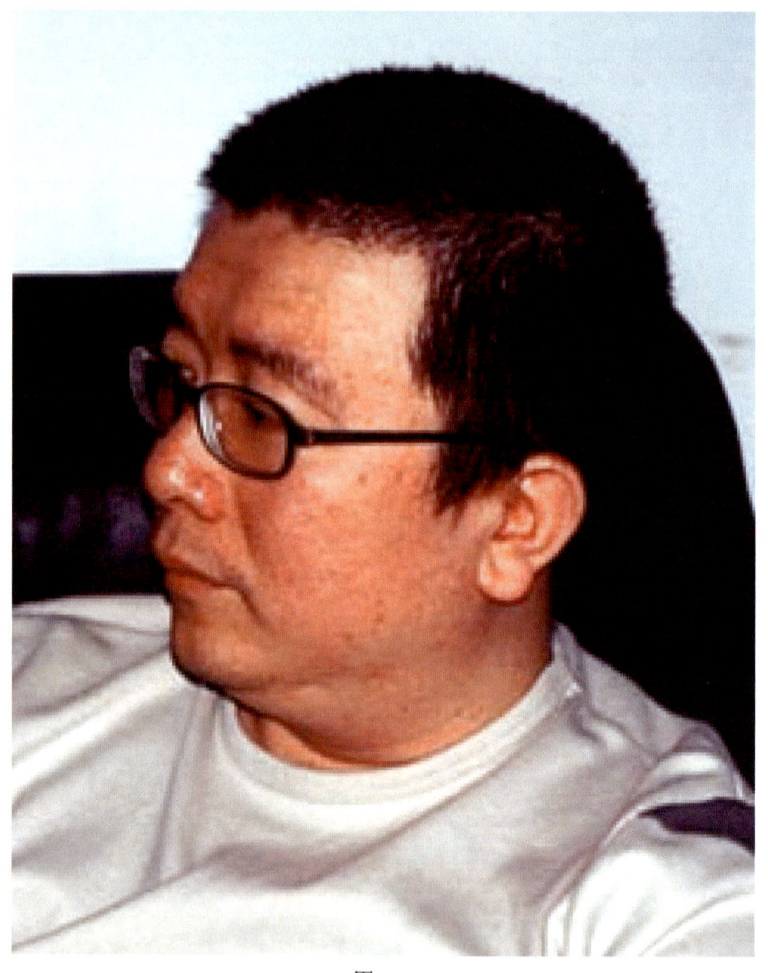

Tang

Born in 1968 in Beijing, Tang Danian was the youngest in the "Class of 1985" of the Beijing Film Academy. Fond of literature when he was a teenager, Tang Danian didn't want to be a filmmaker until his BFA parents asked him to take the BFA exam. In 1985, Tang was admitted to the Script-writing Department of BFA and graduated from there in 1989. Tang's writing talent was first displayed in *Good Morning, Beijing* (1990), a film on which he was credited as the sole scriptwriter. His career as a scriptwriter was further polished as Tang began to work with his former classmates, writing scripts for such acclaimed films as Zhang Yuan's *Beijing Bastards* (he also played a role in the film) and Wang Xiaoshuai's *Beijing Bicycle*. Tang also won an International Script Award at the 1996 Sundance Film Festival for *Crazy Guy*, although it was never made into a film.

A "paradise" far from home
in Tang Danian's *City Paradise*.

Tang's directorial debut, *City Paradise*, was shot without government permission and its post-production was finished on the editing table of an American university. Automatically categorized as an "underground" film, *City Paradise* depicts a bleak picture of Beijing, a post-socialist metropolis that alienates both migrants and local residents. Since *City Paradise*, Tang Danian has been actively involved in directing and writing for television dramas. He also co-wrote the script of Zhang Yuan's 2003 feature *Green Tea*.

Tang Danian Filmography:

City Paradise (Du shi tian tang), 1998

WANG CHAO
(1964-)

Wang

Born in 1964 in Nanjing, Jiangsu Province, Wang Chao grew up in a working class family and worked in three different factories after high school graduation. Although Wang failed the college entrance examination, he kept his dream alive, writing poems and reading literary magazines in his leisure time. In 1990, Wang made an attempt to enroll in the regular program of the Beijing Film Academy, but didn't succeed. In the following year, undiscouraged by the failure, Wang managed to get into the evening program of the Beijing Film Academy, taking classes taught by regular BFA faculty. It was also during his three-year studies at BFA that Wang began to write stories. Four of his stories, two short stories and two novellas, were published in literary magazines.

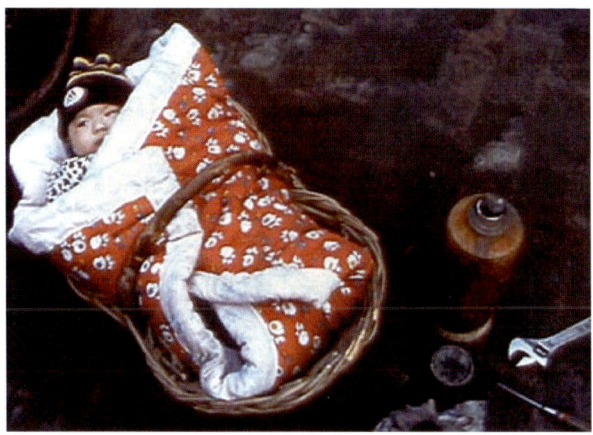

An abandoned baby leads to
an unpredictable story
in Wang Chao's *The Orphan of Anyang*.

In 1995, Wang Chao's filmmaking dream came a step closer as he started to work for the Chen Kaige Film Workshop, assisting internationally acclaimed filmmaker Chen on the makings of *Temptress Moon* and *The Emperor and the Assassin*. The hands-on training at the Chen Kaige Film Workshop eventually led Wang to the making of his debut feature, *The Orphan of Anyang*, an "underground" film about a humble factory worker whose life intersects with an abandoned baby and the child's mother, a prostitute. The film won Wang a slew of international awards, and it was celebrated in Cannes, Rotterdam, Telluride, Toronto, Vancouver, and elsewhere. Three years later, Wang made his second feature *Day and Night*, this time approved by the censors, and the film was hailed at the 25th Three Continents Film Festival in Nantes, France, winning the Best Director award. Wang's third feature, *Luxury Car*, was shown at the 2006 Cannes International Film Festival.

WANG CHAO FILMOGRAPHY:

The Orphan of Anyang (An yang yin er), 2001

Day and Night (Ri ri ye ye), 2004

Luxury Car (Jiang cheng xia ri), 2006

Lu Xuechang
(1964-)

Lu

Born in 1964 in Beijing, Lu Xuechang attended a high school affiliated with the Central Academy of Fine Arts, where he studied painting for four years. Due to his painting background, Lu was admitted to the "Class of 1985" of the Beijing Film Academy, majoring in directing. He was soon assigned to the state-owned Beijing Film Studio after grduating from BFA in 1989. In the early 1990s, when his classmates were making their first films, Lu stayed at

WANG GUANGLI
(1966-)

Wang

Born in rural Sichuan Province in 1966, Wang Guangli never received any professional training in filmmaking. He enrolled in the Education Department of Shanghai's East Normal University after passing China's 1985 College Entrance Exam. Despite his lack of formal filmmaking training, Wang shared similar intellectual background with the "Class of 1985" of BFA. He habitually skipped his own department's classes and sneaked into the lecture rooms of radical young professors. Perhaps an indication of his future career choice, during college years Wang was an active supporter of the "anti-Xie Jin model"campaign, a limited intellectual movement in the mid-1980s that attacked the melodramatic tradition of Xie Jin, then the most renowned Chinese filmmaker. Zhu Dake, Wang's intellectual idol and then a professor at Shanghai's East Normal, was the initiator of the "anti-Xie Jin model" campaign.

Laid-off state employees enjoy a moment of limelight in Wang Guangli's *Go for Broke*.

After graduating in 1989, Wang was assigned to the Youth Political College of the Central University of the Communist Youth League in Beijing, teaching psychology. It was in Beijing that Wang became acquainted with independent documentary filmmakers and decided to become a filmmaker himself. Wang left his post as psychology professor in 1992 to pursue this goal. His first foray into directing, the video documentary *I Have Graduated* (1992), chronicles post-Tiananmen changes in student life at six prominent Beijing universities. From 1993 to 1996 Wang cut his professional teeth working for Dalian and China's Central Television before gaining the opportunity to direct his first film, *Maiden Work*, a docudrama about a painter's prolonged process of getting his first film made. While *Maiden Work* was completed outside the official system, Wang's second film, *Go for Broke*, a fictional reenactment of the efforts of six laid-off state employees in Shanghai, was made "legally" within a government studio system that is marred by censorship and red tape. Wang's third feature, *Karmic Mahjong*, features an international cast and crew and was theatrically released in China.

Wang Guangli Filmography:

Maiden Work (Chu nu zuo), 1997

Go for Broke (Heng shu heng), 2001

Karmic Mahjong (Xue zhan dao di), 2006

Dangerous Game (Bang zi lao hu ji), 2007

WANG QUANAN
(1965-)

Wang

Born in 1965 in Yan'an, the cradle of the Chinese Communist Party, Wang Quanan joined a song and dance troupe before graduating from high school, which enabled him to travel around the world, a rare experience at his age at that time. He stayed in France for more than half a year and decided to return to China to study film. In 1987, Wang was admitted to the Acting Department of the Beijing Film Academy. Not a good student in his own department, Wang nevertheless developed an interest in scriptwriting. His graduation work in 1991 was a well-controlled performance as an ordinary Beijing bus driver in *Good Morning, Beijing*, a neo-realist-style film by the late female director Zhang Nuanxin. After graduation, Wang worked for the state-owned Xi'an Film Studio for seven years; there he made a TV soap opera called *Years* (Niandai).

A mysterious call pulls
the unlikely couple together
in Wang Quanan's *Lunar Eclipse*.

In 1999, Wang Quanan received national and international recog-nition for writing and directing his debut feature, *Lunar Eclipse*, an enigmatic film about a girl's discovery of her alter ego. This elegant film about identity confusion, desire, and betrayal is mixed with a touch of noir mystery and told in a cinematic language rarely seen in Chinese films. *Lunar Eclipse* was invited to over twenty international film festivals and forums in such countries as Germany, Italy, Korea, the United States, and Russia. In 2000, *Lunar Eclipse* won the critics' award for best picture at the Moscow International Film Festival. In 2001, the lead actress in *Lunar Eclipse* won the best actress award in Deauville, France. Wang Quanan's second feature, *The Story of Ermei*, although not as stylistic as *Lunar Eclipse*, emphasizes the difficult living conditions Chinese migrant workers have to deal with both in the countryside and in the city. Wang's *Tuya's Marriage* won the Golden Bear prize for best picture at the 57th Berlin Film Festival.

Wang Quanan Filmography:

Lunar Eclipse (Yue shi), 1999

The Story of Ermei (Jing zhe), 2004

Tuya's Marriage (Tuya de hun shi), 2006

WANG XIAOSHUAI
(1966-)

Wang

Born in 1966 in Shanghai, Wang Xiaoshuai moved to Guiyang, the capital of Guizhou Province, with his relocated parents during the heyday of the Cultural Revolution. He spent his childhood in the isolated city, and then moved again in 1979 to the city of Wuhan, where Wang lived for two years. In 1981, to pursue his childhood dream to be a painter, he went to Beijing and entered the high school affiliated to the Central Academy of Fine Arts. Upon graduation, Wang, partly inspired by the films of the Fifth Generation, decided to give up his childhood dream and become a filmmaker instead. In

1985, Wang enrolled in the Directing Department of the Beijing Film Academy. It was during the days prior to BFA graduation that Wang and several of his classmates began to deliberate the possibility of a "new wave" of Chinese cinema independent of the influence of the Fifth Generation.

After graduating in 1989, Wang Xiaoshuai was assigned to the state-owned Fujian Film Studio, a small unit in China's southern province of Fujian, far away from Beijing, the nation's cultural center. Frustrated by the lack of opportunities at the studio, Wang returned to Beijing in 1990 and decided to go "independent". His first feature *The Days,* arguably the first truly independent film outside the state film apparatus,

Troubled adolescence in a troubled time in Wang Xiaoshuai's *Shanghai Dreams*.

was made on a shoestring budget. It was followed by *Frozen*, a film about the Beijing avant-garde art world. Wang emerged from "the underground" with his next two films, *So Close to Paradise* and *Beijing Bicycle*, both of which were heavily censored by the Film Bureau. *Beijing Bicycle* established Wang's status as an internationally renowned *auteur*. The film won the Silver Bear Award at the 2001 Berlin International Film Festival, and its two leading male actors received Best Young Actor Prize. Wang's eighth feature *Shanghai Dreams*, in many ways his toughest in terms of sensitivity and heaviness, received the prestigious Jury Prize at the 58th Cannes Film Festival.

Wang Xiaoshuai Filmography:

The Days (Dong chun de ri zi), 1993

Suicides (Da you xi), 1994

Frozen (Ji du han leng), 1995

So Close to Paradise (Bian dan, guniang), 1997

Suburban Dreams (Meng huan tian yuan), 2000

Beijing Bicycle (Shi qi sui de dan che), 2000

Drifters (Er di), 2003

Shanghai Dreams (Qing hong), 2005

In Love We Trust (Zuo you), 2007

Xu Jinglei
(1974-)

Xu

Born in 1974 in Beijing, actress-turned-director Xu Jinglei was interested in Chinese calligraphy and painting since she was young, but had never imagined she would have anything to do with filmmaking. In 1992, Xu was admitted to the Acting Department of the Beijing Film Academy, where she later acknowledged she learned nothing but acting. She was given a chance to act in a few television series and films even when she was a student at BFA, but her acting career didn't bloom until after her graduation. Since 1996, Xu has starred in quite a number of television series as well as in well over a dozen feature films, including *Love Spicy Soup*, *Spring Subway*, *Dazzling*, *I Love You*, and *Last Love First Love*. With such impressive acting credentials, Xu quickly becomes one of the hottest pop-idols and superstars in China. Her fan base crosses several age groups, with university students being the most loyal.

Memory and amnesia
in Xu Jinglei's *Letter from an Unknown Woman*.

 Xu Jinglei's breakthrough came in 2002 when she wrote and directed her debut feature *Me and My Dad*, an independently produced and financed film about a widowed father and his relationship with his emotionally traumatized daughter. The film won her China's Best First-Time Director award at the 2003 Golden Rooster Awards ceremony. Xu Jinglei's second feature, *Letter from an Unknown Woman*, is a loose adaptation of Stephan Zweig's 1922 Viennese novella of the same title. The nostalgic and beautifully shot film won Xu the Best New Director Award at the 2004 San Sebastian Film Festival. One of the few visible and internationally acclaimed female directors in China, Xu turned a celebrity blogger in 2005 and quickly attracted an astonishing 10 million hits on her site. She has also published a book based on her blog entries, appropriately titled *Xu's Blog*. The book contains 130 articles and 20 photos from her website.

Xu Jinglei Filmography:

Me and My Dad (Wo he ba ba), 2002

Letter from an Unknown Woman (Yi ge mo sheng nu ren de lai xin), 2004

Dreams May Come (Meng xiang zhao jin xian shi), 2006

ZHANG MING
(1961-)

Zhang

Born in 1961 in Sichuan, Zhang Ming spent his childhood among the green mountains and clear rivers of his hometown Wushan, located on the banks of the Yangzi River's Three Gorges. As a little boy, Zhang liked to paint and draw. This talent in art enabled Zhang to get through the competitive examination of the Fine Arts Department of Chongqing's Southwest Normal University and became an oil painting student in 1978. It was during his college days that Zhang decided to become a filmmaker instead of a painter.

He read everything he could find on the topic of film, including Eisenstein's writings, and saw every film that was shown, regardless of quality. His enthusiasm for film was somewhat dampened upon graduation in 1982, when he was sent back to his hometown to teach at Wushan Teacher's College. But Zhang didn't give up his dream. He kept reading books about film and watched a lot of films from the 1950s, 60s and 70s by directors like Buñuel, Tarkovski, Antonioni, and Bergman. In 1988, Zhang was admitted to the graduate program of the Beijing Film Academy, majoring in directing. Zhang secured a teaching position in the Directing Department after graduating in 1991 with an MFA degree, and he has been teaching film directing at BFA since then.

The quiet light station and uncompromised expectation in Zhang Ming's *Rainclouds Over Wushan*.

From 1991 to 1994, Zhang Ming made a number of short TV series, while at the same time teaching classes in Audio-Visual Language at BFA. In 1995, with the help of his friends, Zhang Ming completed his first feature-length film *Rainclouds Over Wushan*, which won Zhang a host of international awards, including the New Currents Award at the First Pusan International Film Festival and the Fribourg Award and IFFS/FICC Prize at the Eleventh Fribourg International Film Festival. After nearly six years, Zhang Ming made his second feature, *Weekend Plot*, a film that was first conceived as a horror/thriller but had to be changed considerably because of censorship.

Zhang Ming Filmography:

Rainclouds Over Wushan (Wu shan yun yu), 1996

Weekend Plot (Mi yu shi qi xiao shi), 2001

Zhang Yang
(1967-)

Zhang

Born in 1967 in Beijing, Zhang Yang grew up in a filmmaker's family. His father is a veteran filmmaker, known to be one of the earliest martial arts directors in post-1949 China. From the very beginning, Zhang wanted to become a filmmaker. He planned to get into the Beijing Film Academy after high school, but BFA stopped recruiting new students that year. Failing the exam of the Central Academy of Theater Art, his second choice after BFA, Zhang Yang went south and enrolled in Guangzhou's Zhongshan University, majoring in Chinese.

At Zhongshan University, Zhang was an active member of the school's amateur troupe and a devoted amateur playwright. His talent in scriptwriting caught the attention of the CATA faculty and, two years after Zhang's study at Zhongshan University, he was granted permission to retake the CATA entrance exam. In 1988, Zhang transferred to the Directing Department of CATA, where he spent much of his time studying film, drama, and rock music.

Hand-shaking between two generations in Zhang Yang's *Sunflower*.

After graduating from CATA in 1992, Zhang joined the Beijing Film Studio and began to prepare his first film. His debut feature, *Spicy Love Soup*, a tender romantic comedy about a city couple's love life, was a domestic box-office hit, and its soundtrack even sold more than 500,000 copies in China. Zhang established his name on the international stage with the release of his critically acclaimed second film, *Shower*, which examines the tense relationship between tradition and modernity in China, as seen through the eyes of a father and his estranged son. The film won him many international awards, including the Best Director award at the 1999 San Sebastian International Film Festival. Zhang's third and forth features, *Quitting* and *Sunflower*, continued to examine the father-son relationship against the background of the historical transformation of contemporary Chinese society. *Sunflower* took home again the Best Director and Best Photography awards at the 2005 San Sebastian Festival.

Zhang Yang Filmography:

Love Spicy Soup (Ai qing ma la tang), 1997

Shower (Xi zao), 1999

Quitting (Zuo tian), 2001

Sunflower (Xiang ri kui), 2005

Getting Home (Luo ye gui gen), 2006

ZHANG YUAN
(1963-)

Zhang

Born in 1963 in Nanjing, Zhang Yuan had an interest in painting and photography when he was young. In 1985, Zhang was admitted to the Cinematography Department of the Beijing Film Academy. Since graduating in 1989, Zhang Yuan has been a professional filmmaker, directing and producing documentary and feature films. His first film, *Mama*, financially supported by Zhang's business friends and independently produced, was made in 1990, a time when the idea of independent filmmaking was unheard of in China. Zhang's next four features were all archetypal undergrounders: *Beijing Bastards* examines the dissipated Beijing rock scene of the early 1990s; *The Square*, a documentary, is a cinematic contemplation of the Tiananmen Square, the largest "public space" in China; *Sons* tells the story of a dysfunctional family brought to ruin by an alcoholic father; and *East Palace West Palace* slowly reveals a young, gay Chinese man's obsession with a police officer. While Zhang's international recognition cannot be separated from these films, they also brought him troubles at home. In 1997, Zhang was at one time under house arrest as a result of his homosexual-themed drama *East Palace West Palace*. Frequently alternating between documentary and drama work, Zhang resumed his filmmaking career in 1999 with the release of *Crazy English*, a documentary about a dynamic and motivational English teacher. The documentary marks a turning point in Zhang Yuan's film career: he sets out to make films that would be approved by the censors but at the same time tries to maintain his independent spirit. His next four features, *Seventeen Years*, *I Love You*, *Green Tea*, and *Little Red Flowers* were all green-lighted by the censors. *Seventeen Years* won Zhang the award for Best Director in Venice and Singapore, and *Little Red Flowers* won him the International Confederation of Art Cinemas prize at the 56 Berlinale.

Taught to be part of organized communal life in kindergarten in Zhang Yuan's *Little Red Flowers*.

Zhang Yuan Filmography:

Mama (Ma ma), 1990;

Beijing Bastards (Bei jing za zhong), 1992

The Square (Guang chang), 1994

Sons (Er zi), 1996

East Palace West Palace (Dong gong xi gong), 1996

Crazy English (Feng kuang ying yu), 1999

Seventeen Years (Guo nian hui jia), 1999

I Love You (Wo ai ni), 2003

Green Tea (Lu cha), 2003

Little Red Flowers (Kan shang qu hen mei), 2006

Lights!
Camera!
Kai Shi!

In depth Interviews with China's New Generation of Movie Directors

CHAPTER ONE

BFA, CATA, AND BEYOND:
THE ROAD TO FILMMAKING

The understanding of how the "sixth generation" departs from the previous ones and is able to reshape the landscape of Chinese cinema begins with an understanding of the filmmakers as individuals and the part cinema plays in their lives. Therefore, the first question the interviewers posed to the 21 filmmakers was: how did you start your film career, and what was the defining moment or factor that led you to filmmaking? Not surprisingly, education played a large role in their career choice. With the exception of two, all the interviewed filmmakers are graduates of the two Beijing-based institutions (some from their special training programs): Beijing Film Academy (BFA) and Central Academy of Theater Art (CATA). Despite the fact that in recent years there has been an exploding growth of film schools in China, these two colleges continue to be the cradles of Chinese filmmakers.

* * *

Guan Hu

People often say that I was born into a family of film, but if you take a closer look at my life, you would understand that there is little connection between my career choice and my family background. My parents had nothing to do with film before I was fifteen or sixteen. Labeled as "Rightists", they were first sent to a labor camp in Beidahuang [in China's northeast] and then assigned to a medical research center in Beijing. During that time, I became an everyday friend of various kinds of medicines. Did that life experience lead me to medical science? Not at all. Later on, my mother joined the Youth Theater Art Academy and lived in the Academy's residential complex. I had never been to that complex until I was about fifteen or sixteen.

If you must find some connection between my family and my career choice, then there is one incident worth mentioning. I remember one night when I was about fifteen my father came home and grabbed my arm, saying, "Hurry up, hurry up, let's go see a '*neican pian*!' [films for a privileged group and not accessible to the public]" My memory of that night is especially clear. The film shown was Yugoslavia's *The Battle of Neretva*.[xii] My mother and sister took this event quite seriously. They behaved as if they were spies. We sneaked into a bus heading for the General Political Department of the Chinese Navy. Because my mother served as an interpreter, we were able to sit in the front row. As a child growing up with the *Eight Model Operas*, I was overwhelmed by the mesmerizing power of this film. If you still remember that film, you would understand what I mean by "mesmerizing power". Suddenly, you feel the real charm of film as an art form. It has the magical power of leading you to another world, giving you the feeling of "otherworldliness". To be frank, my interest in filmmaking was aroused because of this event, although coincidentally there might have some inevitability in it. After moving into the above-mentioned residential complex, I got more opportunities to see films. The most important thing was that a growing number of friends surrounded me, and most of them shared a common interest in film. In addition, almost every one of them aimed to enter college or graduate school. Living in such an environment, therefore, I naturally followed suit. But I had one disadvantage: I was not a good student in high school, and there was little chance for me to enter a regular college. At that time, the admission score for art colleges was relatively low. So, I decided to take a shot at BFA. Of course there were other reasons for me to choose BFA. I vaguely felt that I could have a more relaxed and laid-back experience by studying film. Most importantly, I felt I could do what I really wanted to do. You could say my nature led me to this road.

I am quite interested in a wide range of subjects, such as that of the Qing dynasty and of the "Anti-USA, Assisting Korea" campaign. But at my age it is quite difficult to control such subjects. Besides, because you are not well prepared for these subjects, no one will let you have a try. My only hope was to first cultivate myself and then fulfill these dreams in the future. To be frank, I was quite ambitious in the past, hoping to do some outstanding things. But at the same time I was not quite certain about the concrete goals of my future. Now I feel I am becoming more mature day by day. Every month I can feel there is something different in me. This process makes me feel deeply that I am only a film fan when encountering each subject. Who can be called a "professional director?" A professional director is the one who is able to masterfully handle the subject he/she doesn't like. I don't have this kind of talent. I can only handle those I like or am interested in. In recent years, therefore, I've only found a few projects that fit my nature. Although one could make a fortune out of filmmaking, I have little concern for pure profit or fame. I am telling you the truth.

Jia Zhangke

I grew up in Fenyang, Shanxi Province. I was studying painting when I first saw *Yellow Earth* in 1990. Originally I dreamed of becoming a fine arts student at Shanxi University, but after having seen *Yellow Earth* I decided not to study painting anymore. At that time, my conception of film was something very formulaic. To be frank, my understanding of film then came entirely from the long period of propogandistic official films. I thought film should be always dramatic, didactic, and formulaic in dialogue and characterization. I couldn't imagine other possibilities except for the official version I repeatedly saw on the screen. But as soon as I saw *Yellow Earth* I suddenly realized that film could be made in different ways, and there was also a place for films like *Yellow Earth*. This film all of a sudden stimulated my imagination, making me feel the unlimited potential of film as a medium of sight and sound. Because of this, I could no longer be satisfied with the flatness of painting. As a matter of fact, back then, I often spoke to my friends about my innate urge and desire for narratives. At the time when I was studying painting I'd already started to write stories. I began with poems, and then devoted much of my energy to fictional writing. Some of the stories were actually published. Since my original intention was to go to a fine arts college, I often blamed myself at that time for digressing from painting to the "secret" practice of fiction writing. Now I understand that the reason for such a shift was because painting could no longer fulfill my narrative desire. At this critical juncture, it happened that I discovered cinema.

I was admitted to BFA's Literature Department in 1993. During the sophomore year, I initiated the Youth Experimental Film Group of BFA. I felt that being attached to BFA would add special appeal to this group. Members of the group included students from the departments of literature, cinematography, sound, and management. Everyone brought his or her own talent to the group. Because we were students back then, our contacts and resources were limited. In spite of the fact that each individual's power was limited, I felt we could achieve something collectively.

I started my first film when I was twenty-seven. Although I lived in Beijing, I spent most of my working time in Shanxi. It seems to me that the age of twenty-seven was the most critical turning point in my life. Most of my friends got married, had babies, and started families at that age. In the past, they were reckless fellows, riding on motorcycles and idling away their time without much to worry about. But their lives underwent a considerable change after marriage. Since I still maintained a good relationship with them, I often went back to hang out with these longtime buddies. I was intellectually inspired. Although I hadn't bound myself to that kind of relationship yet at that time, I saw my friends entangled in a web of problems, including that of family, marriage, and child. It was during that period that I felt that the my scope of contemporary life was suddenly broadened. It is no longer a simple issue of adolescence, but an issue of responsibility and life's burden. After witnessing such changes and transformations, I feel contemporary life is extraordinarily fresh and alive. Why shouldn't we make films about contemporary life in China?

Chapter One

Jiang Wen

I loved to watch films when I was little. Actually it was my parents who made me fall in love with film. They liked to watch movies, and I always followed them. When I was a little kid, I was fond of war films. I didn't like love stories and had no interest in women characters. My role models were all bad guys. Horseriding and battle scenes were my favorite. I guess this childhood fantasy has left traces in my subconsciousness, which explains why my films are more energetic, punctuated by points of excitement.

My passion for film was re-ignited when I was in college. I entered the Central Academy of Theater Art (CATA) in 1980. During the period when I was close to graduating [in 1984], I saw quite a number of films. At that time, students at CATA enjoyed the privilege of seeing many "reference films" (*cankao pian*), even including the privilege of attending some weekly film events at the China Film Archive. During that time, week after week, every Monday, Wednesday, and Friday, I went see films. Interestingly enough, when I later on reexamined the lists I made in the 1980s, the "must-see" films were all made by Martin Scorsese. After that, I started to develop a growing interest in this particular director as well as in film directing. Therefore, it was only after having seen many of Scorsese' films that I developed my interest in film and started directing films. The movies I saw before Scorsese', including Chinese films, served only as a base upon which my interest in filmmaking developed. I was particularly overwhelmed by *The Godfather*. I said to myself: this film is darn good and interesting. Then, I started to think about making a film of my own.

Frankly speaking, during the time when I was a student at CATA, many of us were opinionated about BFA's Directing Department and directing itself. It was often the case that a candidate failed to pass the CATA examination one year but somehow would become a BFA student in the Directing Department next year or the year after. This being the case, how could you be not opinionated about directing? Hence, we generally felt that directing was a major only suited for those who were kicked out of other schools or departments. At that time, no one wanted to be a director. In addition, to tell you the truth, if you ask BFA students about the curriculum of these two institutions' directing departments, they would say there were little differences. The only difference was that CATA students might be younger and trendier.

I was "tempted" into directing due to another factor. Although I majored in performing arts, I occasionally went up to the fourth floor of the CATA building, staging self-selected or self-directed short plays there. I remember some professors once commented: you are very good at stage directing and *mise-en-scene*, even more skillful than students of the Directing Department. To tell you the truth, I didn't quite understand these comments. What I did was all out of instinct: when one is required to climb a tree, I ask him to climb a tree; when one ought to dive into a trench, I ask him to dive into a trench. Why did you make a fuss about it? Because I didn't see any taboos on stage, I was alleged to have made use of depth and cross walking. I said to myself: where could this guy go if he didn't climb a tree? From this I began to realize: first, I could one day direct a play of my own; second, I began to question what the students of the Directing Department were being taught. What I did was quite simple, so how could they come up with such complicated theories? I therefore discovered that some education is actually quite formulaic and dogmatic. Such an education tends to limit or condition people within certain frames. Things are not so complicated, but they would measure your work according to their principles of judgment. I feel such a practice is quite ridiculous.

Jin Chen

I was born during the last days of the 1960s, at the threshold of the 1970s. Occasionally, therefore, I share the residual anxiety of the people born in the 1960s.

The reason I chose filmmaking as my profession is probably due to my interest in painting during childhood. I learned Chinese painting when I was a child. After graduating from a professional school, I started my work at a TV station and developed an interest in editing. There was also a time during childhood when I loved acting. Although not a child star, I was quite frequently called upon to act. So, I have had relations with film and television since childhood. Originally, I had never thought of going to college after beginning my work at the TV station, but I changed my mind as my fondness for Beijing grew. I visited Beijing in the year of 1989, and coincidentally experienced that historical event. Then, I became obsessed with Beijing, and wanted to become a Beijinger by in all ways. With this goal in mind, I started to prepare myself for college examinations. During those years, BFA had already stopped recruiting students; thus the only option left for me was CATA. In 1992, I entered CATA, majoring in directing, which naturally led me to the path of being a director after graduation in 1996.

Studying directing at CATA is different from BFA, and the education I received at CATA changed me a great deal. It has made me intellectually more sedate. What probably benefited me most was the literary quality of drama. I've been developing a very strong sense of lens and visual images since I was young, but I was more interested in technique at that time.

Chapter One

Drama, however, pulls you back from that and redirects your attention to characters and the overall nature of a work. These are the strong elements drama can offer. In other words, the key issue here is whether form stands above content or content stands above form. In the end, I've returned to the latter. Because I studied painting when young, I always felt structure and form should stand above content. But the education at CATA transformed me. I read many plays in college, and all of them were classics, just like classical works in literature. Their artistic charm was irresistible. As a result, I was literarily molded and enhanced. Because of its emphasis on classical training, I think CATA is a pretty good school.

Certainly I feel we should draw a clear line between film and drama. Perhaps film and drama share the same origins, but they are two entirely different forms. It doesn't mean that the two can't be combined. Sometimes the combination could also generate works in good taste. But such a combination would always contain something that is artistically puzzling. I am more and more convinced, therefore, that film is film. Film as a form of expression can achieve many things that drama can't. Conversely, drama also has unique characteristics that film doesn't possess. I have more contacts with the people in theatrical circles, but it should be pointed out that drama has indistinctly cultivated me in other areas of knowledge, not in the area of film. Furthermore, drama can even obscure ones cinematic thinking. Film is an independent language. If you don't enhance your training in film language, you are merely a director good at storytelling, not a film director, because as a film director, you need to equip yourself with more mature technical training and exploration of the language of film. Or, possibly, you could contribute to the improvement of film language. This is what requires a film director. The main purpose of drama is storytelling and characterization. It relies, therefore, more on actors and actresses. Compared to drama, film demands less of acting. Many issues could be solved through cinematic devices. My co-workers, including art designers and actors, therefore, are all required to reach certain level of understanding in film language.

Li Xin

I was born on the third day of the Chinese New Year of 1969 into a family of Shanghai filmmakers. My father is a veteran filmmaker of the Shanghai Film Studio, having made such "main melody" films as *Celebration of the Founding of the People's Republic of China* and *Out of Xibaipo*.[xiii] My sister, who is several years younger than I, is also a director, whose feature debut is *Flying High with You*.

In my pre-college years, I was always uncomfortable with my poor academic performance at elementary and high schools. This uneasiness became more acute when the date of the college entrance exam approached. What was my plan for the future? What kind of college did I want to go? These issues troubled me a lot at that time. Luckily, although I was no good in the subjects of mathematics, physics, and chemistry, my Chinese composition was ranked quite high in class. Whenever I started to use a new composition book, my essay always turned out to be a model one, which was read aloud in class. I didn't know why, but a new composition book stimulated me. I felt especially comfortable when writing in a new composition book. As the new composition book turned shabby from repeated use, the quality of my composition also deteriorated. But strangely enough, my last essay in a composition book would become a model once again. Maybe it was because I figured it was the last opportunity to pay tribute to traces of something in me.

I became a Shanghai Film Studio director in 1991, right after my four-years of study at BFA. In 1995, I made my feature debut, *Your Black Hair and My Hand*. You can say I was lucky to have this opportunity, but it was also due to the hard work. My sister Li Hong was even luckier. She made her debut feature only one year after graduation from BFA. Therefore, I feel that one's quite fortunate to be a film director in China. As long as you don't give up your dream, with a little help from the unknown, you can eventually reach your goal. The most difficult thing, I think, is to find financing. Labeled as the "Class of 1987", we were confronted with a very real problem after graduating in 1991, that is: we had to raise money ourselves to get our films made. For instance, although my debut feature, *Your Black Hair and My Hand*, was released by the state-owned Shanghai Film Studio, I was the one who found the production money. It seemed very clear to me that, because I raised the financing myself, I was responsible to the film's investors and had to make sure the film would be shown domestically. In other words, I couldn't simply do what I wanted to do. However, I have been quite firm on one issue. I won't make any films I don't feel like, no matter how much I am going to be paid. To generalize this attitude, I think we as a group, labeled either as the "Sixth Generation" or simply as the "Young Generation", actually view individuality as the most important thing in filmmaking. We must first make sure our films reflect who we are and what we want. On the other hand, however, we have also gradually discovered a certain "middle road" that not only guarantees the presence of our personal touch but at the same time gives our films a very beautiful look. To me, finding such a road is not too difficult, the road that leads to acceptance by the government, by the market, as well as by the ordinary Chinese people.

Chapter One

Liu Bingjian

I was born in October 1963 in Dangshan, Anhui Province. When I turned five, I started to develop an interest in drawing, a hobby that has never left me since. Even today, I still have many friends in the fine arts circle and often attend their activities and exhibitions. My little daughter is also an amateur painter now.

After high school, I was offered a job in the Publicity Department of the Bengbu Municipal Government in Anhui. I soon became bored with that job and decided to go to Beijing to study film. Fortunately, because of my background in painting, I was admitted in 1985 to BFA's Cinematography Department. In 1989, right after my graduation from BFA, I was recruited to CCTV, China's largest TV station. But even that job failed to rein in my restlessness. I soon quit and decided to work as an independent filmmaker. It so happened that a subsidiary company of the Shenzhen Baoan Investment Group wanted to invest in filmmaking, and I was one of the candidates they approached. So, I responded with the script to *The Stone Bed*. I still can't quite figure out how and why they reached the decision that *The Stone Bed* was the one they wanted to finance. Of course the whole process was not just a simple "Yes". Several scriptwriters were called in to revise the draft, and it took quite an effort to finalize the shooting script. Despite this, however, I must say that my road to filmmaking was not particularly bumpy. Following *The Stone Bed*, my debut feature, I made *Men and Women*, *Crying Woman*, and, most recently, *Plastic Flowers*.

Lou Ye

I have been studying painting since I was a child. Before entering BFA in 1985, I attended a vocational high school for fine arts that had been set up by the Shanghai Animation Studio to train new talent for animation films. Because of my love of painting, my dream was to attend CAFA. When taking the entrance exam in Beijing, I was told I could list another school as my second choice. Coincidentally, BFA was also recruiting students at that time. I therefore added its name. As it turned out, I was rejected by CAFA in the first round, which made me quite depressed. But the road to BFA was exceptionally smooth. There were four rounds of examination, and one by one I passed them all. Since I majored in film at BFA, it was natural for me to choose it as my profession.

Certainly my family also had some influence on me. My parents taught stage and theater performance at the Shanghai Academy of Theater Arts. So, I was able to see many films that were not open to the public, such as Alfred Hitchcock's and Japanese black and white films, including *Twenty*

Four Eyes.[xiv] I was young back then and didn't understand too much of what I saw. But when these films were shown at BFA, I thought, "Yes, I've seen these films before!"

When studying at BFA, I habitually skipped classes and went to see films. Wang Xiaoshuai and I, our entire class even, saw so many films that Zheng Dongtian[xv] once remarked: "Few Chinese directors could compare with you in the quantity of films seen at BFA." But the number of films we saw back then no longer seems especially remarkable, now that pirated DVDs are widely available. There are not too many old films on pirated DVD, though. [At BFA] we saw a variety of films considered historically important, many of them in black and white.

Lu Chuan

My childhood dream was to become a writer, a fiction writer. I entered a military college in 1989. The reason I enrolled in a military college was quite simple. I had witnessed the whole June Fourth Movement, which my parents also experienced. Knowing my temperament quite well, they felt I would be unsafe if I enrolled at a regular public university and was left alone in society. They thought it would be much safer for me to be in a military college, just like putting me in an iron box. Therefore, out of the concern for my safety, they chose a military college for me. At that time, this college only had an English major in its Foreign Language Department, so I majored in American literature. My graduation thesis was on J. D. Salinger, author of *The Catcher in the Rye*.

Although I come from an English studies background, I always have an obsession with film. My close contact with film came from watching movies outdoors on the military drill ground. When I was in high school, I saw films by the Fifth Generation filmmakers. The films that had the greatest impact on me were Zhang Yimou's *Red Sorghum*, Chen Kaige's *Yellow Earth*, and Zhang Junzhao's *One and Eight*. I was tremendously inspired by these three films. From then on I made up my mind to become a film director. Ultimately, therefore, my engagement in filmmaking was due to the influence of the Fifth Generation. This is probably the reason why up to today I still think film must be powerful in expression. Such an expression should not be individual whispers or solitary conversation, but a powerful voice of the times.

My passion for film led me to the decision to take the entrance examination for BFA. God helped me, offering me the opportunity to study at BFA. Since I was still a serviceman at that time, I only had one chance to take the exam. I actually tricked my working unit and got the letter of introduction with the official seal. As a result, I was admitted. But even after

Chapter One

I was admitted into BFA my unit wouldn't let me go. In the end, I was kicked out of the military. Taking off the uniform was quite painful for me because I was working in unit that paid quite well, as it was involved in military businesses. Besides, my colleagues and the people I dealt with were the smart ones with high IQs. They belong to the productive force of society. In comparison, artistic creation doesn't constitute a productive force and therefore can't determine the progress of a society. It is not something that requires backbone. At best it may be regarded as the spiritual backbone of a society. But up to this moment no one has ever reached that level, and the one who could serve as both the societal and spiritual backbones has yet to be born. Since I joined the film circle, therefore, I've always had the feeling that there are plenty of people in this circle who do not possess the ability to uphold society spiritually, although they claim to. This is at least true of me as an amateur-turned filmmaker. I feel I was motivated to take up filmmaking as a profession because I was not satisfied with what I'd seen. In other words, I think I do have something important to say, and I feel what I was going to say ought to be more meaningful. At least I can prove that people like me are capable of fighting for their cinematic voices. Back then, there were heated debates about whether BFA should take graduate students who had no training in film at all prior to their entry. I feel such debates are pointless. What you need to pay attention to is exactly this group of applicants, because they are the ones who have things to say. It would be meaningless if you always entrust the rights of filmmaking to those who have nothing to say or who have no passion for what they say.

I was assigned to the Beijing Film Studio after my graduate study at BFA and have been an active director at BFS since 1998. I don't think too much about being a studio director. To me, working in a state-owned studio is quite simple since the rules of the game have long been established. As a filmmaker, I should act in accordance with these rules.

Lu Xuechang

I was born in 1964, old enough to dimly sense the residual taint of the Cultural Revolution. It is analogous to the novel *How the Steel Was Tempered* in my film *The Making of Steel*. It seems to me that we are among the last group of people who have read that novel. Those who are two or three years younger seem to have little interest in the book. Our coming of age coincided with the period during which China underwent tremendous changes, the years 1966, 1976, 1978, for instance, and then the profound social transformation that is still taking place. I feel the forces that have had an impact on us are innumerable but somewhat chaotic. To be frank, we have our own conservative side, but there is also some kind of rebellious spirit in us, especially when we were just out of college. My own feeling, therefore, is that we are a group of people full of contradictions. Although eager to embrace a lot of new things, at the same time we also feel that among them many are quite decadent. It only took us several years to associate marijuana and cocaine with corruption and rottenness.

I was into painting at the beginning, but later was disappointed with myself. I was admitted to the high school affiliated with the Central Academy of Fine Arts, and it was quite natural that my next step should be CAFA. But I spent too much time on gouache, which soaked my oil painting with light colors. Because I felt one must master oil painting in order to have a career in painting, I became discouraged. I have always been good at Chinese. I have won various awards in essay competitions since elementary school. I didn't give up writing even when I was focusing on painting at the CAFA-affiliated high school. Later, by chance, I became acquainted with a teacher at CATA. who is also a stage director. After we got to know each other, I once went to see him rehearse a play. I was fascinated. Then, I organized an amateur dramatic group at the CAFA-affiliated high school, putting on short plays adapted from works of Japan, Sweden, and other countries. Thanks to these experiments, I gradually fell in love with performing arts. Afterward, some of my senior friends were admitted to BFA, mainly majoring in Art Direction. Thus, I got the opportunity to hang around on the BFA campus. At that time, there were film screenings every Thursday at BFA, and I went with my friends. I said I was initially influenced by the French New Wave, especially films by Francois Truffaut, and by Michelangelo Antonioni. As a matter of fact, I saw their films even before I went to BFA. After seeing their films, I felt overwhelmed. Their films made me feel that filmmaking was what I wanted most. But I didn't make up my mind right away until my comic strip mentor, He Youzhi, gave me a push. "Since you are good at both writing and painting", he said, "you should give BFA a try". Weighing several factors, therefore, I decided to go to BFA.

I studied film directing at BFA. At that time BFA happened to have implemented something called "Two-Four System". Based on the number of units you earned, you would be either qualified for four-year studies or kicked out after two years if you ranked among the last four or five in your class. I remember there were two female students in our class, but they were kicked out after two years. They learned smoking and drinking at BFA and disappeared. They are doing fine right now, however, working for various departments of the Central Television Station (CCTV).

I graduated from BFA in 1989. The unit I originally intended to join no longer took college graduates after the June Fourth incident. Thus I stayed at home for more than a year. After this waiting period, I was assigned to the

Chapter One

Beijing Film Studio. But within a year or so at BFS, my health suddenly deteriorated. I got a kidney disease and was hospitalized. I almost felt I won't have anything to do with film during that period. When I returned to film after an operation and recovery, three years had passed. I still can't figure out why things changed so fast in these three years. Three years ago we were buddies, but everybody looked entirely different when we met again. Marijuana smoking, partying, and other weird things had emerged while I was sick. The initial motive of my first film, therefore, was actually to express this sense of shock and bewilderment. I hadn't walked out of my home one single step in more than three years. Yes, literally, I didn't go out of the door at all and refused to see any friends. Thus I was tremendously shocked when I was suddenly exposed to the outside world. Stimulated, I began to write the screenplay of *The Making of Steel*.

Ma Liwen

I've been writing stories since I was a teenager. After entering CATA, I gradually fell in love with film. However, I was clueless about film in the beginning. It was the education at CATA that really shaped me. I learned many things there. I was admitted in 1993 to CATA's three-year program in film and television directing. It was the first time CATA had such a program. Most professors came either from CATA or from BFA. We also had many opportunities to meet with experienced directors, who were invited to give talks at our program. Besides, we watched numerous films, either on DVD or on tape, when studying at CATA. As for practice, our works were mostly shot with M7, M9, or M3 cameras. There were also classes about two-camera shooting, etc. I am probably the first one in my class to make a feature film.

I read Zhang Jie's *Gone Is the One Who Held Me the Dearest in the World* as early as in 1996.[xvi] I discovered the novel at a bookstand outside Beijing right after graduation in 1996. The long title of the novel attracted my attention. I quickly finished it and was overwhelmed. It reads like a poetic essay, simple and tranquil. I didn't even know how I could covey its greatness to other people. Then, I sent the novel to my mom, who at that time was taking care of my grandmother in Tianjin. She called me immediately after finishing the novel. Sad and uneasy, she told me that she also shared many of the guilty feelings of the protagonist. Before long, my grandmother passed away. This had a strong emotional impact on mom. Certainly it was not completely due to the influence of the novel, but the book made her more emotional and repentant. Even today, she still can't get escape from regret and guilt. Then, I also passed the novel on to my close friends, who more or less loved it. Encouraged by the positive response, I came up with the idea of adapting it into a film. I really felt there are many details in the novel that could easily be translated into images. Simple and tranquil, the novel expresses a lot of views I share. For example, a lover can be replaced, but there is only one mother; life is in fact a process of continuously losing one's loved ones, one by one, and this is human beings' greatest pain. In addition, the novel depicts the daughter-mother relationship from a fresh angle.

Having decided to make the book into a film, I met with the author, Zhang Jie. It turned out to be a difficult task to persuade Zhang to grant me the rights to adapt her book into a film. She simply disagreed. Why did she disagree? She told me that it was a personal experience shared by her and her mother. She regretted about what she did to her mom, and therefore didn't want to turn it into a public topic. Besides, her works had never been adapted as either film or television drama. She believed all films and TV dramas that are based on literary works tend to deviate from the original. If the adapted film failed to convey the right feeling, it would indeed hurt her mother. Also, she thought a person of my age couldn't possibly understand the relationship between a sixty-year-old daughter and an eighty-year-old mother. Even today, she is still bothered by the moral burden of "mistreating" her mother. This guilty feeling will surely be with her the rest of her life. She sleeps on her mother's single bed, and her study room is so dark that there is only one small window decorated with her mother's photos.

I tried and tried, but my persistence went nowhere. Zhang Jie was still unconvinced and won't grant me the rights. Inexperienced, I pushed the matter too hard and was adamantly rejected. I felt very sad at that time because I really loved the novel. The book almost fell apart after repeated readings. She left me with the impression that nobody was capable of adapting it into a film, even Zhang Yimou. Actually, there was no such a need at all. She simply didn't like the film form. Sadly, I walked away.

As it turned out, it would take me three years to finally win her approval. I left a note at her door when I stopped pushing her, saying that I liked her work no matter what happens. In 1999, Zhang dialed the number I wrote on the note and asked me if she could meet with me. She asked me if I was still interested in the adaptation. Of course, I said. Then she wanted me to first finish the script. If the script was satisfying, she said to me, she would grant me the film rights. Because the script was the key to the successful execution of the plan, I locked myself up for more than three months and eventually got the job done. I was extremely nervous about how she would respond and therefore hesitated to show the script to her. What if she didn't feel right about the script? That would mean the death sentence of the whole project. Unexpectedly, however, she called me on the following day: "OK, go find money. You are the only one authorized to do the adaptation." It was as simple as that.

Chapter One

The long process of securing funding followed. I didn't anticipate that I would encounter so many obstacles along the way. I first found a production director, asking him how much I would need to get the film done. I said to him: you must help me with this. This is not about me pursuing the dream of being a director. To be or not to be a director is only for reputation's sake, but what I really want to do was make people accept the story. Then, I called Siqin Gaowa, asking her to play the leading role of *Gone Is the One Who Held Me the Dearest in the World*. I wanted her because I had seen an interview program on a small TV station in which Siqin Gaowa talked about her marriage and family. I had never seen Siqin Gaowa acting like that before, totally relaxed and being herself. From her facial expression, I discovered contradiction and complexity. It was a heavy topic, and the interviewer asked thought-provoking questions. I felt this was exactly what I wanted from Siqin Gaowa. Thus, I dialed her number. Siqin Gaowa's voice sounded very low, but she agreed to meet me the next day. At the meeting, she told me that she was quite busy and asked me to leave the script with her and she would get back to me in two weeks. I remember she said to me: you are so young. I left without much discussion. To my surprise, she called me the following day, asking me what I needed from her besides playing the lead. I said I was still looking for more investors. In the whole filming process, Siqin Gaowa gave me a lot of help, including introducing me to her friends familiar with the copyright issue.

After the film was screened, some people said that the film's theme has social significance and universal appeal. As a matter of fact, those things didn't even occur to me in the process of filming. I only wanted to tell a true story. I didn't want to make a superficially sentimental film. Ideally, each viewer would respond differently after watching the film. One day, I invited several friends to watch a test screening. Originally, we planned to dine together after the film. But everyone silently went home afterward. It is a simple but powerful film. Although it took me almost five years to finally get the project done, I felt I did a worthy thing. Having studied film directing, I felt it is quite natural for me to take this road. As for the audience, everyone has his or her own way of looking at things. It is quite normal for them to differ from each other.

Meng Qi

I was born in 1972. My father teaches drama and literature at the Shanghai Academy of Theater Art. When I was a child, I had little interest in drama and film. I used to hang out with the shooting crews as a teenager, and many of the crew members asked me to play roles in their films. But I refused. Then, they showed me some camera tricks, and sometimes I was lured into assisting the cameraman. Because I was young then, everybody treated me well, which made me feel a little spoiled. It was quite an enjoyable experience hanging out with the crews, because everyone acted like family. As for filmmaking itself, however, I indeed had no interest at all.

After retiring from active military service, I opened a small restaurant in Shandong. It was quite a life lesson for me. Every morning I got up between 5:00 and 6:00 to buy fresh meat and vegetables, and it was not until 1:00 or 2:00 AM that I was able to go to bed. During business hours, whether willing or unwilling, I had to welcome every customer with a big smile. In no time I became a self-taught expert of public relations. My old friends from the military came to the restaurant and couldn't accept the fact that I'd changed so much. They asked me where I'd learned this kind of false courtesy. I also didn't like the way I lived. It was simply being too hypocritical.

Fortunately, at that time, I was also able to live another life in my own advertising company. When sitting by the editing table, I was always troubled by the feeling that each product had to be summed up in a very short period of time. It was terrible that time could become such a menace to creativity. The practice in advertising, therefore, made me quite appreciative of films that unfold gradually and smoothly. Just like what slow running does for a healthy person, films that unfold without hurrying also bring one a smooth and joyful sense of rhythm. You can therefore say that the idea of making a film of my own emerged from my dissatisfaction with advertising. Before engaging in advertising, like many others, I watched movies only for fun. The idea of making a film never came to my mind. Having accumulated some knowledge of advertising, however, I suddenly developed a special feeling toward shadow images. Increasingly, I felt I watched films more from a creator's point of view than from that of the viewer. What inspired me most were the big screens at nightclubs and bars. Images on those screens confronted your eyes without sound. Whether it was a feature film or a sports event, because of the absence of dialogue or commentary, the images acquired their own rhythm. They were pure and live images. Experiencing the flow of those images from a different angle, you felt that they were telling you a different kind of story.

After realizing that film is the best medium for self-expression, I decided to give filmmaking a try. I of course had to do a lot of the pre-production work. I started first with the selection of an adaptable novel. I thought of writing my own script, but one of my friends reminded me that one's life experience and age determine the depth and quality of his/her works. His advice enlightened me. Without enough accumulation of real life experiences, one always tends to view the world with too much ego and emotion. Why can one tell the difference between a masterpiece and a

Chapter One

mediocre work almost from the very first sentence of a novel? That's largely because of life experience and age. Young and inexperienced, therefore, I turned to the library for help. During a short span of time, I read a great number of novels and stories. As a matter of fact, I discovered Liang Xiaosheng's short story "The Tired Man", which I based my film *What a Snowy Day* on.[xvii] The story left such a deep impression on me that I could retell almost every detail of the story to my friend when we met at a restaurant. My friend said to me: "You want to be a filmmaker, right? Why don't you make a film based on this story?" From then on, I made up my mind and worked hard toward that goal.

The process of adaptation was a difficult one. The script changed four times. After the first version was finished, both I and my partners were jubilant. Every one of us was talking big about the future of the film and our contribution to film art. We immediately submitted the script to the censorship committee and begged them to give us feedback as soon as possible. But I guess the committee was quite busy at the time, and it was not until before the Spring Festival of 1998 that the "verdict" arrived. The comments were quite simple, just saying that the script failed to meet the requirements of a standard screenplay and must be rewritten in accordance with the standard format. Now I feel we shouldn't be so dogmatic and formulaic in this respect. But at the time, I immediately started to rework the script. I summoned a group of friends and we convened in a conference room to discuss how to revise the script. They were my longtime buddies and none of them had anything to do with film: some were restaurant owners, some were taxi drivers, and some were my comrades from the military service. It was quite interesting for this group of people, during our leisure time, to sit together to discuss something serious. I said to them at the meeting: Now I want to make a film. Although none of you is a writer or artist, I value your opinion highly on this matter. It turned out that everybody in this environment offered his opinion, including some suggestions on the script. To be frank, there were few constructive suggestions, but I think it was conducive to the whole creative process.

Then, I started to revise the script. I first found several college students and asked them to come up with the first draft. But the result was far from what I expected. My sister was then a student of the Literature Department of the Shanghai Academy of Theater Art. She also attended several meetings about the revision of the script. So, I asked her for help. It turned out that her version was a satisfying one. We then submitted the revised script to the censorship committee. We were even more anxious this time, hoping to get an immediate answer. But after another long wait, the answer still didn't come. Troubled by the slow response, we took the script to Liang

Xiaosheng, author of the original story. Liang told us that the script was quite impressive, good enough as a basis for shooting.

Encouraged by Liang's words, we began to solicit investors without waiting for the green light from the censorship committee. Certainly this was quite an exhausting process. We presented our ideas to nearly 100 potential investors but none of them was willing to take the risk. It was not until after eleven months that we were finally able to convince several investors. I don't think we succeeded by coincidence. I believe the famous Chinese proverb: No difficulty is insurmountable if one sets one's mind on it. The key to persuasion is whether or not you can win your partner's trust and showcase your own potential as worthy of further development. Also, you need to show them your seriousness and spirit of devotion. My investors didn't give much thought about making money from this project. They knew filmmaking was not a profitable business in China, but they were persuaded by our persistence and sincerity. We were told later that what impressed them most was our passion and devotion, which they too had in their youth. Although they had succeeded in their businesses, they were still very grateful to those who had supported them before. Now it was their turn to lend a hand to us. Until today, I still feel I owe them a great deal. After all, it is not easy to get something done, and it is even more difficult to make a film. Although I had accumulated some experience in advertising, I was a blank sheet of paper in filmmaking. But even in this situation, they still trusted their judgment. So, what should I do except express my deep gratitude?

Shi Runjiu

I was born in Shanghai because my father is a native of Shanghai. When I was a little child, I traveled between Shanghai and Beijing quite frequently for my parents work in Beijing. When I was about to graduate from elementary school, my parents took me to Beijing and I settled down in there permanently.

My earliest dream was to become a traffic policeman, because traffic policemen look quite cool in uniform when maintaining order of the streets. Then, I dreamed of being a translator. Finally, I wanted to be a director. The director's dream was nourished at the time when I was a freshman at high school. As an outstanding student, I attended a summer camp, which included a program that featured speakers from all walks of life. One of the invited speakers was a female teacher specializing in children's plays. I started becoming increasingly interested in drama since then and gradually fell in love with it.

I passed the entrance exam of both CATA and BFA, but entered CATA because it was my first choice. Even today, I still think drama is purer than

Chapter One

film in expressing human beings' inner spiritual world. I directed a few plays while at CATA, including *Fast Runner or Nowhere to Hide*, which was included in Meng Jinghui's anthology *Archives of Chinese Avant-Garde Plays*.[xviii] Certainly my interest in film didn't wane. When I was a sophomore, many professors from BFA came to our school to teach. Besides, because I almost became a student of BFA, I knew quite a few students there. Every weekend, I hung out with them at BFA.

I shifted my focus to filmmaking because the demand for drama is simply sluggish. When I was a college student, there were many theatergoing audiences. But around 1991, when I was about to graduate, there were few stage plays. With the popularization of television and the further opening-up of China to the outside world, more and more forms of entertainment, such as karaoke, TV series and discos, became readily available to the general public. In the past, people had few choices in entertainment. Because there was no television, people spent most of their time listening to radio or going to stage shows. But as the society embraces all kinds of new entertainment forms, the market for plays has gradually dwindled.

I started out as a MTV director and documentary filmmaker. For a period of time after graduation, I traveled all over China making films about various kinds of people. Most of my MTV films were about underground rock bands in Beijing. As a matter of fact, I still make MTV today, sometimes two or three songs every year, sometimes five or six, but I only do those I find interesting. Money is no longer my concern. The process of making MTV is quite experimental. Although investment is small and time is limited, making MTV allows me to do all kinds of visual experiments and technical explorations. It is a pleasurable process, during which I can express the inner quality of music without worrying too much about things beyond music itself.

I started to make feature films with the support of Peter Loehr's Imar Film. Both *A Beautiful New World* and *All the Way* were financed by Imar Film. Because of my love for MTV, my original plan was to make a film about rock musicians as my feature debut. But since the cost of making such a film would involve not only filming but also composing, which could easily exceed the 3 million RMB mark that Imar Film agreed to invest, I had to give up the plan and made *A Beautiful New World* instead. This film was based on a true story I read about in a newspaper. A farmer in the Guangdong Province bought a lottery ticket and won. So he went to Guangzhou to claim his prize, which was an apartment. But the apartment building was not finished yet. He had to either wait or convert the prize into cash. I was attracted by the news because the farmer's dilemma was shared by most Chinese in the mid- and late 1990s. This was the time when the government just implemented the new housing policy and ordinary Chinese had to rely on themselves to buy apartments in the housing market. To own a house or an apartment became a dream of many people. I felt the story accurately reflected the collective spirit of that time. Therefore, I settled on *A Beautiful New World*. Of course I changed the story's setting to Shanghai.

If I succeeded in conveying the peculiar "Shanghai" flavor of the main character, Jin Fang, I must thank the two screenplay writers, Wang Yao and Liu Fengdou. Wang Yao was especially keen at grasping the characteristics of the Shanghai girl. Although a native of Beijing, he seems to have a good understanding of the Shanghai woman. When I took the screenplay to Shanghai, an idea suddenly came to me, which was to add some Shanghai flavor to the dialogue. Thus, we found a student at the Shanghai Academy of Theater Art and asked her to re-read the screenplay. She told us that the main character felt like a Shanghai girl but her dialogue didn't. She then spent three days making changes here and there. After her revision, Jin Fang not only behaves but also speaks like a Shanghai girl.

Tang Danian

When I was in high school, literature was my favorite subject. At that time, I felt film was an "uncultured" thing. But my academic performance was extremely poor back then, often five out of six points below a passing grade, with the exception of Chinese, in which I usually scored a "C" or "C minus". My only hope for a college education, therefore, was BFA. Certainly family origin also played a role: my father worked at BFA, and my mother taught in the Literature Department of BFA. As a matter of fact, I had no idea that BFA's Literature Department was going to recruit new students that year. The news was brought back by my mom. I therefore started to prepare myself for the entrance exam. After entering BFA, I slowly developed an interest in film and later on began to fall in love with it.

I entered BFA in 1985. It was a special year because all departments of BFA, including Directing, Cinematography, Art Directing, Sound, and Literature, admitted new students. This was the first time after 1978 that BFA accepted new students for all majors. The years 1987 and 1989 also saw the full recruitment for BFA, but there was a seven-year lapse between the class of 1978 and that of 1985. Between 1978 and 1985, BFA recruited new students each year, but those recruitments didn't cover all majors in a single year. For instances, in 1984, only the Performing Arts Department admitted new students; in 1983, although the Cinematography and Art Directing departments had new students, the Directing Department didn't accept any new students. It was not easy, therefore, for these students to form a creative team. The class of 1985 was different. At that time, the class of 1978, or the

Chapter One

so-called "Fifth Generation", had already graduated in 1982, and only a scattering of students were admitted before the class of 1985. There was occasional cross-level teamwork, but most cooperation took place among students of the same level. We took classes together, lived together, and, more importantly, did our student works together. In addition, the Class of 1985 was the only one to which the so-called "Two-Four System" was applied. This experiment stipulated that each student's academic performance would be carefully evaluated after two years of study. Those who didn't pass the evaluation would only be awarded an associate degree and asked to leave the Academy. Those who passed the review were allowed to continue their studies for another two years. At that time, each major normally had 16 students. After two years, however, almost half of them were eliminated. The relationships among students, therefore, were often tense and quite unpleasant. The problem is that there is no settled standard to measure the success of art. How could one possibly decide who could stay and who should leave? They should have just admitted eight students in the first place. After one year's practice, therefore, the system was abolished.

After graduation in 1989, I've maintained contacts with many of my classmates. I began working with Zhang Yuan. Later on, I also worked with Wang Xiaoshuai. I wrote an outline for Zhang Yuan's *East Palace, West Palace*, but Zhang later asked Wang Xiaobo to finish the script of that film. As for cooperation with Wang Xiaoshuai, I helped him write the outlines of *Frozen* and *Beijing Bicycle*. Then, I joined Lou Ye's ambitious project "Super City". Lou of course was the one who initiated the project. I didn't know how Lou got acquainted with a "Beer City" boss in Shanghai. This beer boss wanted to promote his business. So, he asked Lou Ye to make a TV series. But Lou managed to talk him into dropping the TV series plan and investing in a 10-film project. The idea was to find 10 young directors to make 10 films, and each of them must use the Beer City as the setting. To coordinate such a project was itself a complicated matter because it concerned about 10 individuals with strong personalities. Besides, since there was only one producer in charge of the whole project, it was quite difficult for him to individually manage 10 different crews.

It turned out that only three films were eventually completed. Lou Ye made *Suzhou River*, which was shot on film, I made *Jade*, and Guan Hu completed *Midnight Walker*. Guan Hu's and mine were TV movies shot on digital video. As a matter of fact, besides these three, there were two other films almost completed, but the Beer City boss stopped funding after the first three, which left those two films uncut. The Beer City boss terminated the contract because he didn't see what he wanted in the first three films. Guan Hu's *Midnight Walker* tells the story of one night of a murderer's life in

Shanghai. It consists of dubious scenes like drug addiction and prostitution, even including the scene of a runaway ape from the Shanghai Zoo. Mine was more or less experimental, with disordered space and time. It is about a young couple of the 1930s traveling through time and coming to contemporary Shanghai. It is in fact a hoax, and the film ends with the couple returning to the 1930s. The Beer City boss, of course, was not happy with what I described above. He stopped the funding and the project was never completely finished. As digital films, the *Midnight Walker* and *Jade* were once shown at the Pusan and Hong Kong film festivals.

Most crew members of my first feature (shot on film) *City Paradise* came from the Class of 1985: Meng Fan was the cinematographer, and Wang Lin was the sound recorder and mixer. Wang studied film at Ohio University in Athens, Ohio, after graduating from BFA. The rough cut of *City Paradise* was actually done at Athens. Because we didn't have enough money for postproduction, Wang took the film to Ohio. The university offered AVID equipment for free. In return, Wang used the film as part of his graduate work. After that, we got some money from Rotterdam, which enabled us to finish the final cut of *City Paradise* in Australia.

Wang Chao

I was born in Nanjing in 1964 into a working class family. My parents are factory workers, and I used to be a worker myself for five or six years. Consciously or unconsciously, this working class background is always in my blood.

During my teenage days, I was frequently sick. I had a problem with bronchitis. Because I was always sick I spent a lot of time thinking, using my imagination. Before the age of twenty-seven, I was a young man fond of literature. Influenced by Bei Dao's[xix] theory and practice, I was first drawn to poetry. At that time, Bei Dao and his circle claimed montage was the proper method of writing poetry. My poems, therefore, were dismissed for their "un-montage" characteristics. They liked fragmented sentences, parallel and contrasting images, and the interaction and conflicts of images. This kind of poetry was impossible to me. I was good at repetition and variation in a limited way, but an apple in my writings was indeed an apple. It was impossible for me to associate an apple with a tractor. Later on, having read André Bazin's theory, I spoke to myself with a sense of relief: Isn't it true that my writings reified Bazin's long-take theory in poetry? At that time, I never thought of either filmmaking or scriptwriting. What I intended to do was to apply these filmic concepts to poetry writing. Regrettably, not a single poem of mine was officially published, although occasionally one could find my poems in unofficial publications. I did better in story writing, though. I

Chapter One

started to write short stories in 1994, three years after I was admitted to the evening class of BFA. My first short story "The South" is about a high school student from a small county of Hunan Province who, after becoming a big city construction worker, becomes acquainted with a single mother from the North who sells cigarettes for a living. The story appeared in 1995 in the prestigious literary magazine, *The Story Circle*. Actually, prior to my debut feature *The Orphan of Anyang*, I'd published four stories—two short stories and two novellas.

I've also had a long obsession with film. My love for film was nearly equal to that for literature even before I came to Beijing to study film. I remember buying film cartoons was a regular act of mine at junior middle school. As long as there was a new foreign film-based cartoon book for sale, I would rush to the bookstore to get hold of it. Immediately after entering high school, I subscribed to the magazine *World Cinema*, then called *Film Translation Series*. The look of the magazine underwent several changes. In 1979, it became black and white, but the quality of paper remained fairly good and glossy. Nowadays the magazine is larger in size. In addition to *World Cinema*, I was also a regular reader of a few other film journals. The early exposure to these materials made me no stranger to Western film theories.

Watching film was a significant part of my life in Nanjing. I remember watching many Japanese films during the initial implementation of the "open-door" policy in the early 1980s. Later, I was able to see Truffaut's *The Last Metro*, Roman Polanski's *Tess*, even including Steven Spielberg's *Duel*. I didn't know who Spielberg was at that time, but the film was simply awesome. As a matter of fact, at the time of my junior and high school years, we were able to see a variety of films in addition to Soviet cinema and television programs. For example, Fassbinder's *Lili Marleen* was publicly shown at theaters. There was also this Hungarian/German film called *Mephisto*. I remember watching this film three or four times. I went to almost all the screenings of this film. Another film that impressed me was *Paris, Texas*. This cinematic diversity, in my opinion, has disappeared nowadays.

Because of my passion for film, I applied for admission to BFA's regular BA program in 1990. I passed all specialized exams, but failed general subjects. At the age of twenty-six, it was hard for me to pick up those materials. In the following year, however, I decided to register for the evening program of BFA, because I no longer felt there was a big difference between the regular and evening programs. I only wanted to come here to experience the life at the academy and to watch as many films as possible. I was a late starter; I got into the school when I was twenty-seven. But I think I went in with a lot of life experience. In a lot of ways, compared to other young students I was more mature in my writing and social skills.

Unconsciously, though, I probably also wanted to see my childhood fantasy through. Aloof and unsociable in character, I tended to keep things to myself. When I was in my teens, my health deteriorated. I coughed endlessly and vomited blood. It was a strange disease, and no doctor was able to tell whether it was bronchitis or tuberculosis. It came every other year. Fortunately, it was not life-threatening, only a few mouthfuls of blood. But the disease made me fantasize about death, both physically and philosophically. Although poetry is supposed to be fantastic, and film narrative, I didn't view them that way. My poems tended to be narrative, and I viewed film as something resulting from fantasy. I felt film had this ability to penetrate one's mind and psychology. I found active and dream-like fantasies in film. This is probably why I wanted to become a filmmaker in the first place.

This being said, I didn't set my goal to become a filmmaker in the first two years after I came to BFA. My urge for self-expression was channeled through story and poetry writings. It was not until the last two years of BFA study that I started to seriously think about making films. I muddled along on the BFA campus for four years, spending a lot of time auditing classes in various departments, particularly in the department of cinematography. My attendance for some classes was even better than that of regular students. As for film screenings, I usually watched a film twice, once in afternoon, once in evening. In 1994, I made up my mind to become a filmmaker.

In the following year, I was confronted with a crucial decision. I could either continue my work at the small studio I had signed on to manage, which looked like a plum advertising gig, or join the Chen Kaige Film Workshop. The workshop was not a school. If I didn't do well, I could be scolded or even expelled. There was also no guarantee of getting paid. Because the workshop was just set up, the financial situation seemed very shaky, and the monthly stipend was quite low. But there were also a lot of advantages to working with Chen Kaige. At least I could get hands-on training in filmmaking. The practical aspect of filmmaking was exactly what I lacked. My passion for filmmaking, therefore, made me decide to join the Chen Kaige Film Workshop. It was a turning point for me. It turned out that I picked the right people at the right time. When I first came to Chen's workshop, *Temptress Moon* was in its postproduction stage. I remember recording the discussions between Zhao Jiyun, the film's second composer who replaced Xu Xiaofeng, the film's original composer, and the director. I felt I had suddenly entered a very solid and concrete space. There were no discussions or arguments over film as an art form, only practical issues about how to get things done. Art is another matter. Everyone could have an

Chapter One

opinion about art. Professionally speaking, I think Chen Kaige is an extraordinary filmmaker. His professionalism and rigorousness, in my opinion, is superior to that of Zhang Yimou.

After *Temptress Moon*, the workshop did Chen's *The Emperor and the Assassin*. I learned a lot during the process of working on this film. If it was a film about contemporary life, I think I wouldn't have gained so much, because cinematic elements tend to decrease for films about contemporary society. As a period drama, *The Emperor and the Assassin* required a high standard for costume, make-up, props, and sets. For example, to build the sets for the film, we started with the blueprint and then had several lengthy discussions with the art designer, who modified the blueprint a few times. Close attention was even paid to the designs of earrings and spoons. The whole process made me realize the importance of pre-production work. It took eight months for the workshop to edit the film and three-and-a-half years to complete it. During this process, I truly acquired something tangible about filmmaking. The operational skills of a professional director provided me an excellent example. Before that experience, I really didn't have a clear idea about what I was going to do for a living. I had been a confused person, neither a real worker when working in factory nor a real student when studying at BFA. But suddenly the road became clear when I commuted between my place and the workshop: I want to express my view of the world through film.

I was drawn to filmmaking for another reason. In 1995, I became interested in Christianity. I used to be very narcissistic. At the age of eleven or twelve, I started to write poems. Those poems actually resulted from my ultra-narcissism. But you don't find this narcissism in *The Orphan of Anyang*. Why? It is possibly due to the fact that I didn't make my first film until I was more than thirty. But another more important reason, I think, is related to my encounter with Christianity. It is Christianity that transformed my sense of self-pity to compassion for other people. Before coming to BFA, I'd already read a number of Western philosophy books in translation. I reread them while studying at BFA. One book that particularly appealed to me was Liu Xiaofeng's *Toward the Truth on the Cross*, which utilized Western theology to explain the notion of the truth.[xx] Because of Christianity, and because of the notion of God, my reflection and compassion on the outside world has acquired another shining dimension. I became more interested in other people than in myself.

Wang Guangli

I was born in 1966 in Meishan, Sichuan Province, the birthplace of the Song poet Su Dongpo. I was not a graduate of BFA, but studied at Shanghai's

East Normal University from 1985 to 1989. At that time, I was very much influenced by several young teachers at East Normal, including Zhu Dake and Li Jie.[xxi] They may be regarded as the ones who enlightened me about film. It was just the time when the atmosphere in Shanghai film circles was quite dynamic, and one of the signs of this dynamism was the critique of the "Xie Jin Model". New to college, I was a little self-important, always sneaking into the classes taught by Xu Zidong and Xia Zhongyi. Both of them were professors at East Normal and really active back then. Suddenly, I was intellectually enlightened. Before, living in Sichuan, I was relatively uninformed. I had never been out of Sichuan, not even out of the county where I was born. Then, from an isolated place, I came to Shanghai. I was naturally excited. Before long, the education I received in the past completely collapsed. It couldn't stand a single blow and collapsed easily. After the old was gone, my mind became empty. It was almost natural for me, therefore, to accept their teachings unconditionally.

During that particular period of time, the intellectual environment in China was extremely conducive to the growth of new ideas. I think the most important achievement at that time was the critique of the false ideology that had plagued the Chinese people since 1949. At college, I was very active, one of the most active students on campus. My major was Education. There were also several other active students in the department, such as Zhang Xiaobo and Yao Fei. The reason why it was easier to become motivated in the Education Department was due to the fact that the department's curriculum was extremely boring. We could easily pass those courses even without attending them. Therefore, we had a lot of time. I spent my time almost entirely in the Chinese Department. Furthermore, mostly I hung around with the graduate students in the Chinese Department, including novelist Ge Fei, poet Song Lin, and critic Li Jie. Li Jie lived upstairs. Hence, I hung out with them every day. We were really radical at that time, from the "Anti-Spiritual Pollution" movement between 1987 and 1988 to the student movement in 1989. This explains why I made the documentary *I Have Graduated*. But I was very fortunate. I studied in Shanghai, yet I was in Beijing throughout the 1989 student movement. East Normal, therefore, had no idea about what I did during that period. Unlike most bright students in Beijing whose dossiers were stained, my dossier was completely clean. After graduation, therefore, I was assigned to the Youth Political College of the Central University of the Communist Youth League. Several prominent figures were at the college, including Yuan Zhiming and my best colleague Wang Xiang. Wang was later thrown into jail and did all we could to help while he was in prison.

When studying at East Normal, I organized some film-related activities,

Chapter One

including the Shanghai College Student Film Festival. I didn't have a clue about what I wanted to do after coming to Beijing. At that time I felt film was something quite mysterious. How could it be possible for me, a person without formal training in filmmaking, to make films? But after settling down in Beijing, I found there are quite a few documentary filmmakers in Beijing. I also got the opportunity to see some non-mainstream mini films by young filmmakers affiliated to CCTV. Having seen these films, I said to myself: oh, they can make this kind of film, why can't I? I was quite poor then, but I happened to know a French writer who owned a video camera and let me use it. Every day, therefore, I carried the camera to the places I am most familiar with: schools. I hung around university campuses. At this juncture, I discovered something that moved me most: the revelation of students' true feelings and emotions. It was 1992, just before the graduation of the last group of students who had taken part in the 1989 student movement. I took advantage of this particular moment and started shooting. The shooting lasted six days, from July 1 to 7, 1992. I titled the film *I Have Graduated*.

On a functional level, I did what I was capable of, which was to convey my creative ideas to the crew. My conception at that time was to realistically record what I saw and heard without any polishing. As soon as I walked into the school gates, therefore, the camera started to roll. Although campus lives seemed to be simple, in reality there were various kinds of people. I used almost 50 tapes in six days, which was about 1,000 minutes-worth of film, and then cut them into a 60-minute-long final product. This is a film based on the unpolished materials I recorded. To make the film accessible I clearly divided it into five sub-themes. The film was meant to be a warm-blooded student work, but won praise later from professionals and experts in film circles, which had a tremendous impact on me. Some professors backed me at that time, including one at the Beijing Broadcasting Institute [now named Communication University of China]. I had a good cameraman who later shot several great documentaries, including one about Deng Xiaoping. He graduated in 1991, just one year out of the Beijing Broadcasting Institute when I approached him. He was then working at the Tianjin Television Station, and I invited him to be my cameraman one day after the shooting started. Because I was then completely ignorant about filming itself, I made many mistakes on the technical side, such as taking the sound controller to the shooting location. In the beginning, my cameraman was a graduate of BFA, whose specialty was feature films. Later, I sensed something was not right but didn't know where the problem was. Puzzled, I consulted a CCTV director named Shi Jian, who enlightened me to the fact that I was not making the documentary the right way. Then he recommended the Tianjin

TV Station cameraman, who reported to me the next day. A BBI instructor also joined the crew, and he later became the executive director of the Phoenix TV Station. As you can see, an excellent group of people supported me behind the scenes. Most importantly, I slept little during the entire seven-day shooting period. I was high-spirited and hyper excited, as if there was a revolution going on.

I Have Graduated came out in 1992. I was young and impetuous at that time and didn't know how risky it was to make the film. It was not until 1994 that the film became widely known to the public. It was also in that year that I was singled out by name. What happened was that seven Chinese underground films were shown at the 1994 Rotterdam Film Festival,. This was the so-called "Seven Gentlemen" incident. In April 1994, the then State Administration of Radio, Film and Television issued an announcement, in which six of the seven were mentioned by name. Apparently they didn't know who made *I Have Graduated* at that time. I met Tian Zhuangzhuang in 1994, who said to me: "So it's you missing from that list! We tried in vain to figure out who made the film. Some people thought it must be Xia Gang!"

I still value this film highly today. I often feel that the great impact this film had on my individual development, on my understanding of film and television, and on my future will be always there. Because of the content of the film, everyone knew it was impossible for me to list their names in the credit. In the beginning, therefore, the film came out without the names of the crew. As for those who were interviewed, I only listed their last names. After the film came out, things got a bit out of control. Many foreign film festivals showed the film. To tell you the truth, I never heard of some of the festivals. I had never been out of the country, because at that time I didn't even have a passport. Because of all the excitement I was later investigated by the authorities. As a result, a warning note was issued. I was not forced out of Beijing, but I felt I could no longer stay in the city. Therefore, I left. Because I had little training in film and television technology, my original plan was to get some hands-on training on this subject after the film was completed. But the then president of BFA joked to me: "Guangli, I think you could even give lectures at BFA. There is no need for you to study filmmaking further." He said that the important thing was not to be proficient in film technology, because every area had its own problems. Instead, I should really focus on thematic issues. Since I was just out of Beijing and had the opportunity to work at a small television station, however, I decided to make up the "missed lesson". The TV station's equipment was excellent. I stayed at the station for a year and a half, and eventually became comfortable with the technical aspects of television, from shooting to editing, including even carrying equipment.

Chapter One

I know it is very hard to make documentaries in China, because documentaries demand truth. But it is something that our fragile system and ideology are afraid of. So, partly because of this, I started to think about making feature films. You can make up things in features. In other words, it could be purely fictional. Besides, I thought many creative ideas of mine could be brought to life in feature films. To try something new is both challenging and exciting. Therefore, I wrote a screenplay. Although I was completely ignorant of film, I was lucky enough to be able to solicit a limited amount of money to start shooting. The day the shooting began was the first time I saw real film stock and film cameras. Thus, I made my first film in 1996, properly titled *The Maiden Work*. To be frank, it was quite difficult for me to make the film, simply for technical reasons. I made mistakes in some key aspects, particularly in the technical aspect, because I thought in the beginning that it was sufficient for the technicians to only understand issues related to film technology. For example, I thought it was enough for a cinematographer to know how to focus the lens and measure aperture. But after we arrived at the shooting location, I found things were not as simple as I had thought. Since all the actors in my film were nonprofessional, after the cameraman got the perfect aperture and focus, and I shouted "OK, Action", what I wanted had already gone. It was a disaster. Halfway through, I found I could no longer follow the script. Thus I threw away the script. I told the crew: "Forget the script. Let's make a docudrama about ourselves." Originally, *The Maiden Work* was about a painter who in the creative process found his ideals could be no longer expressed through painting in modern society. So he wanted to try the film form. Since it was no longer possible to follow the original idea, I decided to shift the focus to our crew and to the difficulties we encountered. Thus, all the crew members appeared in the film, which in the end became a story about the painful birth of a Chinese independent film, addressing the artistic, technological, and ideological issues we confronted.

To summarize, I originally planned to finish the shooting in 19 days. But it became apparent after eight days of shooting that that was impossible. Thus, I used the remaining ten days to film us, which transformed a would-be fictional film into a documentary. At the last stage of postproduction, I found I needed to re-shoot some of the scenes. But there wasn't enough money left to do this make-up work. The whole film, therefore, is only 60 minutes long. In order to participate in some film festivals, however, I put in a few tape-to-film TV news scenes, which lengthened the film a bit. To my surprise, *The Maiden Work* received great responses abroad. Many festival jurors spoke highly of the film, but nothing could top *Variety*'s comments. To be frank, attending film festivals was not even on my mind before the film was finished. The worldwide critical success of *The Maiden Work*, however, did give me added confidence. I began to realize that film, as an art form, has no fixed set of rules. The most important thing is creativity.

Having finished *The Maiden Work*, I began to read some film books. In the past, I had intentionally avoided these books. Why? There were several reasons. First, I had a certain prejudice against film students. I thought they had IQ problems because back then I was under the impression that only those students with the lowest scores wanted to study at BFA. I would easily meet the "cultural" requirement of BFA even if you divided my total score on the College Entrance Exam by two. Second, I thought inbreeding was a trademark of the film circle. Many people became filmmakers simply because their parents were industry insiders. In my heart, therefore, I somehow frowned upon them. Third, I happened to have some film friends. I felt they had read few books, and I couldn't even have meaningful conversations with them. Besides, they were very dogmatic, always claiming that I didn't understand film. For instance, when I was in Shanghai, I went with Zhu Dake to the Shanghai Film Studio, criticizing the Xie Jin model. Xie's assistant said to us: What do you know about film? Film is such and such. We felt quite ridiculous back then: Look at the films you made. They show nothing but low IQs. How can you teach us about film? At that time, therefore, I was very biased.

After I began to read books about film, especially after I gained some knowledge about things beyond China (mainly through pirated discs), I felt I was not so right. What I said in the past was a bit naïve. Besides, I finally got my passport after finishing *The Maiden Work*. My view widened due to overseas trips: So Hollywood and European cinema are not the only ones in the world! There are so many alternatives! At that moment, I made up my mind about my own future: I wanted to be a professional filmmaker. It is hard to take this road in China, but the path was even harder to walk after I decided I would make no compromise in matters of individuality but at the same time make films that would pass the censors. This is what I decided. After *The Maiden Work*, I felt that the so-called "underground films" could perhaps win some awards overseas, but the feeling resembles that of refugees. The whole process is full of refugee even colonial flavors. It is you who are catering to their taste. On the surface, it looked like I was treated quite honorably, but I felt very uncomfortable. As a dignified Chinese, I couldn't bear the feeling of being a refugee. Besides, sometimes I felt Western critics and artists are no better than their Chinese counterparts. We are in no way inferior to them. I decided back then, therefore, I must make sure my future films pass the censors and come out openly and legally.

Chapter One

Wang Quanan

If my film has some features that set me apart from other young filmmakers, it is probably because I am less educated. At the time I should have been in school, I joined a song and dance troupe, which enabled me to travel around the country and the world. That was 1983, and I was less than eighteen. Between staying in school and joining the troupe, I decided to choose the latter. At that time, I thought it was perhaps more valuable for me to see the world and to be maximally enlightened.

After giving up my normal schooling, I traveled to various places in the world. To me, it was a spiritually painful period, because I didn't know how to sort out the perceptual knowledge I accumulated through these trips. It was not until after a long period of time that I was able to finally "awake" from this tangled experience. It seems I had a painful transformation and, after that, I started to slowly construct a value system of my own. I could have stayed in the West, but it was hard for me to completely identify with the West. I stayed in France for half a year, uncertain about whether I should remain there to study film. I don't know if it was due to my preference or due to some other force that was beyond my control, such as fate; I decided to come back to China to prepare myself for BFA. We human beings should not be so arrogant as to deny the existence of such a force. This force endowed me with the witty realization that since I had decided to study film and wanted to become a filmmaker, it was too late for me to be a "French" filmmaker. I asked myself: What kind of film do you want to make? If I chose to study film in France and then come back to China after graduation, it would be too hard and too late for me to understand my fellow Chinese and be in tune with the times.

I entered BFA in 1987. My father is president of a Communist cadre school, specializing in philosophy. Probably due to my rebellious attitude, I felt that some of the subjects I tested in, such as philosophy and history, were just waste of time, having no value at all. I had no appetite to study those subjects, which are stained with erroneous thinking. This kind of so-called "knowledge" will eventually become extinct. But I love Chinese, and I love fine arts. The reason why I chose the Performing Department was because it required lower scores on the entrance exam. The most important thing was to get into the Academy and get close to film. After I was admitted, I immediately started to write screenplays. I remember that I was on the verge of being kicked out twice because I always audited classes that were offered in other departments. At that time, I had already learned how to take advantage of the loopholes in the system, just like finding loopholes in today's film censorship. I understood that you couldn't completely turn your back on that, but to me it was merely a technique, not a matter of prime importance. For example, if the rules stipulate that you will be kicked out after skipping 30 classes, then you could just skip 29. I felt I would gain nothing if I spent my time on improving the system of rewards and penalties at the Academy. Besides, I was completely powerless to change the system. But what I could do is to use the time of the 29 skipped classes to write several screenplays. This turned out to be quite interesting. When penalties were announced, every penalized student cried and cried, but I treated every act of discipline, including severe ones, with calmness, just like signing a contract with instructors. I knew I gained something from it.

I graduated in 1991 with some direct experience of the June Fourth Incident. My graduation work was a role in Zhang Nuanxin's film *Good Morning, Beijing*, which I had to take on in order to graduate. Zhang was somewhat influenced by French cinema. Perhaps I am wrong, but from my point of view, *Good Morning, Beijing* appears less pure. No question I had a good working relationship with Zhang Nuanxin, and I was heavily involved in the creative process of the film, from consulting on the script to discussing how to shoot the film. I also tried very hard, through my performance, to polish my character. But it was very hard for me to persuade a person like Zhang Nuanxin to accept my conception of the role. My understanding of the character was that although he is a good-natured, well-behaved, and honest man in the classical sense, such a man is out of tune with the times. He had abandoned the moral education he received from his father's generation, which was inherently valueless. I felt the film should have focused on his dilemma, or his unattractive side. Taken one step further, it is quite possible that such a character would be psychologically traumatized and become increasingly sinister.

Wang Xiaoshuai

I grew up in the province of Guizhou, and later moved to Wuhan with my family. I spent two years in a Wuhan middle school and came to Beijing at the age of fifteen. So, you may call me an "old Beijinger". My father was a stage actor. However, he told me that a person would have much more independence working as a painter. Since I'd had a long interest in painting, I joined the Fine Arts School affiliated to the Central Academy of Fine Arts in Beijing. I became a BFA student in 1985, probably out of "sudden enlightenment". It took little time for me to realize that I was not particularly talented in painting. I felt my painting was not bad, but my teacher didn't think so. He gave high scores to several of my classmates, but claimed he didn't understand my work. I figured from this that my career in painting was doomed.

Chapter One

But it seems I have a natural love for film and film-related books. My friends and I often gathered together to share stories. When telling stories, some of us, including me, would suddenly do some improvisations and mimic certain characters. This was of course quite different from painting, and I discovered I did have some talent in story-telling and spontaneous performing. Another strange thing that led me to BFA was the fact that, although I was studying at a fine arts school, I suddenly realized during the College Entrance Exam period that the books I read in my four-year middle school education were mostly film-related, books on film history, biographies of film directors, etc. Therefore, I asked myself, why can't I set my sights on BFA?

I studied film directing at BFA from 1985 to 1989. At that time, outside the academy, it was almost impossible to see non-Chinese films. So, the most critical advantage we had as film students was the opportunity to see a variety of films. Besides, the China Film Archive was also open to BFA students, where we sometimes watched five or six films a day. As far as teaching was concerned, there seemed to be a strong emphasis on film as an art form during my study at BFA. Most messages I got were art-related. Looking at this from a purely artistic angle, I think this emphasis on film as an art form has had a tremendous influence on me. When I was making my first feature, *The Days*, this conception of film never escaped me. Even today, I still think this influence has played a positive role in my filmmaking, and I am grateful to the teachings I received at BFA.

In 1991, two years after graduation, I was assigned to the Fujian Film Studio. With one suitcase, one sleeping bag, a table lamp, and a tooth brush, I left for Fujian on my own. I stayed here and there and felt extremely lonely. Besides the fact that I didn't have a sense of belonging in Fujian, what saddened me most was the impossibility of making my own films. There was a long waiting list of directors at the state-owned Fujian Film. If I stayed in this line waiting, I would never have been able to make a film in this lifetime. Suddenly, therefore, I felt hopeless about my future, as if my life had been abruptly cut short after graduation.

Fortunately, I didn't give up. I had a strong urge to express this feeling of hopelessness through film. Since the chances of making a studio film were next to none, I decided to create my own opportunity. I slipped out of Fujian and came back to Beijing, turning myself into an independent. Then, using borrowed money, I made *The Days*. I remember the first time I saw *The Yellow Earth* at BFA. It was quite an encouraging experience. The film's individuality strengthened my idea of making a film of my own. A Hollywood commercial movie might look exciting, but there's no incentive to make that kind of movie. The case with *The Yellow Earth* is different, however. As an alternative work, the film looks unique, with simple composition and storyline. When you see a Hollywood movie, you are excited, but you feel there is a distance between you and the movie, and you couldn't imagine yourself making a film like that. With *The Yellow Earth*, however, you feel you are closely connected to it and feel that you yourself are capable of doing the same thing. As a former student of painting, I didn't think the composition of *The Yellow Earth* was that extraordinary. Certainly it was a little edgy, but I felt I could do the same thing, probably even more impressively than *The Yellow Earth*. *The Days*, therefore, was inspired by this kind of "alternative cinema". Many BFA graduates actually started to make their independent films after having seen *The Days*, including Jia Zhangke, as he told me privately. The videotape of *The Days* was circulated among those who shared my views at the time, just as one would share an unofficial hand-copied novel.

Both the male and female leads in *The Days* are my Fine Arts School classmates. We know each other quite well. The film is actually a reflection of our emotional and spiritual status of the time. Of course it is somewhat fictionalized. For example, the film ends with the girl leaving the country, therefore one remains in China, the other goes abroad. In real life, this would generally not be the case. After *The Days*, my creativity was stimulated. I wanted to make another film immediately. Luckily, I was able to borrow money from various sources, which enabled me to finish my second independent feature, *Frozen*.

Xu Jinglei

Before attending BFA, I had had absolutely no training in acting. Sometimes I practiced calligraphy and drawing, but always felt I was only an amateur. I studied performing arts at the Academy, but there were no classes offered in the Acting Department about filmmaking itself. Filmmaking classes, such as classes on cinematography and related subjects, were offered in other departments, but the Acting Department was an exception. We only learned acting. Sometimes we were taught how to create mini plays, but that was it. Students from other departments at least had hands-on training in shooting MTV and other minor genres, but I was indeed completely ignorant of filmmaking. If you ask about acting, I might be able to tell you something. As for filmmaking, however, I was never exposed to things such as cinematic language, neither the theory nor the practice.

I became a celebrity, made money, and accumulated a lot of experience through acting. But I always feel that acting is not what I really want to do. In fact, I always ask myself: if I am tired of acting, what should or can I do? Business? It seems I have no interest. For several years, I couldn't really come up with an answer. On the one hand, I felt acting was probably not a

Chapter One

lifelong career. On the other hand, I couldn't figure out what I was capable of besides acting. Since 2001, however, I have tried to write some screenplays. After one of them was completed, I decided to turn it into a film by myself. I would have felt rather disgruntled had I let somebody else make it. It is just like having a baby of one's own. I wouldn't let other people raise it. Even if I were not able to raise it well, the baby would be better off in my own hands.

I didn't try to find a financier or an investor. Instead, I decided to use my own money to make the film. By so doing, I wouldn't feel pressured. Since I have been in the entertainment business for quite a number of years, I think I know pretty well the nature of filmmaking. I don't want to be under the control of anybody, but prefer to make whatever I feel like. Now that the film was made I felt quite relieved. Whether it was good or bad, I felt I've learned a lot through the filmmaking process. I began to realize that many things can't be easily acquired without learning. Unlike acting, directing indeed requires a person with comprehensive knowledge. In acting, what you need to pay attention to is only the character or the rhythm of acting, but actors or actresses are powerless in controlling the overall rhythm of a film.

I don't feel anything special about being the youngest director in China as well as the first to try filmmaking after the "single feature" policy was implemented. The news made a fuss about it, but I really feel nothing special at all. My original intention was only to find something more meaningful, and I feel I've found it. This is what makes me happiest. Now I feel I know what I am capable of, and I can work in that direction. This time I worked both as a director and a scriptwriter. In the future, I might find directing itself requires more attention. If that's the case, I don't have to write script myself. I might direct a film written by someone else. Adapting fiction is an option, because it is relatively convenient and easy. Besides, fiction already contains strong literary qualities. As a matter of fact, I feel the screenplay is the most difficult part in the whole process of filmmaking.

I start my film career with acting, and I still feel that acting is not entirely uninteresting. But I have to say that sometimes I am a bit tired of acting. Now that I have ventured into directing, I think I have more options. For example, in the future, I don't have to worry about how many roles I should take each year. I can devote more time to studying new things, such as editing, which is quite interesting. Also, I will spend more time on pre-production when making my next film.

Zhang Ming

I was born in the small town of Wushan in Sichuan Province where the Yangzi River runs through it. When I was a child, I often saw kids using slingshots to hit the swelled bodies that calmly flowed downward from the upper reaches of Yangtze. As a little boy I liked to paint and draw, and I think painting, drawing, and art in general have a lot of similarities to film, so I guess that's why I became more and more interested in film. Later on, I went to Chongqing's Southwest Normal University to study oil painting. In college, I read a book by Sergei Eisenstein, and that's when I really developed a deeper interest in film. The images of his films in the book had a great impact on me. I could see that his films were much different from Chinese films. That was at the beginning of the 1980s, when Chinese film went through so many changes. So I thought I might try to change things as well. After graduating from Southwest Normal, I really exerted myself to pass the entrance exam to the Beijing Film Academy. I watched a lot of films of the 1950s, '60s and '70s by Luis Buñuel, Andrei Tarkovski, Antonioni, and Bergman. Finally, I was admitted to BFA's graduate program in directing in 1989. After graduation, I became an instructor of BFA. I've been teaching film directing since then.

Filmmaking, I believe, is highly related to one's experience. It is a manifestation of your view of the world, of your reaction to the immediate environment, and of your response to the things that stimulate you. Those who grew up in Beijing or Shanghai would feel more attached to the two cities, and their inspiration would most likely come from Beijing or Shanghai. My experience is quite different. Born in a small county, my inspiration comes mostly from the milieu of that place. I spent my childhood in the isolated environment of Wushan, which is surrounded by mountains. I knew little about the outside world until I left the place. Although the Yangzi flows far, what passed before ones eyes are the boats, boats that seem to have no destination. In this isolated environment, the flowing Yangzi and the boats moving by bring many dreams. These dreams, I think, have left enduring traces in my filmmaking. You can find these traces in the two films I've made so far. Both *Rainclouds Over Wushan* [a.k.a. *In Expectation*] and *Weekend Plot* visualize the dreams I had at that time. You can call it "way of expression" or an "individual style", but what I want to reiterate is the close tie between one's work and one's environment.

But things have certainly changed for me. In the past, I felt the countryside was the most "Chinese" landscape where metropolis and the rural scenes converged. Besides, about 90 percent of China's population lived in the counties and the county-administrated countryside. Thus my first feature, *Rainclouds*, is set in Wushan, the small county that will soon be inundated by the river after the first stage of the completion of the famed Three Gorges Dam. Nowadays, however, the boundary between metropolis and small city are increasingly blurred. On the one hand, millions of people

Chapter One

from small towns and the countryside come to Beijing or Shanghai to find a better-paying jobs. The metropolis is being transformed by this "floating" population. In the past, only urbanites could afford to fly. But nowadays many people from the countryside also travel by air. The streets of Beijing and Shanghai are packed with these people. On the other hand, there is also a trend of reverse "migration". Many urbanites flock to the countryside, either spending weekends or vacations there. This is a grand spectacle of contemporary China. The two-way "floating" is a testament to the ever-changing China, a China that is drastically different from the one when *Rainclouds Over Wushan* was made.

Zhang Yang

I was born in Beijing in 1967. My father, Zhang Huaxun is a veteran director of the Beijing Film Studio. Specializing in martial-arts films, he made a few films in the 1970s and '80s, including *The Mysterious Buddha*. When I was thirteen years old, I went along with my father to shoot the film *The Mysterious Buddha* in Sichuan, and I got a small part. It was a kung-fu movie, so I had great fun. At age fourteen, a friend and I played the emperor's grandsons in an Italian film shot in China called *Marco Polo*. Your classmates were very impressed if you acted in a film, so I was very proud of myself. Since my father was a director, I could also watch many great films, including foreign films that people outside the industry couldn't see. When it came time to choose my major in the high school, my parents wanted me to choose medicine and become a doctor, but I chose the arts and humanities. After high school, I knew I wanted to be a director, so I decided to go to the Beijing Film Academy.

But BFA didn't recruit new students that year. So, I aimed at CATA instead. But I failed to pass the entrance examination of CATA and therefore went south and enrolled at Zhongshan University [in Guangzhou], majoring in Chinese. At Zhongshan University, I became a key member of the school's amateur troupe. I wrote many plays myself and later came back to Beijing with one of my own plays. A number of teachers and students from CATA came to see the performance. After the performance, I was asked whether I wanted to transfer to CATA. So, I retook the entrance exam and officially transferred to CATA's Directing Department two years after I entered Zhongshan University.

When studying at CATA, besides drama, I was also interested in rock music. I was young back then and felt music was the most direct way to express oneself. Both drama and film couldn't fulfill my needs in this respect. But after almost half a year, our rock band couldn't even produce a single song. Thus, we stopped practicing and I came back to drama. In addition, my love for film also started to pick up.

Two steps, therefore, led me to filmmaking. The first was family influence. Because my father is a filmmaker, I often went to his movie sets, finding filmmaking quite interesting and playful. The second step was after I transferred to CATA, where I began to learn that inside me there are so many ideas and feelings I'd like to express. For me, the most important thing is self-expression. To choose which art form, either music or drama or film, is only secondary. It is only after a long period of soul-searching that I found cinema to be the form that suits me best. Since childhood I've been good at organizing people, and my calm and rational character makes me see things relatively objectively. All these qualities are necessary in a director. I love music, architecture, and painting. Although I'm not an expert in any one of these art forms, as a whole, I am above average. So, after graduation I decided to become a filmmaker. I believe the role of director fits my character relatively well.

Zhang Yuan

I was born in Nanjing in 1963. Photography and painting were what I loved in high school. In 1985 I was admitted to the Cinematography Department of BFA. I was drawn to cinematography because I thought at that time that image and composition were the most important elements in filmmaking. Indeed, this was my conception of film at BFA. Moreover, studying cinematography guaranteed me more shooting opportunities and more working experience on celluloid. It was not until I'd seen more films that I began to learn that filmmaking involves other issues and ideas that may be closer to our feelings and views of the world.

I finished my study at BFA in 1989. Although majoring in cinematography, I've never worked as a cameraman for any director since graduation. Working independently after graduation, I made not only feature films, but also documentaries, music videos, and TV commercials. I even directed some stage plays. In 1990, I produced and directed my first feature, *Mama*. It is also the first Chinese independent film [made] since 1949. It was financed by my business friends, as were many of my other films. It was done in a time when the idea of independent filmmaking was unheard of because all films made in China back then were made by state-owned studios. Private individuals making films was something hard to imagine in China at that time. I had never heard of the expression "independent films" until somebody at a European film festival described *Mama* as an "independent film". It was reported that only three copies of the film were sold domestically. To be frank, I didn't even expect the film could be released at that time in China. So, I was not disappointed with the poor sales of the

Chapter One

film. On the contrary, I benefited tremendously from *Mama*. First of all, the film provided me with a starting point from which I was able to launch my filmmaking career. Although fresh out of college, I discovered a fresh angle and a focal point to examine Chinese society. Unlike many directors my age, who tended to tell their own stories, I made a film not so much about myself or about people of my age. I examined Chinese society from the point of view of a mother raising a mentally handicapped son. It was a theme of social significance. So, the film actually provided me a good point of entrance into both society and filmmaking.

In addition, I was quite fortunate that this film opened many opportunities for me. *Mama* was screened in more than 100 countries, and I traveled all over the world and attended almost all the film festivals in the world. It also won many awards in, for example, France, Great Britain, and Germany. *Mama* made festivals and audiences abroad realize that there are other directors, cinemas, and genres in China besides Zhang Yimou and Chen Kaige and their films. It is fortunate that I was able to study at BFA, and it is even more fortunate that I am able to continue making films after graduation. Filmmaking is quite an interesting career. Life may be sorrowful and unbearable, but film creates a world of happiness.

CHAPTER TWO

CHINESE CINEMA AFTER YELLOW EARTH:
TOWARD A WORKING DEFINITION
OF THE "SIXTH GENERATION"

*Unlike the term "Fifth Generation", which is widely accepted both domestically and internationally, the "Sixth Generation" is at its best only a convenient label. If the "Fifth Generation" refers to the "Class of 1978" of BFA (graduated in 1982), then, in a strict sense, the "Sixth Generation" only applies to BFA's "Class of 1985" (graduated in 1989), as the class's collective essay "The Post-*Yellow Earth *Phenomenon in Chinese Cinema" indicates. But Chinese cinema after* Yellow Earth *presents a much more complicated picture, with many young filmmakers emerging from non-BFA institutions. This being the case, many critics have suggested dropping the term entirely or replacing it with such terms as the "New Generation", "Generation X", or the "Young Generation". The 21 filmmakers interviewed responded to the questions "What defines the 'Sixth Generation'" and "Is there a collective identity that sets you apart from the previous generations" with divergent answers. Some readily accepted the label, but others (such as Lu Chuan) vehemently denied having any connection with the "Sixth Generation". The disagreement among the filmmakers themselves is another indication that differentiating Chinese filmmakers in generational terms becomes increasingly problematic.*

* * *

Guan Hu

My understanding is that, in the early 1990s, the graduates of the classes of 1985 and 1987 of BFA began to make their first films with self-raised money. Although each of them worked independently, it turned out that they shared the same interest and walked the same path. Not only were they presenting similar subject matter, but what they felt about the city and the cinema itself were very uniform. Then, the accumulated energy started releasing, and the result was the making of a few films that seemed to demonstrate a certain kind of collective spirit. In fact, there is nothing unusual for this kind of uncoordinated collectivity. Around the world, young filmmakers often rely

Chapter Two

on autobiographical materials to launch their careers, materials they can manage and feel intimate with. As they become more mature and established, they begin to go separate ways. It is just normal.

To the people of BFA, it is a common understanding that the so-called "Sixth Generation" is a natural formation. This creative group has never issued a manifesto or intended to form a particular school. An artistic school first requires a few representative works. As a matter of fact, if you take a closer look at this generation, they have already gone their separate ways. They are making different films. I think the notion of the "Sixth Generation" has more to do with the naming itself. Back then, this group of young filmmakers had to make certain amount of noise to get their first films done. Compared to this noise, their works became secondary. Of course the result is the formation of this group of young filmmakers who shared their view about the city and who were concerned with the emotion, fate, and puzzlement of the individual. Naturally, the phenomenon of a peculiar "generation" began to emerge.

Quite a few years have passed since the notion of the "Sixth Generation" was circulated. In my opinion, this notion has now become obsolete. In addition, I don't think this notion provides any help for Chinese cinema. Only if it could in some way help advance national cinema would it be a good thing to keep promoting. Since this group has in fact disintegrated, let bygones be bygones. Besides, personally, I've never taken the notion seriously, and I've never thought of myself as being a member of the "Sixth Generation" while making films. I seldom compare myself "horizontally" with the filmmakers more or less the same age. Rather, I like to examine my works "vertically" to see how I've progressed. If compared to others I lack individual characteristics, then I am in a weak position. Other filmmakers have accomplished great things, and their films are quite mature. I need to learn from them. The only advantage I have is my ethic of hard work. You can make a difference as long as you devote yourself wholeheartedly to what you are doing. A long journey begins by taking the first step.

Jia Zhangke

I don't think most filmmakers have a clear conception of or even care about the notion of the "Sixth Generation" because it is increasingly the case that each one of them works quite independently. Besides, their production methods are also drastically different. Although most of them are making independent films, they differ greatly from each other. It is like the famous Chinese saying, "Eight Immortals crossing the seas, each displaying his/her ability". In addition, they also differ in their views of film as a medium as well as in what the things that concern them. Speaking for myself, I don't hold a clear view of "generation" either. On the other hand, however, because I also studied film theory at BFA, I understand that grouping filmmakers together in generational terms is a convenience for researchers and scholars. Therefore, I don't have a particular dislike for such a notion. Fortunately, it seems that most filmmakers have not been constrained or burdened by this classification. If they had a clear consciousness of which "generation" they belonged to, it would be harmful rather than conducive to their filmmaking. It would make them constantly search for things in common, or push them to the extreme of setting up an imaginary enemy in film production. In this aspect, I think the younger the filmmakers are, the less burdened or constrained they seem to be. The negative elements of traditional Chinese culture seem to have less impact on younger filmmakers.

Jiang Wen

I don't like the term the "Sixth Generation" at all, because it is far from reasonable. It offers little insight for film appreciation, film judgment, and film criticism. It also narrows people's field of vision. Those who emerged after the "Fifth Generation", because of the divergence of their backgrounds, social environment, and character formation, cannot be bound together with a single thread. Prior to the emergence of these filmmakers, it might be excusable to name a number of filmmakers as a "generation", because where they came from and what they'd accepted made it possible for some to paint a coherent of color tone. But it is no longer possible to do the same for the filmmakers after the "Fifth Generation". As a matter of fact, the notion of the "Fifth Generation" is already questionable. It is therefore quite ridiculous to name the people after the "Fifth Generation" the "Sixth Generation". I've discussed this with many people, and none of them found the term agreeable. But the term is still being used and circulated despite strong disagreement from many people. I feel quite puzzled by this. If the term only provides convenience for some people, then the very notion of "convenience" is exactly what we need to avoid in filmmaking, film appreciation, and film criticism. Convenience can't produce quality films. If film does possess artistic quality, then it ought to be sensitive, even unique, and sometimes ambiguous. It is from this ambiguity that one could find different characteristics of each film. Therefore, the notion of the "Sixth Generation" is actually against the principle of film criticism.

Let's go back to these newly emerged filmmakers. Why do I feel these young filmmakers have made considerable progress after the Fifth Generation? Take a look at Jia Zhangke and Lou Ye. One thing I admire about them most is that both seem to have achieved a certain level of thoughtfulness through the creative expression of their life experience and

Chapter Two

perception. Although the two are totally different, they have one thing in common: things flow naturally from their hearts. No matter how petty-bourgeois and colonial it appears, Lou Ye's Shanghai didn't prevent me from enjoying his films. It doesn't matter whether or not you like Shanghai. What matters is the truthful expression of a Shanghai native's obsession and perception. In other words, I sense a certain level of purity from watching his films. There is a certain luminance in his films, not awkward at all.

I feel the films of the Fifth Generation are sometimes a little awkward: what do they want to say exactly? You have few clues as to what it is they want to achieve. Sometimes they are self-contradictory. In other words, I think the Fifth Generation is not as pure as these two directors in expressing themselves. They are also not as powerful as Jia and Lou in touching people's souls. The difference between Jia and Lou and those before them is twofold: First, the latter have little to say. But since you allow me to express my opinion on this, I ought to try. Saying for the sake of saying is quite uncomfortable. Second, even though a few of them do have something to say, what they say is quite awkward. I feel none of them do as well as Jia and Lou in this respect. What Jia and Lou have achieved is to make you want to see their films again. Simply put, their films are powerful and attractive. Jia's attitude toward filmmaking and his view of life and the world are quite powerful indeed. Indeed, both of them have reached a certain level of freedom in artistic expression. I find this extremely valuable. Most people before them were unnatural in expressing themselves.

Jin Chen

My personal view is that the "Sixth Generation" refers to a group of newly emerged filmmakers who have neither a clearly defined banner nor share any well-defined belief or attitude. It starts with the Class of 1985 (graduated in 1989) of BFA, and ends with those who graduated at the turn of the century, including the year 2001. They have only one point in common: they are all young. Except for this, they have almost nothing in common. There are many factions or subgroups within this generation. Each individual strives for change and at the same time attempts to differentiate himself/herself from other filmmakers through nurturing an individual voice. To look at this generation from another angle, however, because they are close in age and have been nurtured by a common cultural milieu, there must be something they commonly share. For example, their main goal is to examine the surrounding world from the point of view of an individual. This individual-based cinema tends to be more interested in the lives of people on the edge of society or of the so-called "unimportant" characters. To me, the conceptualization of the "Sixth Generation" is more sociological than aesthetic. It is social change and cultural diversification in post-"Fifth Generation" China that has hastened the emergence of this group of filmmakers.

To classify this group of filmmakers as a generation is only a matter of convenience. It does not do justice to the fact that BFA is no longer the only institution that produces filmmakers. When the pioneers of Chinese cinema made their first films, there were no such things as film schools or film as a discipline. Many of them were engaged in film simply out of passion. They were eager to express themselves through the new medium of film. In other words, there was no such a faction solely affiliated to some institution. When it came down to the second and third generations, many of them came from a theater background. It was not until the emergence of the Beijing Film Academy that defining Chinese filmmakers in generational terms became a habit. Thus we have the notions of the fourth and fifth generations, and the latter is especially resounding. As Chinese culture becomes increasingly diverse, however, I feel it is even less necessary for us to categorize Chinese directors on the basis of a film academy or a single art school. People from other backgrounds can also bring fresh look and rich imagery to Chinese cinema. This is actually a clear tendency in today's China. Students of Chinese, dramatic arts, and other disciplines are now making films. This trend, in my opinion, is very healthy.

To sum up what I've just said, if we must apply the "Sixth Generation" concept, I think we should expand it to include the non-BFA young filmmakers from diverse backgrounds. It is not only because the first, second, and third generations of filmmakers had nothing to do with BFA, and it was not until the fourth and fifth generations that BFA became the main players in Chinese cinema, but also because film is only a part of a bigger cultural map. No matter where we come from, either BFA or CATA or other institutions, we make films not for film's sake but for the creation of a cultural phenomenon. I think this is why film as a medium still charms us, completely independent of the "aura" of any prestigious film academy. As long as you are passionate about film, you will find your place in filmmaking.

Li Xin

It doesn't really matter whether we have formed a distinct generation of filmmakers. The simple fact is that a group of young people are making films today. Whether or not we can be labeled the "Sixth Generation" is not my concern at all. I have no idea when I was classified as a member of this generation, but I figure this is due to the fact that many young people with similar life experiences started to make their first films in a short span of time. It might also be because we had a strong urge to differentiate ourselves

Chapter Two

from the previous generations when we were students.

Since the beginning of my career as a professional filmmaker, however, I've become more and more doubtful about the practice of enthroning a particular group of filmmakers, as if they'd started a brand-new school of their own. I've never had the feeling that we ushered in a new era in Chinese cinema, partly because you have little time to think about it once you throw yourself into an actual project. Of course there is a thread between your current work and what you liked in college. Looking back, for example, I still like what I liked at BFA as a student. But it does not mean that each of us, or of the so-called "Sixth Generation" filmmakers, thinks the same way when making films. This difference in thinking, I believe, has led to a variety of cinematic directions within our "generation". To me, being 100 percent clear about what you are going to do is not always a good thing. If I were absolutely clear about where I am supposed to go or which group I am supposed to belong to, I would be no longer Li Xin, but Wang Xiaoshuai, Jia Zhangke, or someone else from this "generation". So, I didn't have a clear idea about what I was going to achieve when making *Dazzling*. Many details were decided on location. As I was monitoring the scenes, performances, and costumes, sometimes fresh ideas suddenly popped into my head. I don't think this method suits every film, but *Dazzling* is quite unusual. With minimum plot, it does not have a central character dictating the beginning, climax, and ending of the film. Xu Jinglei, who plays a large role in the film, does not even utter a single word. It is precisely because of the different nature of each film that I hesitate to accept the notion of the "Sixth Generation".

Liu Bingjian

The notion of the "Sixth Generation" is largely a product of media frenzy. I've never connected myself to any generation, be it the "Sixth Generation" or the "X Generation". I suspect that this notion also provides a certain critical angle for film scholars, which is why it has been widely used and is still alive today. But to me, this term, label, is completely meaningless. It is my belief that the richness of contemporary Chinese cinema can't be generalized with a simple word like "generation".

Lou Ye

Actually, our styles vary greatly. I think there is a rich variety of films by the so-called "Sixth Generation" directors. Each of us has his/her own distinct taste. Consequently, our films also look different. [Wang] Xiaoshuai likes this, but Jia Zhangke may like that. This individual taste cannot easily be changed. I actually feel quite good about this diversity. Starting from our generation, everyone is working individually. This individuality is also reflected in the creative process. Many of us write our own scripts, a practice that differs entirely from that of the Fifth Generation directors who, even today, may still depend on other people's scripts. I myself cannot bear even the thought that my film could be based on another person's script. How tiresome!

But it has always been my belief that having such a label is a good thing. This is at least better than the situation in which the Fifth Generation was the only group that dominated Chinese cinema for ten or fifteen years. This label makes me feel more optimistic and confident, because it would be disastrous if a country like China had only one school of filmmakers. Some people call us the "Sixth Generation"; others call us the "New Generation". To be honest, I feel quite gratified. It is surely a good thing to have these labels because they reflect the richness of Chinese cinema, and the film industry will benefit a great deal from this richness. If the "Fifth Generation" alone dominated, would it be different from the previous era when film circles were controlled by official ideology? Fortunately, therefore, these confusing labels reflect nothing unhealthy.

Speaking of collective identity, I think the essay "The Post-*Yellow Earth* Phenomenon in Chinese Cinema" is of vital importance. It is a result of casual talks several classmates and I had before our graduation in 1989. Several of us, including myself, Wang Xiaoshuai, Lu Xuechang, and a few others, drank and chatted at a Beijing friend's home. We stayed there for two days and spoke of nothing but film. At that time, none of us had yet to make a film. It was just empty talk. [But] Someone took notes on our conversation and afterward gave them to Hu Xueyang.[xxii] Hu might have been the one who sorted out the notes and later sent the article to the magazine.[xxiii]

We talked about a lot back then, but gradually came to feel that the situation was not quite right: there was only one kind of film being made by one group of directors and one set of producers. This was not what we had imagined when we thought about Chinese cinema and the Chinese film industry. We also debated what the future of Chinese cinema would be. I remember Wang Xiaoshuai said to me: "I absolutely won't be influenced by the Fifth Generation [directors]." I replied that this claim itself reflected the influence of the Fifth Generation directors, because if you say "I am not the same as him", you in fact have some relationship with him. Perhaps you are opposed to the Fifth Generation tradition, but it cannot be denied that you will somehow continue it. It is impossible, therefore, to completely dismiss the influence of the Fifth Generation directors. But this does not mean that there isn't indeed a dramatic difference in age and life experience between the Fifth Generation directors and us. There have been astronomical changes in the period that separates the two groups of directors. The generation "gap",

Chapter Two

so to speak, is quite wide. In France, this ten-year period [1980s-1990s] probably does not separate two generations of filmmakers in terms of style, because the recent development of French society has remained relatively stable. This is also the case for the whole of Europe. But China is quite different. I believe ten years of change in China perhaps equal thirty or forty years [of change] in Europe. If you select any two French directors today who have a forty-year age difference between them, they will surely differ greatly in style. In China, those forty years are compacted into just ten. To compare the Fifth Generation with us, then, I must say that we are miles apart. Even though some of us are making films at the same historical moment, we in essence are two different species. I think we are as far apart as the sky and the sea in our views of society and the human race. This is no longer an issue of just two *generations*.

To come back to the label itself, however, I think the so-called "Sixth Generation" is actually not a school, and there is no commonly shared manifesto among us. The above-mentioned article cannot be viewed as a manifesto, because I remember that nothing was said in it about what kind of film we would make. It didn't spell out a clear and firm view of filmic art. If the "Sixth Generation" were an artistic school, it would at least have a manifesto as well as a clear position on art. But we did not have any such thing. At the beginning, there might have been the inclination to become a school, but it quickly vanished. No school was formed. If this inclination had been followed through, a school would have been formed. Generally speaking, therefore, the "Sixth Generation" is only a label to me, but this label is not bad at all. It is good for the whole film industry. Variety is always good.

As a matter of fact, the term "Sixth Generation" itself has already been darkened with the shadow of the Fifth Generation. BFA did not recruit a full group of new students for seven years [since 1978]. We were the first full group of students to matriculate after recruitment resumed. As soon as we entered BFA, therefore, some people began to call us the "Sixth Generation". The first full recruitment [following the Cultural Revolution]—when all BFA departments, including directing, cinematography, sound, art directing, and literature, admitted new students at the same time—was in 1978. This became the Fifth Generation. Seven years later, we became the beneficiary of the second full recruitment. It seems to me that there is a close lineage between these two groups.

As for the fact that some young directors without a BFA background are also being counted as members of the "Sixth Generation", I am not surprised at all. Because the "Sixth Generation" is not a school, it is very hard to define who is a member and who is not. The definition of the "Sixth Generation" is open-ended. If someone claims to be a member, then let it be so. To a great extent, it is very similar to that of the French New Wave. The notion of the French New Wave is quite inclusive. It is almost impossible for you to clearly define who belongs to the French New Wave, partly because the number of directors in France at that time far exceeded that of Chinese directors today. Can you count some of the later works, including plays and films, of the typical New Wave directors as part of the New Wave? To come back to the issue of group identity, however, it is very clear that directors like Truffaut and (Jean-Luc) Godard indeed lived through the New Wave period. They succeeded in setting a general trend, one that could not be easily detected from their films but which determined the direction of the whole of French cinema. This is the most important thing.

Lu Chuan

I think there is indeed a group of filmmakers collectively called the "Sixth Generation". We are doubtful of such a group because they differ from each other considerably. But from the point of view of those latecomers like me, the common traits they embody are sufficient for the formation of a group identity. First of all, their way of expression and textual features are very similar. Second, the perspective from which they observe the world is almost the same. Even the decibels of their cries are hard to differentiate. So, I feel they belong to the same generation. But I am certainly not a member of this generation. Thematically, my film is not city-centered. *Ke Ke Xi Li: The Mountain Patrol* is set in China's northwest, and my next film will use small town as a backdrop. I therefore think of myself as being pan-Chinese.

To tell you the truth, I have little personal contact with these "Sixth Generation" filmmakers. It seems only meetings could bring us together, at which I sometimes am able to learn what they are doing and how they view certain things. In my opinion, they are a group of "pure" filmmakers who share the same professional background. No matter what they've done later, their first films were all about themselves. This is the same when you examine the films of Zhang Yimou and other Fifth Generation filmmakers. You can't judge them by looking at what they are doing now. The situation is just like a broom. Although the top of the broom is tied together, its end splays out in all directions. To examine them as a group, you should only concentrate on the first films they made in their career. When they embarked on filmmaking, I feel, the "Sixth Generation" filmmakers all wanted to make either their personal films or films about their immediate environment. They felt that that was reality, at least from their point of view. They succeeded because of this and, also because of this, they've been criticized by many. Although I've only seen a few of their films, comparatively speaking, I find them not too exciting. You don't feel overwhelmed after watching their

Chapter Two

films. Or, you might have the feeling that this group of filmmakers is only capable of making a certain type of film. They only serve me as an axis, warning me not to follow their footsteps. Because I view myself as someone who has already walked out of their circle, if somebody still tried to include me in their category, I would feel very put out.

Lu Xuechang

My understanding is that the notion of the "Sixth Generation" is tied to BFA. We entered BFA in 1985, and the Class of 1978 entered BFA in 1978. After the class of 1978 graduated from BFA in 1982, some film theorists started to view them as a distinct group. Those immediately before them, such as Zheng Dongtian, were labeled the "Fourth Generation". Consequently, the Class of 1978, whose members include Chen Kaige and Zhang Yimou, was collectively called the "Fifth Generation". This group of filmmakers started to make their first films in the mid-1980s and gradually became known to the national and international audience with such works as *One and Eight*, *Yellow Earth*, and *Red Sorghum*. After the Class of 1978 entered BFA, however, what happened between 1979 and 1984 was that the directing department didn't recruit new students until 1985. In other words, we were the first group of students admitted to the directing department of BFA after the Class of 1978. Naturally, therefore, the term "Sixth Generation" started to float around. Since there is a Fifth Generation, there must be a generation after that. But who are the members of this generation? Because BFA had just recruited a group of directing students, the answer to this question was logically tied to them.

I remember that Professors Zheng Dongtian and Ni Zhen[xxiv] began to promote this notion even before our graduation. At that time, we hadn't made a single film. I don't know the situation in other schools, but all of us, particularly the directing students, felt the so-called "Sixth Generation" referred to us, although none of us had made a film yet. As a matter of fact, I am sometimes also doubtful of this notion, but it can't be denied that we did feel that way at that time. Some of the theoretically active professors, such as Zheng Dongtian and Ni Zhen, also thought that the directing students of 1985 had the natural duty to continue the tradition of the Class of 1978 as a generation. At least I feel that way. As for later critiques of the "Sixth Generation", such as the argument that they are too self-centered and only concerned about marginal figures in society, that is another issue. Based on my own experience, the origin of this notion, or how this notion became associated with this particular group of people, can be traced back to the directing students of the Class of 1985 of BFA.

Certainly I also agree with the idea that to group a number of directors of a similar age together is sometimes only a convenient way for film theorists and scholars to study them. However, no matter how different each director of the "Fifth Generation" and "Sixth Generation" is, there are also many common traits shared by the same generation of filmmakers. Age and life experience are something you can't escape. For example, the Fifth Generation lived through the most turbulent years of modern China. They experienced this turbulence when they were coming of age. So, no matter what subject they choose, I feel this experience has distinguished and will continue to distinguish on their work. This is also true for our generation. As a group of people of a similar age, we came out of the same class. Therefore, it is quite natural that our life experience and what interests us are somewhat similar. I think those who graduated from CATA also share our views of the world. Although it is also true that each of us is different if examined more closely, our common traits are quite obvious. First of all, because we grew up in the city, in my impression, almost 99 percent of us deal only with life in the city. I am not very good at theorizing and generalization, but I feel some of us, including myself, were affected by this lack of a broader life experience. Therefore, from my point of view, it is understandable that some of our works were alleged to be too individual-centered, immature, and divorced from reality. To look at this from another angle, however, you could also say that this emphasis on individuality also reflected our common wish, which was to make our films as cinematic as possible. Today, I think most of us have already freed ourselves from this limitation. Their works are becoming more and more relevant to ordinary people's lives. This transition, I believe, is also another manifestation of our common traits.

Ma Liwen

I am fond of Jia Zhangke's films. What I love most are those films you can feel the presence of directors, the presence of their minds and souls. This is a must. Of course I also like another kind of films, such as *Run Lola Run* and *Amelie*. Although these films lack soul, they represent another kind of style, cinematically pure. I hope my films will also work toward the above two directions, but whether or not I can achieve that goal remains to be seen. Speaking of Jia Zhangke, I feel he is very consistent, including the consistency of perception and intellect. I've also seen a DVD by a woman director. I can't wait to acquaint myself with her. The film is called *Old Men*, shot in black and white and with no score on the soundtrack. I saw the film in a bar. The screening was meant only for a small group of people. I remember I was extremely sleepy on that day, but somehow couldn't fall asleep. I saw the film after midnight. Sleepy and absent-minded, I watched

Chapter Two

the whole film. Strangely enough, after the film was over, I regained my spirit and became really energized. I immediately wanted to watch it again. You simply felt the presence of the director's soul. Simple and pure, the film consists of little cinematic tricks. What you can feel is the humanistic concern of the director. This concern, in my opinion, is the soul of any artistic work.

As for me, I don't think I can identify myself with any particular group. It is impossible to put a fixed label on someone who has only made one or two films. The first films of mine may resemble the works by those of the same age group, but my next film might be totally different. I also don't see myself as a member of the "Sixth Generation".

Meng Qi

I think dividing Chinese filmmakers in generational terms implies that the latter generation has rebelled against the former and achieved some breakthroughs. But the term "generation" in China has exclusively referred to the succession of the trained directors from BFA. The Fourth Generation refers to the BFA graduates of the directing department in the 1960s. The Fifth Generation consists of the 1982 BFA graduates, and the "Sixth Generation" includes the BFA graduates of both 1989 and 1991. There are a lot of misunderstandings in the West surrounding these labels. Many are simply parroting the words of others. Indeed, I think it is no longer meaningful to use the label "generation" again after the "Sixth Generation" because filmmaking is no longer limited to a small group of BFA graduates anymore.

To be frank, I am really not an authority on the works of the Fifth and "Sixth Generation" filmmakers. I've seen only a few of them. Among the films of the Fifth Generation directors, I love *Red Sorghum*, *Yellow Earth*, *To Live*, and *Farewell My Concubine*. I view directors of the "Sixth Generation" as my big brothers. I've seen some of their early films, which many people haven't seen, such as *Xiao Wu* and *Beijing Bastard*. The reason why I refuse to see too many films is because I want to keep a fresh sensibility to the surrounding environment. I am afraid that watching too many films would tire me. This is also what I do with reading. I always try to keep my reading appetite under control. Reading stories every day, I think, would dazzle one's eyes and make good things slip away. To keep a sense of freshness, I only read stories occasionally. This "occasional-ness" often strikes sparks with me.

Shi Runjiu

My understanding is that the line between generations is drawn in accordance with the different classes of BFA. The Class of 1978, who graduated in

1982, was labeled the "Fifth Generation" and, naturally, the Class of 1985 was called the "Sixth Generation". I have no idea who invented this term, but it has floated around for some time. I think the term the "Sixth Generation" refers specifically to the Class of 1985 of BFA, whose members include Zhang Yuan, Wang Xiaoshuai, and Lou Ye. I entered CATA in 1987. So, I don't think I have anything to do with the "Sixth Generation".

On the other hand, it seems to me that young directors in general, including the "Sixth Generation", are especially interested in the real life of today's China. They think film should focus on today instead of yesterday. The Fifth Generation filmmakers like Zhang Yimou and Chen Kaige made a number of films that are concerned with Chinese history and tradition. Although I myself also have a fascination with history, I feel the Fifth Generation's obsession with history is closely connected to their education. In those days, they were sent down to the countryside as so-called "intellectual youths", and most of them dreamed of transforming China and the world. The education they received emphasized social responsibility and a sense of mission that traditional Chinese scholar-officials were expected to have. But this idealism has largely faded. To be frank, I personally still believe in this idealism. This is probably because the education I received still consisted of some lingering lessons on those high morals, including Fan Zhongyan's [989-1052] work "To Be First in Worrying the World's Worries and Last in Enjoying Its Pleasures". But most young people changed their world-view and direction after June 4, 1989. I believe they also had that idealism and sense of social responsibility before then. After that incident, however, many of them completely changed. I am not sure whether this transformation has anything to do with their films, but I guess the answer is yes.

Tang Danian

I think dividing filmmakers into different generations came initially from the Soviet model. I am not particularly supportive of the notion of the "Sixth Generation" because I feel the whole environment surrounding this group of filmmakers is quite complicated. First of all, because of the changes brought about by reform policies, Chinese society has become increasingly open. Second, as a result of this openness, each filmmaker's life experience, the intellectual resources they can draw upon, and the means of self-expression have also multiplied. I thus feel that not only do they differ from each other, but each filmmaker's own style varies from film to film. In comparison, the Fifth Generation filmmakers have a lot of things in common, such as their shared life experience and background. Besides, the overall cultural milieu of China at that time was relatively monolithic. Everyone grew up in that kind

Chapter Two

of environment. As a matter of fact, the practice of dividing filmmakers in generational terms started with the Fifth Generation. It is not a practice that is based on chronological sequence: because there were the first, second, third, and fourth, the following one must be the fifth. On the contrary, because of the emergence of the Fifth Generation, people started to go back to the cinematic tradition of China and rediscovered the previous "four generations". In other words, the naming of the Fifth Generation has awakened the notion of "generation". The emergence of the Fifth Generation brought about the Fourth Generation, and the latter started to search for their common traits and ways of expression.

In reality, the naming of the Fifth and "Sixth Generations" was based on the emergence of two creative groups from BFA. The year 1978 saw the full recruitment of new students of BFA after the end of the Cultural Revolution, and the second full recruitment didn't happen until 1985. No new students were admitted to the directing department between 1979 and 1984. These two recruitments resulted in the formation of two complete groups of creative artists in filmmaking. But as I just mentioned, the notion of the "Sixth Generation", if purely for the purpose of academic discussion, is not quite meaningful. It actually only provides a convenience for commercial promotion and media campaign. Directors such as Huang Jianxin and Sun Zhou can't be easily labeled in generational terms, for example. They definitely do not belong to the "Sixth Generation", and it is also unpersuasive to label them the Fifth Generation. On the other hand, dividing directors in generational terms is also a reflection of our overall understanding of culture and art. We used to be obsessed with the notion of unity, or of the so-called "typicality of times". We often assumed that the essence of this "typicality" could be sufficiently conveyed through a group of people's collective efforts. Traces of this obsession can be still found in the practice of naming the "Sixth Generation". Today, however, more and more people are reaching the consensus that art is actually a form of individual expression.

Wang Chao

When the term "Sixth Generation" was first used, I hadn't started making films. At the time people began to challenge this notion, I had little connection with filmmaking. This context, therefore, explains why I don't see myself as a member of this "generation". If you use the term "filmmakers born in the 1960s", then I am certainly one of them. But if you switch the definition and use the "Sixth Generation" label, then I don't think I belong to this generation. I can't see how I could be connected in that context. Besides, my background is entirely different from that of the so-called "Sixth Generation" directors. On the other hand, my relation with the Fifth Generation is more tangible. It was at the Chen Kaige Film Workshop that I acquired concrete filmmaking experience. Certainly it doesn't mean that my films are similar to those of the Fifth Generation. To a certain extent, my guiding principle is exactly the opposite.

Although I view myself as not belonging to any one of the two groups, I take no offense when people tend to speak of me in relation to them. I feel really relieved that people, including those "typical" Fifth or "Sixth Generation" filmmakers themselves, begin to question these labels. This means they've realized that individualism is more important than group identity. It's just the correct thing to do.

Wang Guangli

As a matter of fact, I went to college in the same year as such core members of the "Sixth Generation" filmmakers as Zhang Yuan and Wang Xiaoshuai did. I am the same age as they are. Therefore, I could be a member of the "Sixth Generation" in its classical sense. But I often deny this label based on the premise that I have no connection with BFA. If the Fifth Generation refers to the BFA students who entered BFA in 1978 and graduated in 1982, then the "Sixth Generation" only means a particular group of filmmakers who graduated from BFA in 1989. Although I am the same age as they are, I am first not a BFA graduate. Second, my films are not quite like theirs. In addition, I don't think it is possible anymore to form a "generation" after the Fifth Generation because each filmmaker is quite distinctive. For the convenience of study and discussion, however, I think there is nothing wrong to group them as a generation. Emotionally, I am quite willing to be included in this generation, because the overall conditions are still very harsh for them. I am more than happy to join this group and to make it stronger. If in any way I can help strengthen the power of the "Sixth Generation", I am emotionally ready to make my contribution. From a rational point of view, however, I feel my filmmaking style is quite different from that of the "Sixth Generation". Besides, the BFA people would probably say: How can you have anything to do with the "Sixth Generation"? You've got a different background!

Certainly, as I've said, emotionally, I am very willing to side with this generation because they are indeed working under arduous conditions. Besides, their luck is not even close to that of the Fifth Generation. Although the films by the Fifth Generation are also stamped with strong individuality, they were hailed by the social elites back then. The filmmakers themselves, on the other hand, were treated the same way as today's pop stars.

Chapter Two

Wang Quanan

In theory, I support any effort to label us in generational terms. First, it is simply convenient. Second, it is also based on the real situation of Chinese cinema. Didn't we come along one group after another? This seems to be customary. But why it becomes a little harder to continue this "custom" when we come down to the notion of the "Sixth Generation"? I believe this is also an objective reflection of the current status of Chinese society. The rapid transformation of Chinese society has made many traditional notions fall apart. Consequently, the so-called "Sixth Generation" can no longer cohere as a group. It is not an issue of whether they are talented. I feel it is the changing society that has nurtured diversity and multiplicity. Since you could use any means to express your view of the world, individuality starts to emerge. It is no longer a requirement for us to be the same; indeed, it is impossible for us to be alike. For example, you and I are two different individuals, and this difference will surely lead us to different views of art and choices of film. This is what I feel about the so-called "Sixth Generation".

However, this emphasis on individuality, in my opinion, only began to take shape recently. It is only the beginning of bidding farewell to a collective era. Spiritual independence is still an infant, immature and unstable. Furthermore, beside you is the grand shadow of the mother. She is strong, solid, powerful, and very utilitarian. It is quite hard to break away from her.

Speaking of my relationship with the "Sixth Generation", I've actually tried very hard not to be affiliated with any collective entities. You could probably detect this from *Lunar Eclipse*. To put it more clearly, you can find the budding consciousness of individuality in my films, and I tried hard to make it as pure as possible. Purely in the sense of resisting the established, I don't find anything wrong with the term "Sixth Generation". You could call it "seizing power", an act that is very Oedipal in the Freudian sense. But if we look at it from an artistic perspective, this group of filmmakers is quite different. It is a combination of both old and new: some of them might find it hard to completely walk out of the shadow of the Fifth Generation, because to mimic the success of the Fifth Generation is simply too tempting; a lot of them, however, want to follow their own path of independence. Under the current condition, I think the latter group of people would find it most difficult to get their films made. It is my hope that truly individualized works, both stylistically and thematically, will come out of this group of filmmakers. This is the best result we can hope for.

Wang Xiaoshuai

The notion of the "Sixth Generation" began to gain momentum after Hu Xueyang, a classmate of mine at BFA, made *A Lady Left Behind*. We felt quite encouraged by this, because Xueyang was the first one to fulfill his silver screen dream. This notion was raised again when scholars and critics started to pay attention to this group of young filmmakers. They researched back to the days of our graduation and dug out the manifesto-like article published in a Shanghai magazine. In reality, however, nothing was so formal or official. We just felt that we needed to get our films made.

Since the very beginning, I'd had the presentiment that the word "generation" would reemerge because it provides convenience for discussion and classification. But I also had the feeling that the nature of this notion would definitely change, and it would soon turn out that the notion of the "Sixth Generation" wouldn't last long, because it's simply inaccurate. So I have repeatedly requested various media not to use the word "generation" to address us. It is every filmmaker's hope that his/her career will continue for a lifetime, or at least for a considerable period of time, but to address filmmakers in generational terms gives one the impression that once labeled their positions were fixed. Besides, it would also mislead people to imply that today's young filmmakers are replacing the so-called Fifth Generation directors and making them irrelevant. I am always against the notion of replacement, because there is no need for us to replace anyone. Once you start to talk about replacement, you are advocating a return to self-isolation, a status that we Chinese are quite familiar with.

It is quite clear that today's China is no longer the one that existed when I made my first film. At that time, each of us was on the same starting line and started running together once the whistle was blown. After this group was done, the next group would line up again and wait for the whistle. In this situation, the line that set one generation apart from another was clearly drawn. But today many different ideas actually co-exist, and films are being made by both young and veteran filmmakers. It is a phenomenon that is both interdependent and cross-generational. To keep using the word "generation" to describe us is, therefore, misleading.

My feeling is that people nowadays are becoming jaded and are constantly in search of new stimulants. This is particularly true for the media and critics. They need something like the term the "Sixth Generation" to stimulate their imagination. As a matter of fact, this notion itself is already a violation of art as an individual endeavor. It assumes that a whole generation had the same experience and shared the same way of thinking. This assumption is evidently against the principles of artistic creation, because art to me is definitely an individual undertaking. I view the film industry in Hollywood more as one that makes consumer products rather than artistic works. Because of this, Hollywood can follow the successful formula of making one model and then duplicating it in large numbers. If this formula were not followed, the audience would respond negatively. After the first climax is over, it must be followed by the second, third, and fourth, and the ending must provide the audience with some sort of satisfaction and have some sort of emotional impact. This is the rule of Hollywood. But non-Hollywood cinemas, such as the French New Wave and "auteur film", are mainly individual-based, no matter what labels are attached to them. There are no formulas to be followed. Besides, today technology has made it possible for more people to make films. In addition to 16mm films, there are also DV films and made-for-TV films. For an artist living in today's society, there are a lot of possibilities. Even purely from a technological viewpoint, therefore, it is impossible to label a particular group of filmmakers in generational terms. It is quite likely that a forty- or fifty-year old person, although having had no opportunity in the past, could make his/her first film because of the birth of the DVD medium. If this is the case, which generation does he or she belong to? As a filmmaker, I feel my goal is only to make good films. I would feel quite content if I were able to create some individual works for critics and society to talk about. Through these individual cases, people may judge for themselves how representative these films are in terms of reflecting life and society.

The notion of the Fifth Generation, on the other hand, is relatively tenable, because all of a sudden there emerged a group of filmmakers who at the time rewrote the history of Chinese cinema. Comparatively speaking, the Fifth Generation appeared on stage in a well-balanced lineup, like a group of people in Western suits walking down the street together. Therefore, I think the notion of the Fifth Generation speaks to a certain truth. Certainly there is no denying that the Fifth Generation has also changed somewhat in both its style and way of thinking. One day, some of them might even gradually become identical with young filmmakers in their way of thinking because everyone is capable of reflection and self-examination. But before reflection there is also subconsciousness or unconsciousness. This is what sets two generations apart. I think the difference between subconsciousness and unconsciousness lies in the fact that when the previous generations started to make films, society left little room for individualism. At that time, therefore, people didn't dare or were unwilling to acknowledge individuality. This is the unbearable sadness of the previous generations. I feel people at that time were closely connected to their social environment. The sent-down youth went to the countryside like a flood and returned to the cities again like a flood. This collective life experience dismantled their individuality, and few of them knew their true selves. The ultimate concern for them was to return to the city, and there was little time for self-reflection and exploration. When they came back to the city and finally had the opportunity to go to college and carry out their creative plans, the Cultural Revolution had just ended.

I think the termination of the Cultural Revolution was a critical moment in Chinese history. All of a sudden, Chinese history seemed to come to a pause at that juncture. Although the situation was quite chaotic prior to this, history was at least in full motion, with one political campaign after another. But this motion came to a sudden pause after the end of the Cultural Revolution. By then, the old generation of Chinese leaders had passed away, and the new leaders started to call for a rethinking of the previous policies. Rethinking the past actually became the dominant theme of the "Roots-Seeking Literature" and "Scar Literature" of the early 1980s. I think this political and literary milieu had a tremendous impact on filmmaking at that time. People gathered together to talk about their common experience and reflect upon what went wrong with China. Thus the Fifth Generation emerged. Having experienced a series of political movements, however, they understood the Communist Party quite well and had a good sensibility of politics. They were therefore quite wise not to directly address reality but to turn to history, suggesting future development through cultural reflections. This is why films like *King of Children* began to emerge. They are more or less still trapped in that mode.

As for us, we as a group no longer have that kind of collective consciousness. Also, we lack the much-needed concrete experience to reflect upon the Cultural Revolution and the previous political upheavals. What we are facing is an ever-changing Chinese society: our view of the world, our morality, and our social surroundings…everything is changing at full speed. When we went to college, the Soviet model still had a lingering effect. But it was soon shelved and Western philosophies and literary theories poured in. Then, there was the 1985 Student Movement. What we got from those theories was an emphasis on freedom: individual freedom, free speech, free press… At that time, the talk on individual freedom was just gaining momentum, and issues like individual heroism also began to emerge. We were indoctrinated with these ideas throughout our college years. We began to realize the important role of individualism in determining one's fate. In other words, the relations between the individual and the family as well as between the individual and the nation began to return to their natural state. Before us, the top priority was the nation. For the benefit of the nation, you were supposed to sacrifice yourself as an individual and your family. But when it comes down to us, we believe you must first protect yourself and your family, and the issue of the nation comes after that. There is a renewed concern for individualism and individual consciousness. When I first started to make independent films, therefore, I always reminded myself to pay special attention to self-expression and the surroundings that are resonant to my own experience.

Chapter Two

Xu Jinglei

I feel the Fifth Generation filmmakers are somewhat burdened by history. They have many complexes: the "Cultural Revolution Complex" and the "Sent-down Complex", for instance. Perhaps they are deeper than us in philosophical and historical thinking. Compared to them, I think the "Sixth Generation", if there is such a group, is sometimes too obsessed with marginal subjects. Certainly this does not mean I disagree with them on many issues. As a matter of fact, I like many of their films, particularly that of Jia Zhangke. Watching his films is almost like experiencing a different life that you otherwise would have never imagined. This being said, however, I have a natural objection to those films in which form overpowers content. It is my belief that content must always determine form, not vice versa. This is also one of the underlining principles that guided the making of my first feature. I dislike many films. It is not because these films are bad in cinematography, art design, or acting, but because form is more important than content in these films. I like Quentin Tarantino's films, though. Although his films are dazzling in form, I don't feel content is overshadowed by form in his films. In other words, the forms these films use are consistent with what they intend to express.

I don't think I belong to the so-called "Sixth Generation". I also don't like to be categorized or set into certain fixed pattern. Where I stand depends on the nature of my future projects. In other words, I must first focus on what I want to express, and then go on to choose the corresponding method or style. It is quite possible that my next film will have a totally different look, because filmmaking to me is both a business and a recreational endeavor. So, I am quite eager to try something new after the first two features. The exploration of the new is always interesting and stimulating.

Zhang Ming

Many people don't agree with the notion of the "Sixth Generation", including me. Although different from the Fifth Generation, this group cannot be named collectively. I think this is exactly the root cause that sets the two groups apart. In the past, it was relatively easy to find a way to summarize a group of directors, but it now becomes quite difficult to name these young filmmakers in collective terms. This is where the difference lies. If you ask me what sets the Fifth Generation and those who are after them apart, I would say that, from the very beginning of naming, their difference has been already revealed. In the long history of China, it has been a common practice to either consciously or unconsciously categorize people in collective rather than individual terms. I feel these young filmmakers should be defined as different individuals. After all, their styles differ greatly from each other. Up to the Fifth Generation of filmmakers, one could probably still find resemblances in visual style, film language, and choice of materials among Chinese directors, but this cannot be applied to those who came on stage after the Fifth Generation. These later filmmakers, as I said, differ in many ways, particularly in visual style. Some favor dramatic elements, whereas others emphasize individual experiences. While the former pay particular attention to casting and dialogue, the latter devote much of their efforts to staying close to life's naked reality, and their films sometimes look more like documentaries.

Furthermore, the overall filmmaking environment in China has undergone great changes since the Fifth Generation. When Chen Kaige and Zhang Yimou came to prominence in Chinese cinema, filmmaking was completely a state operation. Their first films were approved and financed by the state, and they also didn't need to worry about the issue of distribution. The situation is quite different now. The state plays no role in many films made today, including the two works of mine. In terms of financing, at least, the state is no longer relevant for many filmmakers today. This is entirely different from the days of the birth of the Fifth Generation. In the past, to be a filmmaker was considered a privilege, and it was only through official channels that one could possibly become a director. But now there are many channels for film financing, and anybody can be a filmmaker as long as he/she has the money. This is a fundamental change. If you must find similarities among these young filmmakers, then it is exactly that disparity—disparity in background, disparity in education, disparity in their roads to filmmaking—that speaks to their similarity. Enjoying unprecedented freedom unprecedented since the 1950s, these young filmmakers are confronting less control from the state. Or, the state simply finds it harder to control them. Thus, works have emerged that would have been difficult to imagine in the past, and some of them are even made outside the system. These are what some people label "underground films". Maybe China is the only place where you can find "underground films" like these. If the Chinese government and Communist Party didn't exist, then there would be no such "underground films" at all. Ultimately, therefore, the ideological environment has undergone a sea change since the birth of the Fifth Generation.

For the convenience of discussion, however, some people still persist in using a special term to describe this group of filmmakers, and perhaps they also have many followers. But as more and more young filmmakers emerge, I think more people will give this kind of labeling a second thought. Why do we need to find their similarities? I think the more important thing is to find their disparities. If finding one's similarity remained our habit, then it would be another testament to the fact that we really haven't got beyond the ideology of the Fifth Generation era. My original purpose of becoming a filmmaker was to articulate a self that differs from the rest of the world. If you don't try to differentiate yourself from other people, then there would be no basic incentive for artistic creation. To create your own work is actually to provide a contrast or a reference point for a further exchange of views. If everything were the same, then there would be no need for exchange and, ultimately, there would be no need for your work at all. Cinema should be used as a tool for understanding of today's changing society. Your view of the world should be embedded in your films. Through cinema, you let the world hear your individual voice and see your distinct way of expression. It is more important, therefore, for us to search for each director's distinct voice. In the past, we were enveloped by a pseudo sense of "great harmony": our thinking was identical, our language was identical, our expression was identical, and our actions also tended to be identical. I am especially opposed to this kind of sameness: why must I be the same as you? Everybody has his/her own views, which must be fully respected. This world and art itself will become much more colorful if the respect for disparity is properly observed.

Zhang Yang

The notion of the "Sixth Generation" seems to be taken as an act of rebellion, as something quite radical. If this is true, then you might find that the films made by non-BFA graduates have nothing in common with this notion. We are not walking the same path. Latecomers, therefore, will probably find it even more difficult to identify themselves with this notion. Personally, I also have problem with this notion. What I find easy to identify with is the feeling that compared to the works of the previous generation the cinematic world created by this group of young filmmakers is completely different, different both in subject matter and in cinematic perception. If put in this context, then this generation does possess certain common traits and tends to pursue some similar goals. We are concerned about the creation of an urban cinema, and we share our common concern over the existence of modern man. We are also especially concerned with the self and how it communicates with and differentiates from the surrounding environment and lives. In the films of the Fifth Generation, the direct link to life itself often remains invisible. Compared to them, our generation has shown great emphasis on the relations between art and contemporary life.

However, I think our generation of directors also differs greatly in filmmaking. Even in the conceptualization of an urban cinema we differ considerably from each other in subject matter and ways of expression. In addition, in recent years, there has been a trend of diversification among the directors of this generation. In the past, we were against many things, particularly against commercial cinema. We felt being marginal and alternative was something worth pursuing. Today, however, many of us have chosen to go mainstream or to pursue a popular cinema that is outside the "Main Melody" film. We vary greatly in our choices. As far as cinematic style is concerned, unlike the Fifth Generation filmmakers—who often resemble each other in style and disposition—there are also great differences among us. Therefore, if you want to arbitrarily group these filmmakers of diverse interests together according to the standard of "generation" or "age", it is perfectly fine. But such a classification, I believe, is not quite meaningful considering what I've pointed out above.

The reason why the notion of the "Sixth Generation" becoming popular overseas, I think, is due to the fact that people outside of China tend to pay more attention to common traits instead of differences within a particular group of artists. It makes no difference whether one calls it the "Sixth Generation" or the "New Wave". What matters most for them is something they can grasp. I see more differences than similarities. I pay less attention to their "common traits", because I feel quite ambiguous about them. I also feel we don't have enough representative works to be qualified for the definition of the "Sixth Generation". Compared to other young filmmakers, I sometimes feel I don't particularly dislike the works of the Fifth Generation. Going back to two or three years, at least, we hadn't been able to produce anything that could possibly surpass the films of the Fifth Generation. Even at this moment, we as a group are still on the verge of a creative explosion. So far we haven't been able to impress people with a variety of great works. Maybe there are a few masterpieces I am not aware of from our group, but even a few does not qualify us as a distinct generation.

Zhang Yuan

I feel this practice of labeling is quite scary. At every turn the term "generation" is used to represent a group of filmmakers. But who can represent whom? Even my own films look different from each other, to say nothing of comparing them to the works of my friends and other filmmakers. Sometimes, I feel those works done by people younger than I or older than I, even by those who have already passed away or who have no BFA background, are much closer to me. I don't feel particularly intimate with the works by filmmakers of my "generation". So, there is no reason to lump me together with them. Certainly I am also proud that some of my classmates have made great films. I am honored that I used to be their classmate. But this is not to say that my works are similar to theirs.

Chapter Two

I remember when I was a student at BFA the idea that we should not follow in the footsteps of the previous generations was quite prevalent. Even before our graduation, all of us, including those who would have nothing to do with filmmaking after graduation, were labeled as "Sixth Generation". It is sometimes true that the younger generation will usually outdo the older generation, simply because death can't be avoided, and the old must make way for the young. This is natural law. But it doesn't mean the works by the younger generation resemble each other in appearance and nature. The most important thing is to make what you love to make, to do what interests you, and to create the style that suits you most.

It has been more than 100 years since the birth of cinema. After experimenting for 100-years, nothing seems to be new anymore in cinema. If you list the 100 best directors of all time in the world, you will find many great names left out. This is because there are too many great directors and too many good films. As a filmmaker, however, you have no choice but to continue to do what concerns you most. Making a film is just like writing a book. You become interested in a person or a topic. You don't care whether the similar things and ideas have been expressed in other books. You will simply continue writing. To a certain extent, the work has become part of your spiritual and natural life. You don't give up. To me, therefore, each film carries a strong personal imprint. This is why I have a problem with the practice of labeling us a "generation" or a "collective". I don't hang out very often with the friends of the so-called "Sixth Generation", but I maintain a close relationship with friends who have nothing to do with filmmaking. Being labeled a "Sixth Generation" filmmaker, therefore, I feel quite strange.

The same is also true for the "Fifth Generation". I don't think there is such a group of filmmakers called the "Fifth Generation". Who are the members of this generation? This term is used at every turn, as if it consisted of a great number of filmmakers. But whenever this term is evoked, we only hear the names of Zhang Yimou and Chen Kaige. Besides Zhang and Chen, who else have you seen? Why don't we simply address them individually? There have been frequent reports about Fifth Generation gatherings of more than 100 people. But out of this number, how many of them are making films today? Besides, those who are still making films today differ greatly. Each one is distinctive.

CHAPTER THREE

"DANCING WITH THE SHACKLES:" THE (UN)CENSORED VOICES OF THE "SIXTH GENERATION"

Since the beginning of their careers, the "Sixth Generation" filmmakers have been in constant negotiations with government censors. The first films by the generation, Wang Xiaoshuai's The Days and Frozen, *Lou Ye's* Weekend Lover *and* Suzhou River, *Jia Zhangke's* Xiao Wu *and* Platform, *Jiang Wen's* In the Heat of the Sun *and* Devils on the Doorstep, *Guan Hu's* Cello in a Cab, *Liu Bingjian's* Men and Women, *Tang Danian's* City Paradise, *Wang Chao's* The Orphan of Anyang, *Wang Guangli's* I've Graduated, *and Zhang Yuan's* Beijing Bastards *and* East Palace West Palace, *were all banned by the Film Bureau, an official organ of the State Administration of Radio, Film, and Television (SARFT). The hostility began to thaw by the end of 1999, when some of the banned filmmakers, including Wang Xiaoshuai, were invited to attend the SARFT-sponsored "Symposium on Young Directors' Films". In the summer of 2002, two similar symposiums on "emerging directors" or the "New Generation" filmmakers were held in Beijing and Shanghai, paving the way to a more relaxed environment for the "Sixth Generation". By late 2003, almost all the aforementioned directors began to "dance with the shackles" of film censorship (if paraphrasing Chinese poet Wen Yiduo's famous line), i.e., to make "legal" films within the system. For example, Jia Zhangke has developed a cozy relationship with the state-owned Shanghai Film Studio, which partially financed his officially released feature* The World. *Jia also chaired the jury panel for the Asian New Talent Awards at the 2005 Shanghai International Film Festival.*

* * *

Guan Hu

I feel my situation is slightly different from that of some of the young filmmakers. In general, I've been always working within the system, never quite "underground". This being said, I am fully aware of the advantages of being "underground": several like-minded people gather together and the ideas coming from that gathering could soon materialize into a film. As a matter of fact, I also did some "underground" works in the past, not because I wanted to, but because I was forced to. I always feel it's actually not necessary to go "underground" unless the subject one chooses has no hope at all to pass the censors. If working

Chapter Three

within the system does no considerable harm to your work, why would you give yourself a hard time by being "underground?" Besides, working within the system would also guarantee you a much broader audience.

The practice of shooting without your screenplay approved by the censors is certainly an option, but it was more of a strategy that worked in the past. The censors are now increasingly wary of this kind of practice and won't easily let you get away with it. The best strategy in dealing with the censorship apparatus, in my opinion, is probably to shoot the would-be "problematic" scenes two or three times. Then, what you might want to do is to first show the censors the "worst" or the most "problematic" ones. If they have no objection, you consider yourself lucky; if they find it objectionable, then you can easily go to the second or third option you've already prepared. To me, therefore, you can always find a way to negotiate with the censors.

It is quite regrettable that for Chinese filmmakers devoting only 50 percent of their energy to filmmaking itself is already considered quite remarkable, because most of them have to spend a considerable amount of time on interpersonal connections. It is especially frightening if you metaphorically compare the censorship apparatus with a slaughterhouse: you are actually dealing with the butchers of your film. Despite this analogy, I think in the end you will always be able to find a solution to how to deal with the "butchers". In addition, the more experienced filmmakers will also provide you with valuable advice and guidance through the process.

Jia Zhangke

From my point of view, since the days of my first film, I've always hoped that I could have a broader audience base in China. To put it more simply, it is my strong desire to have my films passed. These days there is a misunderstanding about us, the claim that we never intended to go through the censorship process, as if being "underground" was a trademark for us, and we must rely on this trademark to sell our films and achieve personal gains. I think those with this kind of criticism have never experienced what we've gone through. When your film can't be shown in your own country, I have the odd feeling that I as a person was completely absent in China. My films are being screened in Europe, in the United States, and in Japan, but never officially shown in China. It seems all things about me and my films can only happen in remote places. I always say film can't be defined by rumor. But in China, my films are only rumors. Instead of watching my films, people here can only "read" about them. Why do I use the word "read?" because they only appear in magazines. Just take a glance at those magazines: my films are reduced to three lines and two stills. That's why I say my films are only rumors. When your films are equal to tabloid news or rumors, there is no way for you to defend any rumor-based criticism. Be it "postcolonial" or "catering to the foreign taste", I am simply powerless in defending myself, because I can't turn tabloid news into real films.

Platform was once screened at a bar in Beijing through a SVGA projector. Even in optimal conditions, this kind of projection would itself reduce the picture quality significantly. But the projection of *Platform* was much worse. First, rain leaked into the main screening room. We had no choice but moved the projection to the main room, three sides of which were walled by glass. It turned out that the curtains could barely keep the sunlight from entering. As a result, the projected images turned dazzling white, and it was almost impossible to tell who was who. Before that incident, *Platform* was also screened outdoors, but next to the screening site there was a disco club. The disco music from that club drowned out the sound of the film. One could barely hear the characters' dialogue. The audience could only rely on subtitles. I call it *Platform*'s disco edition. I did manage to show the celluloid version of *Platform* at a local drive-in theater. But do you know what kind of screen the drive-in theater had? It was made of a wooden board with white paint. The screen had no reflection at all, and it was absolutely impossible for one to see various shades in the picture.

When one's films are exhibited in such conditions, I think any director would agonize over it. "How could my films turn into such visual fiascoes?" Because of this kind of thing, I don't think any director is willing to purposefully play the "underground" card. Once forced "underground", you will find it impossible to defend yourself. For example, when people criticize my films as being merely focused on the "poor" and "backward" side of the Chinese society, I am simply speechless. I can't say "No. No. My films are not like what you described", because most of them haven't seen my films at their best. My hope is for everybody to experience the feelings that permeate each shot, each cut, each camera movement, and, most importantly, the seemingly coldness or calmness of the surface. It is meaningless for me to vocally defend my films, because one needs to see them in a normal theater to feel their subtlety. If only relying on the storylines or a few glimpses of those films, I myself might also agree with those critics in arguing against this kind of filmmaking. Without a healthy viewing environment, it is unrealistic to expect people to share the feelings of your films.

While all my films were submitted to the Film Bureau, the experience with *Platform* was the most painful. After *Xiao Wu* was finished in 1998, my financing situation greatly improved. Many companies, including some big ones, expressed interest in investing my projects. Later on, I decided to team up with Takeshi Kitano's company. That was the end of 1998. But I didn't

Chapter Three

finish *Platform* until the beginning of 2000. Why so long? That's because I was patiently waiting for the words from the Film Bureau. I went there countless times but heard nothing about *Platform*. The part that saddened me most was that although I'd been to the Film Bureau countless times in a year I didn't even know whom I was dealing with. There was certainly a cadre in charge of my case, but he constantly used the phrase *lingdao* [a top official] to dodge my questions. Who was this *lingdao*? "I can't tell you", he said to me.

Frankly, many people at the Beijing Film Studio were quite helpful during this painful process. When *Platform* was submitted, both Tian Zhuangzhuang, then director of the just founded Filmmaker Workshop at the Beijing Film Studio, and Shi Dongming, then vice president of the Beijing Film Studio, were especially enthusiastic. They were willing to do all in their power to help me. How far did we go? I even paid the administration fees required for a co-production. At one point, I was told that I could start shooting the following week. But suddenly I was called over one day, and Shi Dongming informed me that I must give up the project, because a leading cadre deemed it "inappropriate". There were no actual opinions or suggestions, just the word "inappropriate". How could such a simple and vague word determine my project's future? I felt it was extremely unfair. At that time, most pre-production works, including the selections of costumes and props, had already been finished. In addition, I'd already ordered film stocks and made up my mind that I would use a lot of long takes in *Platform*. How could I simply stop shooting? Furthermore, I couldn't suppress my creative impulse, or my anger. After more than a year's wait, therefore, I decided to start shooting without "official permission" from the Film Bureau.

I feel at this historical moment there is a very dangerous tendency in China. That is: when we are dealing with the very reality of China, some people will jump to the conclusion that you are actually selling life. I think this kind of criticism is quite dangerous. If confronting reality meant selling life or life experience, then the whole culture of China would float down to the bottom. If this was the case, who would dare to face reality itself? What use would art be? I came across some criticism the other day on the Internet, saying that "underground film is just like a perch wrapped in a piece of aluminum foil. Although the perch is cooked, we can't taste it. Why? Because these directors are not willing to calmly cut that piece of aluminum foil open. The solution is in fact quite simple: just cut that piece of paper open." I think this writer has got it wrong. I've spent so many years trying to cut this piece of paper open but completely failed.

Jiang Wen

The system that is beneficial to the development of cinema and warmly received by the people is a good system. Anything that is the opposite of this or affects artists' freedom of expression needs to change. To me, the ideal environment is the one that provides creative freedom for artists. People shouldn't compromise or give up, because without such an environment one would end up losing everything. If you make certain compromises, the nature of your work will change. If this is the case, then it is no longer an issue of compromise. So, I think we must first go back to the roots to understand how we see certain things. I am afraid that a nation that is not accustomed to self-reflection will eat its own bitter fruit. It is quite easy to fool others as well as oneself by claiming that compromise is a necessary act. It is also easy to justify this kind of argument. But what price does one pay?

To compromise or not is actually a matter of choice. I don't intend to accuse anybody. As grownups, everybody has the power and ability to control his/her fate as well as the freedom of choice. But what I want to reiterate is that everyone must take into account the price he/she would pay for his/her choice. If the price is too high, you can't fool yourself by saying that you've succeeded on both ends: censorship and artistic integrity. No sugarcane is sweet on both ends, right? Ordinary people have already realized this for a long time. I feel that for centuries the idea of price has been either absent or overlooked in our moral education. This idea is quite simple: if you want that piece of meat, you must lose some of your money. Otherwise, how do you get that piece of meat? You can't expect to have that piece of meat without losing even a penny, unless you resort to robbery.

Jin Chen

The Chinese film censorship system is a very interesting one. It is a system that every artist resents. I am also annoyed by it. But we can only take things as they are. It is one thing to talk about whether we should get rid of the system, and it is quite another when we face the reality itself. My feeling is that this system will continue to exist into the foreseeable future. As long as it survives we can only accept it as an unavoidable reality. As to whether other countries have similar systems or how film is censored in those countries, I don't really care. Have you seen *Cinema Paradiso*? To a certain extent, this film touches upon the issue of film censorship. I firmly believe one day our system will become better, just like the one in *Cinema Paradiso*. But for now, we have to confront this system and learn how to deal with it.

The current system of film censorship is quite strict and complicated. It has one notable characteristic. That is: if you know the existing taboos for certain but refuse to accept them, then for sure that you will be courting your own ruin. The subjects that are deemed sensitive or directly concern the reputation of the Party or Party-related figures, such as teachers and public

Chapter Three

security officers, will be carefully scrutinized by the Film Bureau. Based on my experience with the two previous films and the just-finished *Three Doors*, I think to dodge sensitive issues does require certain skills. I remember there was one line in the original screenplay of my first film, *Love in the Internet Age*, that got on the censors' nerves. The line appeared when a character in the film jumped into a swimming pool, hoping to pacify her mind after a series of incidents. She looked quite pale and didn't want to talk to anybody. But people thought she was going to commit suicide. So, one of the onlookers rushed into the pool to save her. I remember the original line from her was roughly like this: "There is no quiet place in this world; even when you are under the water, people will still come to disturb you." In other words, from her point of view, this is a world without peace and serenity. This line got on one censor's nerves, a censor who used to be a scriptwriter himself. He became very sensitive and said to me: you can't have this line. How can you say that there is no peace or serene place in this society? You must make changes. I had no choice and therefore changed the sentence. After the change, the sentence reads like this: "There are so many kindhearted people; even when you hide under the water hoping to get some rest, some people will still lend you a helping hand." You can see the tone has completely shifted. Serious doubt is replaced by sarcasm. But it turned out that the government didn't take this sarcasm too seriously. So, in dealing with the censors, sometimes you need to change yourself. In this case, the shift from direct social criticism to sarcastic comments made a difference. The screenplay was then passed. This is what I mean by "skill".

My second film, *Chrysanthemum Tea*, also had some trouble with the censors. There's a line "How about dying together?" in the screenplay. The Film Bureau was quite unhappy with this line, saying, "How can you say 'dying together?' It should be 'living together'." I was dumfounded after hearing this. They had the nerve to make this kind of demand. As it turned out, however, the problem was later skillfully solved. What we did was to first make changes in other places. As for this particular line, although we agreed to follow their suggestion, it remained intact in the final cut. By that time, because the censors felt we had followed most of their advice, this line no longer mattered to them. When facing the censorship system, therefore, we need both firmness and flexibility. Sometimes you want to stand up to what you believe, but other times you may need to make compromises. I feel this is a battle of both wits and courage, because on the one hand you must understand the awkward role this system plays, but on the other keep your spearhead sharpened.

Nor can I dismiss the possibility of so-called "self-censorship", which means that sometimes filmmakers tend to restrain themselves in advance if they foresee troubles from the Film Bureau. In my case, I usually first think it through before making crucial decisions. If I feel it would be impossible for something to pass, I either get around it or simply give it up. Sometimes I even like to prepare two versions, one of them specifically for the censors. This practice, however, has its own drawbacks. What if the censors are more lenient than you expected? In other words, what you deemed "problematic" or "troublesome" may very likely encounter no obstacles in the censorship process. Your "self-censorship" might turn out to be much stricter than the official one. This is especially true considering the fact that the censorship system seems to be loosening nowadays. Ultimately, market forces will determine the direction of the censorship system. The deepening of reform by market forces will eventually bring changes to this system. Take *Big Shot's Funeral* as an example. Originally, I thought many scenes in this film, including the one at the Great Hall of the People, would be heavily censored. But because of the lightness of the film as well as its market potential, these scenes were simply ignored by the censors. Zhang Yang's *Quitting* is another example. If you think in terms of your old view about the censorship apparatus, you would be very surprised to see these films passed. This is at least a positive change, isn't it? We can't say the censors were too stupid to perceive the subtlety of the films. I think this is a reflection of the fact that the system is slowly changing.

    Generally speaking, however, the censorship system greatly exhausts filmmakers' energy. Without its looking over my shoulder, I feel my filmmaking would be much smoother and purer. A clearly drafted production code or rule would be helpful, too. As a filmmaker, if I am unambiguously told what can and can't be said, I will live with that. A film rating system could probably achieve the same goal. Right now, however, the system requires a lot of guessing by the filmmaker. Sometimes you could be overreacting, but other times you could be underestimating. Both are harmful to your film and to Chinese cinema in general. For example, I didn't make any films in 2001 because a screenplay I submitted to the Film Bureau was turned down. Since the screenplay was about kinship in the contemporary Chinese countryside, it was deemed too sensitive and I was asked to make considerable changes. I made certain changes but found the dashing spirit of the film was missing, so, I essentially gave up the project.

Li Xin

Unconsciously, I've been trying to avoid many sensitive issues, such as those related to love and sex. You may say this is some kind of self-censorship. As a matter of fact, I've been trained in this since the early days of my filmmaking. I'd rather "clean up" my screenplay in advance than suffer the

Chapter Three

pain of being forced to cut certain scenes afterward. For instance, love and sex are intimately connected, and the latter plays an indispensable part in love relations. I fully understand that without sufficient expression of sex the believability of love would be severely affected. But as you know, sex, or anything related to sexual intimacy, is a taboo in Chinese cinema and therefore will be heavily censored. My way of dealing with this dilemma is to avoid the direct depiction of sex and to use more suggestive scenes that allude to sex. Of course this practice will bring about unspeakable losses to one's film, because you can't simply replace sexual repression with other kinds of repressions. If you cut the love-making scenes of a given sequence, then this whole sequence would become incoherent and difficult to grasp. What a frightening thing it is! But sometimes there is also the possibility that you can find some alternatives to remedy those losses. Physical contact, for example, could be replaced by suggestive actions that allude to sex. Certainly this is only one alternative among an array of choices.

I don't know if it's because my films are relatively "clean" or because I have been lucky, except for a few minor scenes, my films have so far encountered little problem with the censors. Perhaps this is because my basic premise is that one does not necessarily need to bypass the system for self-expression. Frankly speaking, no one in this business is happy to see himself or herself being excluded from the system, because that means few people could see his or her films in a normal theater. For filmmakers, nothing is more comfortable than seeing audiences go see their films. Besides, I think we can't totally dismiss film's educational function. In the past, this function might have been exaggerated, but it doesn't mean that film doesn't play an educational role in society. When I was visiting some foreign countries, I said to the audience: for some foreigners, especially for some Western critics, because you are "underground", and because your films are banned by the government, you represent truth. "This is wrong", I told them. There are many things that are against the system in every country, including violence, abusive sex, and drug addiction. China is no exception. But those things do not reflect the life of the Chinese majority. To the majority, a life similar to that of *Dazzling* may be more truthful. Being "underground" does not necessarily mean more truthful.

Liu Bingjian

When I was making *The Stone Bed*, my thinking was quite simple and pure: I'll do whatever it takes to get my first film done. Because it was my debut feature, I felt I needed to pay more attention to what other people had to say. I genuinely felt at that time that you can't do whatever you like in filmmaking. As a collective process, filmmaking is conditioned by many factors that are beyond your individual control. This willingness to get other people involved, however, made me pay a heavy price. I started the project in early 1994, and finished this film by the end of 1995. The whole filmmaking process, I have to say, was marked by considerable compromises on my end. Not only was a voice-over added but the whole narrative structure, even including the captions at the beginning, was altered by the Film Bureau people. Because the Film Bureau at that time promised me that they would try their best to pass the film, I didn't complain about the many changes I was forced to make. Originally I used many long takes, and the film was highly individualistic. But just look at the released version: is that my film? I felt terrible after the altered film was released. What can I say? I guess back then I was preoccupied with the urge to get my first film done. Despite the fact that the government was heavily involved in the whole filmmaking process, therefore, I didn't complain.

After *The Stone Bed*, therefore, I went "underground" and made two independent films, *Men and Women* and *Cry Women*. To be frank, I don't like to make "underground" films. Actually, I don't even think there is such a thing as an "underground" film. To me, there is only distinction between independent film and studio films or films made outside the system and within the system. Certainly China is still in a transitional period, during which the system itself and many arbitrary policies will continue to play an important role in filmmaking. Many things can't simply be done according to your individual wishes. Based on my past experience and the lessons I've learned, however, I'd rather sacrifice many other things in order to uphold my own principle of filmmaking. The most important thing for me is not to lose the original spirit of film. I do regret that I've lost many things because of the certain choices, but I've also gained a lot, among which freedom of expression is the most valuable. Perhaps in the future I'll make "above the ground" films again. As a matter of fact, I always try to walk on two legs. All of my screenplays were submitted for official approval. It was only because I was asked to make too many changes that I decided to take another road. If I had a choice I would certainly take the high road, which is to win the approval of the censors. But if my works are altered beyond recognition, I'd rather take the low road, go "underground" and do something more independent.

Lou Ye

I don't think film censorship is simply a film-related issue. Therefore, you cannot just accuse the Film Bureau. It is only part of a larger issue. The current mechanism of film censorship is actually a partial reflection of today's political system and economic environment. If our economic

Chapter Three

environment continues to improve, or, if our political system becomes more liberal, film censorship will naturally disappear and be relegated to history. The fate of film censorship, therefore, is closely connected to the political, social, and economic development of the nation.

    To dismantle the current censorship system also requires a collective effort. Every time I'm interviewed, therefore, I always bring up the issue of censorship. Although I am making "legal" films now, I still cannot let the issue go. If you talk to the people at the Film Bureau, they would also sympathize with me. Sooner or later this problem has to be resolved, if not today, then tomorrow, or ten years from now, because this is the inevitable road that must be taken. When the official document was handed down to me, stating that I was not permitted to make films for three years [after *Suzhou River*], therefore, I didn't feel shocked at all. Why? First, it was nothing new to me. My first film was banned for two years. Second, while always cautious, I am confident that our films will be eventually released as long as we refuse to give up making films. After tireless efforts, for example, the ban on my first film was conditionally lifted two years later and it was granted "limited release". Ten years ago, I did not have such an understanding. I was angry and irritated [about my first film being banned]. Now I am able to remain calm. First of all, censorship is not something an individual can single-handedly smash; second, it is not even subject to the power of the Film Bureau. Like the situation in Korea, the issue of film censorship cannot be resolved overnight. It has close ties to politics and economics. It is determined by a nation's general policy on art.

    After the first encounter with the censorship system, I began to explore its "mystery" and gradually acquired some knowledge of the system. So, I always feel that no one, including veteran directors, has a clearer understanding of China's film censorship than does our generation. In addition, this group of directors is perhaps the most capable in terms of negotiating with the government, because for more than ten years, these directors, both "underground" and "above ground", have been acquiring ample knowledge about what censorship is and where the problems lie. Ten years from now, if you look back, you will feel it is quite ridiculous that these films [*Suzhou River* and others] didn't pass the censors. If the situation changes fast enough, sometime in the future, film censorship will be abolished. Or, it will become more scientific and democratic. If this happens, then I think these directors will be seen as the real heroes, because it was they who began to really confront the censorship system. They would make it so the would-be directors who might just have begun their film careers ten years from today could forget the word "censorship". This is the most valuable thing this group of directors could accomplish. It is my sincere hope that directors younger than I will no longer encounter the problem of censorship.

From *Suzhou River* to *Purple Butterfly*, it seems I have emerged from the "underground", but I do not feel that way. As a matter of fact, both films were forwarded to the censorship department of the Film Bureau. Like a stone dropped into the sea, I heard nothing after the sample tape of *Suzhou River* was submitted. The fate of *Purple Butterfly* was different, however. The script passed the censors without any problem. They didn't ask me to make any changes, and I do not think there will be any problem in publicly showing the film, whether domestically or internationally. If *Purple Butterfly* had failed to pass the censors, I would have simply quit filmmaking entirely.[xxv]

To me, the strong political overtone of film censorship needs to be rejected. We should view film censorship not purely as a political issue but more as an economic one. In other words, the government should weigh the financial gains and losses when making these decisions. If you ban so many new Chinese films and prohibit them from entering the market, then they will definitely find markets overseas. To put it more bluntly, you make these films inaccessible to the most profitable market: the native-language market. If these films are not supported by the native-language market, then you lose a large amount of money. Viewed from this angle, the issue of the market should dominate. We have to be financially savvy about this. If American producers told Spielberg that his films would be allowed to be shown in China after certain cuts were made, he would be more than happy to make those changes. This means Hollywood directors understand the importance of the market. To Hollywood distributors and entrepreneurs, China is just an under-explored market, a special territory that requires censorship. They know their films need to pass the Chinese censors before entering the market. So, it becomes quite simple. It is only a business deal.

Lu Chuan

Almost everybody knows that *The Missing Gun* passed without a single cut from the Film Bureau. This doesn't mean that censorship didn't have any role in the whole process. But we worked hard to minimize it. The screenplay, for instance, had a rough time in the hands of the censors. As you know, part of the censorship apparatus involves the tacit rule that if a submitted film or screenplay concerns some special professions, it must first win approval from the concerned institutions. My screenplay, therefore, was first handed to the Cultural Department of the Public Relations Bureau of the Ministry of Public Security after the Film Bureau received it. It took me quite some time to talk the Ministry into my way of thinking. Having received the green light from the Ministry, I went to the Film Bureau again. The official document of approval from the Ministry of Public Security

Chapter Three

almost guaranteed the project wouldn't be banned by the censors. The screenplay remained in the hands of the Film Bureau for another extended period of time, however. I didn't know whether the project could continue. The only advice I got from the Film Bureau was to make further changes and revisions. This process lasted for about two years. Because I am a director hired by the Beijing Film Studio, and I must rely on the money from the studio to start filming, I had no choice but to wait.

Since I am a studio-hired director, I feel it's my obligation to follow the rules, no matter how arbitrary they are. These rules stipulate that both your screenplay and the final cut of your film must be submitted to the censors for approval. This is what I need to follow, nothing else. With the exception of these rules, it is up to the filmmaker to decide what to express and how to express it. One can't blame the system for not being able to make quality films. Excellent works can be also made within the system. Besides, if every filmmaker tried to bypass the censorship system by every possible means, the rope would surely be further tightened because the authorities would assume every filmmaker was making political films. I strongly believe film shouldn't be used as a political tool. Making "Main Melody" films is an act of political propaganda, so is making "underground" films. In my case, since the June Fourth Incident of 1989, I've grown increasingly weary of politics. To be frank, I am sick of politics. I hope my films can get away from it and instead get near to humanity.

I don't think working within the system means I am afraid of it. On the contrary, because of my state of mind, I feel I am not greatly affected by the system. Perhaps the censors didn't particularly like *The Missing Gun* because a film like this adds no golden color to the current regime. But I insisted on going through the censors, because only by doing so could ordinary people in China see the film in a regular theater. As it turned out, *The Missing Gun* was officially released nationwide. To me, nothing was as rewarding and satisfying as the fact that the audience was finally able to see the film. Furthermore, because of the success of *The Missing Gun*, I think I will have more leverage next time when negotiating deals with the system. In fact, the key to my un-thorny relation with the system lies in the fact that I don't think film is a weapon for student movements or political persuasions. I am tired of film being used for that purpose. In my opinion, film must first return to its original roots, the roots that were nurtured by cinematic pioneers like the Lumiere Brothers and Méliès. At the current stage, this is the most positive thing we can do to Chinese cinema. To me as an individual, film is a religion; but to Chinese cinema as a whole, we must first call for a return to film's original roots.

Lu Xuechang

It took me three years to get *The Making of the Steel* passed. From 1994 to 1997, I did nothing but make changes of the screenplay time and again. After *The Making of the Steel*, I wrote several other screenplays, but none of them was approved. As a matter of fact, even while revising the screenplay of *The Making of the Steel*, I was planning my next project. But this "next project" never materialized because the screenplay encountered some serious problems in the hands of the censors. I think this is partly due to the fact that my first film had such a hard time passing; naturally, therefore, the censors paid more attention to what I submitted thereafter. Although unable to make anything that was based on my own screenplays, I got the opportunity to make *A Lingering Face*. It took three years for *The Making of the Steel* to pass, but it took just three months for *A Lingering Face* because the latter was an assigned job, not my own.

Following the suggestions of the Film Bureau, I revised the screenplay of *The Making of the Steel* thirteen times. For example, the film originally ended with the main character trying to kill the club boss, but the whole sequence was later changed to a dream. This change actually altered the whole nature of the film. In the original screenplay, this character rushed to the club and blinded the boss. As a result, he was sent to prison. This is how the film originally ended. In fact, when I was asked to revise the screenplay the thirteenth time, this ending turned out to be the main problem. I had two options then: either edit out the whole ending or change it into a dream sequence. Back then, I felt I must do whatever I could to make it pass, since it was my first film, and I had invested so much energy in it. If I didn't change the ending, the film would still be banned today.

I guess many Chinese filmmakers tend to prepare two versions of a project, one without a thought for the censors, the other for the censors. As for me, I still hope I can do what I intend to do and shoot what I love to shoot. Of course this will sometimes get me into trouble. But I think everything has its bottom line. Above that line, I am willing to compromise, but below it I would simply quit. There are a lot of other things I can do.

Ma Liwen

My film *Gone Is the One Who Held Me the Dearest* went through the censors without a single word of objection, a very smooth process. I don't know whether it was because I was lucky or because my film's subject matter is not sensitive. The censors only felt that the old Communist cadre character was a bit pedantic: "Why doesn't he do something to help his wife?" But they also felt that the presence of such a character is justifiable. So, the film passed without my even seeing the censors. It was submitted to the censors through

Chapter Three

the normal channel and, step by step, they green-lighted it.

Right now I have two projects, but I suspect they will have a hard time at the hands of the censors. I am struggling to find a solution to this. Maybe what I will do is to first test the water by talking to the insiders to see how they respond. If it's generally all right, I would give it a try; if not, I would probably give up. One of the projects I am working on is quite sensitive in its subject matter. It can't be partially revised to satisfy the censors. It is either "pass" or "no pass", no middle ground at all. I once showed the screenplay to Shi Dongming, who was very interested but told me that the most sensitive issue in the screenplay is the use of allusions. Allusion is more alarming to the censors than in-your-face confrontation, because allusion tends to imply a lot of things, and many people might suspect they are being alluded to. I think what he said is quite right. Many films fail to pass the censors not because of politics but owing to the film's overall attitude as well as what it alludes to.

I've never thought of doing something "underground". It is certainly all right to do a DV film if the project has no hope of passing the censors, but where is the market for a DV film? As a filmmaker, I wish the whole censorship process could be more transparent. If that is the case, everybody would be quite clear in the beginning about what he or she needs to do. I could either walk the normal road or go through the "underground", nothing in between. I don't think "walking the tightrope" would work.

Meng Qi

Although I've had firsthand experience with the censorship system after *What a Snowy Day* was done, I am actually still in the dark about this process. For example, I am not quite sure whether a clear-cut censorship code even exists. Furthermore, if there is such a code, who are the people actually implementing it? To be more specific, what are their personal favorites and viewpoints about certain issues? These things are quite important in the decision-making process. The reason why I think I am still in the dark is because I can't assume their position to figure out why certain decisions are made. This being said, I think what I need to do is not to worry about how they will judge my work but to focus first on what I intend to create. In order to make one's work available for the general audience, sometimes one might be forced to make certain compromises. This is indeed when you have no other options. In any case, one has to first rely on one's own strength to strive for what he/she stands for.

As a filmmaker, I hold certain hope for the current system of film censorship. I hope the censorship rules become more tolerant and flexible. If not concerned about matters of principle, the censors ought to be lenient and tolerant toward filmmaking. There are indeed evil things and people in society, and you can't completely ignore them in filmmaking. If you forbid them to be represented in certain films, these works will become nondescript and awkward. I think the key issue here is how to handle those materials. Ultimately, I believe most of us want to see beautiful things come out of it. Use the American film *The Godfather* as an example. Almost all the characters in the film are professional gangsters. But in the end the main character turns out to be a hero. Although the environment determines that he belongs in the world of gangsters, he comes out as a typical American hero. This character has many good points, such as taking good care of his family.

Shi Runjiu

In dealing with the censors, I certainly want to be a gainer. In other words, I hope my characters are as truthful to life as possible. This is truly a thorny issue every filmmaker has to face. In the process of making my two previous films, the worry that the censors might stretch their muscles was always in the air. Although my films, particularly my debut feature, *A Beautiful New World*, passed the censors without major changes, it doesn't mean censorship didn't play a role. As a matter of fact, we had already made great compromises when working on the screenplays.

Tang Danian

From screenplay to final cut, I've never thought of submitting *City Paradise* to the censors. It was meant to be an "underground" film. Why? In 1996, a screenplay of mine received a prize at the Sundance Film Festival. My original plan was to make that screenplay into a film. But I was never able to get permission. The censors didn't give me a clear "No", but I was asked to make changes. After five or six revisions, the censors were still not satisfied. Perhaps they never intended to pass the screenplay, because they would never say "No" even though that's what they meant. When I was making *City Paradise*, therefore, I simply decided to bypass the censors. Maybe because this film didn't get much attention abroad, I've encountered no trouble in China since making this "underground" film. People of the Film Bureau have never come see me.

I think the censorship apparatus has to a large extent strangled Chinese cinema. In recent years, there've actually been fewer films that are worth seeing. Despite the fact that there's been one or two good ones that have managed to survive the censorship process as well as a few good "underground" films, as a whole, China cinema lacks vigor, the energetic vigor that Korean cinema now exhibits. If you go to Korea, you will be able to feel the enthusiasm of the film audience there as well as the thriving nature of the whole Korean film industry. Although I have no doubt that this censorship system will eventually collapse, to an individual that it persists is quite scary, because an individual's life is measured in years. If the censorship apparatus remains intact for ten more years, then the most creative years of my life will have vanished.

Wang Chao

When attending film festivals abroad, I always emphasize the progress China has made in recent years. In addition, I also speak about the fact that China has at last acknowledged the multiplicity of the society. Of course this acknowledgement is not clearly spelled out in any official documents. The government is not so stupid as to publicly announce what you are allowed to do in art and literature. As you know, although making DV films without permission is not allowed, almost everyone is doing it anyway. Regardless of your view of the system, therefore, you have to acknowledge that there exists a space that provides you certain freedom. At least I've got my film *The Orphan of Anyang* done in this country, right?

What I mean by this is that not only do our ideas and artistic inspirations come from this country and this culture but we also benefit from this space in actual operations. No matter how ambiguous you feel about this space, it is in this space that I made my first film and, moreover, was able to take it to many parts of the world. If you really understand the reality of China, you are in a good position to handle things well. After all, as we've marched in the new millennium and gradually merged into the overall trend of the world, either passively or actively, China is making great progress and its social multiplicity is taking shape. I often use my own example to explain this to the overseas audience: the very fact that I am able to show my film to you is itself a testament to China's progress.

It is every filmmaker's desire that audiences would flock to theaters to see his/her works. I think none would intentionally make an "underground" film that is inaccessible to the general public. It is my hope, for instance, that *The Orphan of Anyang* will emerge from the "underground" and be seen by as many people as possible. If that were the case, I would be overwhelmed with joy. What is my number one wish right now? I've been to more than fifty film festivals around the globe. On average, each festival screened my film three times, which means that *The Orphan of Anyang* was screened at least 150 times in the world. In addition, France also bought the European rights to the film. But these achievements do not satisfy me at all. My number one wish is to have the domestic audience see my film. Regardless of terms and conditions, I would be overjoyed if more Chinese audiences came see my film.

The thing that worries me most at this moment is not the film censorship system, but the issue of self-expression. If my self-expression in art is recognized and allowed to go "above ground" to face the general audience, I would be exhilarated. I haven't given much thought on how to cope with the censors' demands. Up to now, I still think that the issue of self-expression is much more important.

Wang Guangli

I think we must first learn how to survive and not be strangled by the censorship system. This is the most important thing. In other words, you must first find where the fresh air is coming in, and then you may begin to force your way through that opening little by little. You must mobilize all kinds of forces to widen it, regardless of how little you might be able to achieve. Of course, I would weigh the advantages and disadvantages. I am willing to make compromises on technical issues. For instance, there were a few places in *Go for Broke* which the censors found objectionable. If I insisted on keeping them in, the film would never pass. Thematically, this film actually had no problem. How can be a film about unemployed workers be objectionable? But there are several occasions when the film becomes sarcastic and socially critical, but in a humorous manner. This got on the censors' back up.

The film begins with a group of laid-off workers in Shanghai deciding to start a company of their own. Although laid off, they still decide to hire a few migrant workers. These are typical Shanghaiese: even though we've lost our jobs, as "bosses", we must wear designer suits and ties. So the main male characters all wear ties in the film. In the original version, as the film began, these "bosses" and the hired migrant workers are remodeling a fancy apartment. One shot shows the lead actor singing. What song is he singing? It's the most popular song at that time, "Marching into the New Era". Because he sings the song in a high pitch, the singing abruptly stops in the middle, and then he asks his co-workers: where are my pants? After learning his paints are being washed, he rushes to the laundry, wearing only underpants, because there is a lottery ticket in the pocket of his pants. In this sequence, the "Marching into the New Era" song is repeatedly evoked. In the last sequence of the film, after winning the lottery, they treat people from the neighborhood to noodles. Afterward, these people, mostly old men and women, want to entertain them with some songs. The old men sing "We Workers Are the Most Powerful", and two old women picked "Marching into the New Era". Not only do they finish the song but emotionally they are quite into it. One of the old women is quite charming when she sings. She was probably a cultural worker when young. Following their example, the lead actor again sings "Marching into the New Era". Guess what. This time he finishes the whole song.

It turned out that this song, "Marching into the New Era", was the one that got the film in trouble. If not changed, the censors simply wouldn't pass the film. Left with no choice, I replaced the song with another one called "Come Visit Your Family Often". As a matter of fact, the purpose of evoking the song "Marching into the New Era" was to both satirize all the popular songs of that year and express my sarcasm regarding the changing Chinese society. The changed version, you may feel, has lost some of its critical edge. If the censorship system were less up tight, *Go for Broke* could have had broader market appeal.

Wang Quanan

If your ego is not the only thing you care about in this world, you will agree that film is not an individual art form, but a result of cooperation between you and your colleagues. A film can't be made by a single director. You must rely on both actors and all the crew members. With this understanding in mind, you will naturally feel that you need your colleagues' support and creativity to get your films made. This is a negotiation process, during which you must make compromises, right? The same logic also applies to our relationship to the system and the censorship apparatus. To me, this issue is no longer an emotional one, but a technical process, a process you can't avoid. In the United States, I must face the producer. The producer is a capitalist. In order to accomplish my mission, I must learn how to cooperate with the producer and eventually work out some sort of mutual agreement. I must convince him that my art film also has the potential to make money. Or, I could work with him to explore different ways to recoup his investment. In China, what you must face is the Film Bureau. Like you deal with a capitalist producer in America, you must also learn how to communicate with the Film Bureau. You need to first demonstrate that you don't have nefarious intentions. You need to let them know the nature of the film you plan to make and tell them frankly that your film might be very realistic in depicting the actual situation of a particular group of people.

Then, when it reaches the point at which you are asked to present your case in detail, you must come up with language that can be easily understood by the people in the Film Bureau. As they say, "When in Rome, do as the Romans do". Art is always full of ambiguities, and good works could be very ambiguous. The point you want to make can be effectively expressed in different ways.

I have the feeling that the very apparatus of censorship, the Film Bureau itself, is the last stronghold of a power structure that is gradually falling into decay. We can feel that the shrinking power of this apparatus has actually reached the point of collapse. As an integral part of political control and propaganda, this apparatus has been in fact squeezed into a relatively condensed space. Of course the people inside will fight desperately to defend this space, just like the situation before the Berlin Wall collapsed. I bear no ill intention in saying this. What I mean is that because of the current situation this apparatus is full of vigor, but at the same time quite vulnerable. As artists, we must have both confidence and patience. I can fully understand those bureaucrats. They are the last defenders of this apparatus, and the realization of their self-worth depends on it. As human beings, we need to learn how to understand them on a human level. What would happen to them if the censorship apparatus disappeared? Where could they go?

I think sometimes the problem comes from the tension between the two sides. Believe it or not, both of them are still playing their traditional roles. That is: one a rebel, the other an oppressor; or, one a ruler, the other the ruled. All these are classical roles, and there is no space for a role in the middle. In terms of filmmaking itself, not too many filmmakers want to make a feel-good film. Instead, they favor the role of savior or rebel. In response to this, the censors, or the investigators, feel their role is to dig out the rebellious elements of the submitted films. This is where the tension comes from, I think. As a matter of fact, most internationally shown Chinese art films bear the same characteristics: full of anxiety and tension. No matter whether the film is about history or about contemporary China, it is tight and anxious. Because many filmmakers hope to achieve overnight success, they tend to exaggerate or overdo certain things. International art films, on the other hand, are quite relaxed in style and content. You can find both individualism and lightheartedness in them. Of course I am referring to good art films.

Getting back to the issue of censorship. When submitting works to the Film Bureau, we ought to relax and give the censors a clear idea about what we really intend to do. Based on this frankness, it may be easier for both sides to reach a consensus. You need to convince the bureau that except for serious filmmaking itself there is no "hidden agenda" in your work. What I mean by "hidden agenda" is that some filmmakers are still used to playing the classical role of using politics to get international attention. As a filmmaker, you might even be unaware of this. What you deem to be the most serious and purest artworks are in fact the ones most exemplary of this practice. I am not against the spirit of rebellion. On the contrary, I think serious art ought to carry this spirit. But it must be internalized and channeled toward the goal of enlightening people's spiritual world. It is where the power of art lies. Art is not a gun. Once it is being used as a gun, you might be able to achieve certain short-term goals, but not for long. Using art as a gun is actually doing exactly

Chapter Three

what the other side is doing to filmmakers. When you carry a gun to the bureau, how could you expect its cooperation? As artists, I think we must also reexamine ourselves and play down our traditional role as rebels.

When I submitted *Lunar Eclipse* to the Film Bureau, the censors were puzzled. They didn't understand why someone even hoped that the bureau would approve such a film because in the past a film like *Lunar Eclipse* would automatically go "underground" even before the thought of submitting it to the Film Bureau popped up. Even my teachers were surprised: "How dare you send such a film to the censors?" But my feeling was quite different. I didn't think *Lunar Eclipse* was an "underground" film. It ought to be "above ground". First of all, my intention was not to make another "underground" film. I was therefore willing to listen to what the censors had to say. Everything has its limit. When you totally disregard this limit and refuse to accept any constraint, it is also something to be afraid of. To be able to articulate is a form of power, but if this articulation fails to take the rest of the world into consideration, then this power might easily be abused and become vulnerable. Besides, filmmaking is also a business activity. What I mean is this: in a normal and healthy environment, making profits and paying taxes are of equal importance. Like a commodity, your film must be "consumed" by the audience. The beneficial circle of filmmaking must rely not only on artistic exploration but also on the participation of the audience.

As filmmakers, we, I feel, also have the responsibility to constantly exert influence on the Film Bureau and make them see things more positively. Before *Lunar Eclipse*, most Chinese art films tended to emphasize the expression of pain, either painful emotions or painful memories. This alone is worth notice. Why can't our films be a little pleasant? We feel either spiritually liberated or psychologically sublimated after having seen some foreign art films, even including those from Iran. But why is it that so many Chinese art films cannot offer these feelings? Many of us seem to be obsessed with the idea of overnight success. In order to achieve this goal, some of us wouldn't even mind binding ourselves up and then showing our pained bodies to the rest of the world. Sometimes I feel this practice is very irresponsible. Why are there so many young filmmakers having a hard time getting their films passed? Aside from the problem of the Film Bureau, I think they are actually being lured into the traditional role described above. They should be encouraged to free themselves from the oppressor/oppressed dichotomy. I feel that the ever changing Chinese society has opened up a lot of opportunities for today's artists, and there is plenty room for them to create more tasteful works. The world has become better. You can swing your arms and do whatever you want. Let us suppose you are in the United States. Are you talented enough to make a film that could attract a large crowd and emotionally move them? Or, suppose you are in Europe. Are you able to do the same? What I mean by this is that it's time for us to deliberate the issues that concern only film itself. To put it more bluntly, suppose the Film Bureau no longer existed, and suppose the censorship apparatus were gone, what would you be capable of doing? Could you still make attractive films?

When I conceive of film projects, therefore, the Film Bureau or the censorship apparatus is never a concern for me. I am not saying that I am completely free from the shadow of the system. What I am saying is that there are more important issues for me to worry about. Compared to those issues, censorship is not a big deal, because it is easy to solve. I feel it's time for us to stop complaining, either about the system or about money, and focus on film for itself, as an art form. Today political issues are no longer very intense, and the sense of oppression has largely disappeared. The problem China is facing is not so much a political one as a moral one. The moral pressure this country feels has almost reached the point of explosion. When in the United States, I told the audience who came to my film: we Chinese are actually the ones exploring the frontiers of morality, because we've sustained what you could hardly bear. In China, everything is upside-down. When you feel comfortable with something, in an instant, it changes to its opposite. The pressure actually comes from this moral chaos.

In fact, what Chinese filmmakers have never been able to get rid of is precisely what they rebel against. They still think film is a form of propaganda and a powerful tool for political gain. Otherwise they wouldn't be so enthusiastic for the traditional role of the oppressed. Once assuming this role, they tend to become self-important, as if being cheered as revolutionary leaders. While it does feel good to be a "hero", it also alienates you from filmmaking itself. When the new rebel comes, the old "hero" would naturally be denied and abandoned. Then, this would be followed by another destruction and total denial. It resembles the logic of destroying old culture during the Cultural Revolution, the logic of not respecting any value system. Chinese consciousness seems to get tangled in the "oppression/rebellion" dichotomy, as if rebellion and revolution could solve everything: once the pain comes, let's start another revolution! In other words, we always hope to get rid of various tensions through the means of destruction. As a matter of fact, art is not immune to this consciousness in China. Whenever problems arise, we tend to resort to revolution to solve them. This is the legacy of the Mao years. Mao hoped to single-handedly wipe out all the old things and create a new world out of nothing. I remember Mao once said that from the vantage point of view of Tiananmen Square he would like to see the Everlasting Peace Boulevard covered with a forest of chimneys, because this scene would symbolize China's rapid industrialization. In the context of today, what a scary scene that would be! Like the economy, the development of art also requires stability and accumulation. We Chinese are very proud of the Tang dynasty. But remember, it took several hundred years for the Tang dynasty to reach its peak in both economy and art.

Wang Xiaoshuai

The biggest problem of the current censorship system is that there are no set standards. Because this system mostly relies on man-made decisions, no one knows for sure what will happen at any given time. This time you might be able to get through, but next time the feeling of uncertainty will come back again. The development of cinema depends on two things: hardware and software. The former includes investment, movie theaters, and so on. The latter, in my opinion, refers mostly to management and administration. In China, this points very much to the censorship system. Throughout the world, it is a normal practice that, as a government branch, the film bureau or commission's mission is to provide services and conveniences for filmmakers. The brochure prepared by this office usually lays out the details about the application procedures for filming at a particular location. But this is not the case in China.

I've always believed that Chinese cinema will regain its glory if the system changes. Why? The rapid economic development of China explains it well. Just see what Shenzhen has achieved. After an edict from Deng Xiaoping, Shenzhen prospers, and a stone turns into a diamond. Why didn't Shenzhen prosper prior to Deng's edict? It is because of the rigid system that hindered its development. The current system, therefore, is the biggest obstacle preventing Chinese cinema from regaining its glory. Once the system changes, I am confident that Chinese cinema will definitely surpass that of Japan, Korea, or Iran.

There are signs of change, though. In November 2004, the film censors came to me and said we are ready to forget about your past. We want to reform Chinese cinema because otherwise we realize it will die. I told them, "We already know that—we've been saying that for twelve years." They said, "From now on film will not just be propaganda, but film can also be a product. You can sell it and market it." During these past years, a lot of Hollywood films have come to China and are taking over the [film] industry. So the film bureau realized it had to face reality. One question was how to deal with underground film directors [like myself]. They realized things had to change. Before, as a director, you had no control. You might spend US$200,000 making a film, and then it would be censored and you wouldn't be able to earn a penny back.

Everyone knows that China has a billion-plus market, but film directors have been unable to make any money. It's amazing, really.

In the case of *Shanghai Dreams*, the film bureau asked me to send a 1,000-word synopsis. At first I wondered whether I should make it sound softer—in many ways this is my toughest film yet. Then I decided that this should be a test of their new openness. So I didn't make it any softer. Then they asked whether they could take a look at the whole script. They were afraid that I was still a bad guy and was tricking them. [*Shanghai Dreams*] is a very heavy, very sensitive, and very individual story. Actually, I was afraid [the film censors] would say no. They told me, "Your past is past, and we have reformed". And they approved it.

Xu Jinglei

My film *Me and My Dad* didn't encounter devastating censorship. As a matter of fact, to a large extent, I feel I should be thankful to the Film Bureau. Because my film was regarded as the first independent film in China, I got a lot of help from the people at the Film Bureau. I was completely ignorant about the development of independent production in China until they told me that a new regulation had just been issued on February 1, 2002. I went to the Film Bureau with my screenplay and was a little worried about where to find a studio willing to be my production partner. To my surprise, they told me that, according to that regulation, my own company alone is eligible for producing and releasing the film. In addition, the censors sent me back their suggestions for change in no time. Therefore, I feel they were quite supportive of my project. My film was the first one that passed censorship without a studio partner. Along with mine, there were a few submissions with the similar nature. But the Film Bureau thought my screenplay was more mature. So, I became the first filmmaker to get the "Single Feature Permit".

Although some might think my film is a little "gray" [dark], particularly when the four main characters are having dinner together, I don't see it that way. There is nothing especially "marginal" or "pessimistic" about my film. Of course, a few scenes were indeed censored, such as the bar scene. But I have no problem with that. First of all, the original sequence in the bar was indeed a little too long. Second, I felt the focus should be on the relationship between the father and daughter, and a long bar sequence would be a digression. Besides, film shouldn't attend to each and every aspect of a matter.

Zhang Ming

Speaking of film censorship, it is in essence an issue of the system. It is also an issue between the individual and the environment. As a Chinese and a

Chapter Three

Chinese director, since the day of my birth, I've been already chosen and determined. It is not me who has chosen this environment and society. It is due to some holy creatures' choice that I was born into this environment. Therefore, since the day of my birth, I've already learned how to make compromises. Although I was powerless in choosing my own environment and family, I have to make peace with what has been determined for me. This, in my opinion, is the ultimate compromise. Born into this world as a Chinese, it has been already determined that you must live through many years of darkness and repression.

Of course you do have some options later. You can either escape from the chosen environment or live with it and make use of it. To me, escapism is not an option. I think human beings are smart enough to adjust to an adverse environment and, moreover, to take advantage of it by exploring many loopholes in the system.

In order to do this, I think we must first have close contact with this environment, specifically with the censorship system, and explore the limits of the apparatus. For instance, my second feature, *Weekend Plot*, was meant to be a horror film, but I was forced to give up the original screenplay simply because the Film Bureau told me that a horror film wouldn't be approved. If a horror film were set before Liberation [1949] or in ancient China, I was told, shooting permission would be granted. If it were set in contemporary times and somehow related to today's society, then no permission would be issued. Although the result was that I had to literally find another screenplay to replace the original one, I at least acquired some knowledge of the limits of the system.

There are many things we can't do today. Many subjects are simply not allowed to be treated in film. I think it's partly due to the fact that film's role and influence in society have long been exaggerated in China. In actuality, filmmaking is not such a big deal at all. This being the case, if as a filmmaker you decide to live with this environment, you ought to at least abide by the rules of this environment. You ought to learn how to adjust yourself and be flexible in order to survive. Besides, to me, it's very important for my second film to be seen by the domestic audience. It would be devastating and all your efforts would become meaningless if the domestic audience was unable to see your film. Even if your film can only be seen on TV's movie channel, it is still better than being excluded from the domestic market. In this process, therefore, some trade-off might be needed. On this issue, I never feel moral judgment serves the purpose. How to value this kind of trade-off depends essentially on where the director's conscience lies. The most important thing is not to do what your conscience doesn't allow you to do.

Because of censorship, many directors choose to take abroad and market their films there. But for me the most important market is China, so I will definitely give my films to the government for supervision. I think the level of Chinese cinema depends on all Chinese directors, not just some underground directors. If the whole level goes up, then the Chinese film industry can go up. The advantage of having your films approved is that you can show your films to the Chinese people, but the advantage of going "underground" is that you can play your films abroad and have more freedom to film what you find interesting. Even now, I can't say which option is better, but my choice is to play my films in China.

When I was at the 2002 Rotterdam Film Festival, during a meeting with other Chinese directors, I found out that I was the only person making approved films! It is true that the result of making underground films can be much better than that of making approved films. You can get much more support abroad and the revenues could be higher. Even so, I still think that a Chinese director shouldn't give up the Chinese market. Now that China has joined the WTO, it means that the Chinese film industry will face more competition from abroad, and if Chinese directors give up the Chinese market, the whole film industry will be demolished.

Zhang Yang

I think the definition of compromise depends very much on what your original intention is. If your intention is to make a film that is deemed unacceptable to the social majority or the mainstream ideology, then making compromises would be a matter of principle. Your film would lose its integrity because the very nature of this kind of film requires an uncompromising attitude.

Why have I been quite successful on this matter so far? It's because I honestly feel that besides the aforementioned there is another kind of film, the kind of film that is not only appealing to the general audience but also acceptable to government censors. Just use Iranian cinema as an example. The whole environment of the Iranian society is much more restrictive and repressive, both socially and religiously, than that of the Chinese society. But it is in this environment that many great Iranian films have emerged. These cinematic classics, if put in a Chinese context, would have no problem at all in the hands of the Chinese censors. Some of them could be even labeled "Main Melody" films. Not overtly political, these films pay much more attention to the in-depth exploration of humanity and the human condition. As a matter of fact, some of Ang Lee's films, particularly the family drama, *Eat, Drink, Men, Women*, and the like, would easily win official approval of China without any cuts. I can envision myself following the path of Ang Lee and Iranian cinema: making intelligent and socially acceptable films at the same time.

Chapter Three

Since the above is my original intention, I don't think my principle of filmmaking has been compromised at all. To me, there is no life-and-death struggle in today's society, and the real challenge is how to handle a variety of delicate issues in a more skillful way. In fact, I think my films can exist in the current environment. The censors might ask me to make some minor changes here and there, but these changes do not pose any threat to the overall integrity of my films. Of course I understand this is only true to my case. To those whose films are sensitive in both subject matter and characters, censorship is a matter of principle. How can you change the subject matter and characters to please the censors? The issue of censorship, therefore, depends very much on what kind of filmmaker you are. So far I haven't encountered any serious problem with the censorship apparatus. Every film of mine has been slightly censored in some details, but nothing fundamental.

Zhang Yuan

There have been a number of independent or "underground" films made in China that did not win a pass from or simply bypassed the censorship apparatus. My estimation of the number is in the double digits. I've only seen some of them. As for myself, six or seven films of mine failed to pass the censors, including *Beijing Bastards, East Palace West Palace, Sons,* and *The Square*. My first film, *Mama*, won approval from the censors but its distribution was a disaster. In addition, I couldn't even secure a single theater to screen most of my documentary films. I think there are also a number of filmmakers out there whose documentaries or feature films, like most of my earlier works, have no relation with the Chinese film market at all.

The biggest hurdle for Chinese filmmakers today is that they can't just make any film they like if they want their film to see the light of the day [in] their home country. There are too many rules, spoken or otherwise, that are like land mines. When you exercise self-censorship, tiptoeing across the fields, you end up in a place you don't want to be. And of course your project may still get blown up when you step on one of those mines. This being the case, I think a film rating system must be implemented without delay in China. I don't expect teenagers to see the film *East Palace West Palace*. I hope the filmgoers are eighteen and above for this kind of films, because they have the ability to make their own judgments.

There is a censorship procedure in Chinese cinema. This so-called procedure requires each filmmaker to first submit his or her screenplay to the censors. You can't start shooting until the screenplay is approved. In face of such an apparatus, I often find myself being as vulnerable and naïve as a child, because what you are facing is not an individual, not even the Film

Bureau, but a concrete censorship apparatus. As a filmmaker, if you don't follow this procedure you are advised to self-criticize the mistake you've made. I happen to be the one who has written several self-criticisms. It even took seven months for an eventually approved film like *Seventeen Years*, a film accused of being a sellout, to pass the censors. In addition, the screenplay of the film didn't win a pass until one-and-a-half years later. I spent several months alone to get my application for prison interviews passed. This is, therefore, quite a time-consuming procedure.

I have been thinking lately about whether my banned films have any connection with today's Chinese society and culture as well as with the audiences of those films. I usually don't like to watch my own films, but some people once held a retrospective exhibition of my earlier works and I was invited. To me, this was an astounding experience that made me reflect upon the relevance of my earlier works to Chinese society. I don't know how the critics in the United States viewed those films, but I genuinely feel it is only in the cultural context of China that film is given so much undeserved attention. In reality, film is nothing but an art form that has little social impact. I guess even if those films had not been banned they wouldn't have much influence on people's thinking. Why did those people once take away my passport in the first place? It's exactly because they overestimated my importance as well as the social function of film. I know being "underground" or independent is quite a casual notion in the United States, but in China, for ideological reasons, the line between being "above ground" and "underground" becomes extremely political, as if being "underground" meant joining an underground party. With this kind of mentality, they would naturally overrate the importance of film and overreact to the works of those "underground" or independent filmmakers.

After that retrospective, therefore, I become more and more interested in the film market of China as well as in showing my films to the general Chinese audience. In the years prior to the making of *Seventeen Years*, I became a frequent guest at international film festivals, going abroad almost every three or four months and having the opportunity to watch many foreign films. But this experience also gave me a bizarre feeling about the way my previous films were made. I don't like to stay very long in a foreign country. This means I must live in China and abide by its rules. Besides the choice of living here, I also faced a difficult choice in my creative career. This difficulty was exemplified in my decision to make a prison-themed film. If I were to stick to my previous method of filmmaking, not only would this film be banned from domestic release but it would also get my friends who backed my film in trouble. No matter how one looks at it, therefore, it seems to me that I can no longer stick to my previous filmmaking methods.

Chapter Three

Certainly the more important thing is that I want my films to be accessible to the domestic audience. At the very least, I need to maintain a sensible connection to where I live. Hence, when making *Seventeen Years*, I made up my mind that I must get my films through the censors. To me, emerging from the "underground" and learning how to deal with the censors is a road I must take. I love my work as a filmmaker. In order not to have this work interrupted, I need to be supported by large investments. The three films I made in 2002, including *Green Tea*, testify to this necessity. Therefore, despite the fact that the time I spend on dealing with the censors is almost equal to that I spend on filmmaking itself, I will continue to stay "above ground".

CHAPTER FOUR

WAVES FROM THE MARGIN:
CINEMA AS A "NARCISSISTIC" MIRROR

Sometimes used as an accusation, but other times used as a compliment, directors born in the 1960s and 1970s are alleged to be a generation with heightened interest in the socially marginal figures alienated by the rapid transformation of contemporary Chinese cities. Their earlier films were also accused of being "narcissistic", a label that has been frequently invoked since the emergence of the "Sixth Generation". The two features, "marginality" and "narcissism", have been associated with this generation and considered by many as the very characteristics that set this group of filmmakers apart from the previous filmmakers, including the Fifth Generation. Inevitably, the interviewers raised this issue in their talks with the featured directors.

* * *

Guan Hu

From the very beginning I've felt quite ambiguous about the notion of so-called "marginal figures". Who in the world can be labeled "marginal" or "central?" For instance, if your focus is on an old man of the Shanbei [north Shan'xi] plateau who wears a white bellyband and a towel turban, this man could also be called a "marginal" figure. Why? It's because his life is a mystery to you, and you can't really understand him. He doesn't represent the mainstream life of China. This is why you could call him a "marginal" figure. I understand the word "marginal" is usually attached to rock stars and the like. But isn't it true that there is certain historical truth about these people? Actually, from my point of view, they are no more "marginal" than the old man of the Shanbei plateau. Because of this, I wouldn't label them either "marginal" or "alternative". As for me, I see myself exclusively concerned about the life of ordinary people or the "little guys", at least for now. Living at the bottom of society, these ordinary people are often overlooked by the social mainstream. As a matter of fact, if you study them carefully, you will find their life is quite interesting. You will feel rewarded because their life can enhance your work with some gravity. The audience, on the other hand, will usually find it easier to relate to these characters. Besides, financially this kind of film is more manageable.

Chapter Four

Jia Zhangke

I don't agree with the claim that our films are about "marginal" figures in society. Just use my films as an example. I don't feel my works are in any sense "marginal" or about "marginal" figures. On the surface, both the thief in *Xiao Wu* and the Performance Troupe in *Platform* are somewhat "marginal". But both films actually deal with the common issues of human fate and life. I feel these issues actually concern the majority of Chinese. These characters, therefore, are ordinary, not "marginal". The notion of marginality refers to something alienated from the center and the mainstream. Out of the city, however, what is the mainstream of Chinese society? How does the Chinese majority live? If you think my characters are "marginal", then the majority of the Chinese could be also labeled "marginal". This is why I don't agree with this claim.

In the beginning, the so-called "marginal" might pertain to directors like Zhang Yuan and Wang Xiaoshuai. Characters like rock stars and avant-garde artists did give their early films some "marginal" feature. But I think they've undergone great transformations in recent years. Just take a look at *Beijing Bicycle* and *Seventeen Years*. Even when the main character is a convicted inmate, the major concern is still about family values. I think most young filmmakers are working hard to fulfill their shared ambition, which is to truthfully represent the lives of the ordinary Chinese. I don't think this ambition has anything to do with the notion of "marginality". It is not our intention to present something "strange" or "alternative". On the contrary, what we try to do is to use the film medium to explore the common fate, experience, and issues of the Chinese people. Therefore, we are right at the center, not the margin.

Of course, "marginality" has a variety of meanings. If it refers to something outside mainstream filmmaking, then I agree I am a little "marginal" because I view myself as an independent filmmaker. On the other hand, the rapid changes that have been taking place in China since 1989 can be regarded as an ongoing process of marginalization. The working class, whose status as the "master" and central force of our society has been enshrined in our constitution, has been socially marginalized to the degree that a lot of its members can't even get their unemployment benefits. This process of marginalization, I think, is a trend that will continue in the years to come.

As for narcissism, I think every director is narcissistic, and each film is a result of narcissism. I feel there is nothing wrong with narcissism. The real issue is whether your personal point of view can be somehow related to the social majority and whether your films can resonate with the concerns of the majority. Certainly the accusation that young filmmakers are "narcissistic" has something to do with the fact that a great number of our films can't be shown in public. If you put fifteen young directors' films, including mine, into the broader spectrum of the Chinese film scene and let them seamlessly and equally merge into it, then there would be no such thing as "narcissistic" at all, because our films would only prove the richness of Chinese cinema. But since our films are now put in a box and isolated from the rest, it does not surprise me at all that they've been treated differently and the accusation that we are "narcissistic" has won a certain legitimacy. In a healthy film market, there should be a variety of films, and ours is only one category of them. If you put them together with films like *The Lion King* and *Kong Fansen*,[xxvi] you would only feel they are "unique" in style and taste. That's all. But when they are deemed "problematic" and "special" and isolated from the broader context, you can't easily fend off such criticism.

Jiang Wen

I don't quite understand the notion of "marginality". Or, to put it in another way, this notion itself is rather "marginal" to me. In my vocabulary, there is no such concept at all. I also don't like people using this concept to define a work. The quality of a film or a literary work doesn't simply depend on the choice of character. Whether your work is about emperors, feudal lords, or scholars and beauties, they can't determine its quality. Even when your work is about a "marginal" figure, it could be also quite mainstream. Conversely, even though your focus is on "mainstream" people, the result can be quite "marginal". Crude life may be transformed into a masterpiece, but fine life may be turned into a tasteless and crude work. This is why I feel this notion is quite misleading and dangerous. It is not important as to what kind of people you will feature. The most crucial issue is how you will feature them and what you really want to express through the featured characters. What I've featured actually serves only as a medium. It doesn't really matter whether your film is about Mao, migrant workers, Japanese "devils", or the Red Guards and teenagers during the Cultural Revolution. As a filmmaker or scriptwriter, you are only "borrowing" their voices to express things that are hidden inside you.

Because of this belief, I don't start with the concern over what kind of people I want to feature, but with the question as to what I really want to express when making a film. Only after that will I worry about the suitability of a given story. I personally think it's impossible for a director to avoid expressing his/her inner self. No matter how twisted or indirect it might be, a director's inner world will always leave deep imprints on his/her works. My conception of a film director is always the one who passionately pursues what he/she really wants to express. Certainly the materialization of this self-

Chapter Four

expression requires a certain medium or channel.

When making my first film, *In the Heat of the Sun*, I had doubts and hesitation. I had an inner urge for self-expression, an urge to revisit the childhood experience of the Cultural Revolution. It wasn't so much about the Cultural Revolution, however. To me as a filmmaker, the most important thing was not the "revolution" itself, but the psychological and emotional traces left by this "revolution". My memory of the Cultural Revolution has been dominated by a sudden eruption of unrestrained passion. During that period, this passion reached the boiling point of an ultra-idealism that felt almost surreal. On the one hand, this passion carried with it the great power of destruction, from which we may be able to sense how human creatures could be easily carried away by ideology and propaganda. On the other hand, passion and ideals are also something humans can't do without. The importance of passion and ideals can never be overstated in human life. It was this mixed feeling toward passion during that particular historical period that inspired me to make *In the Heat of the Sun*.

Compared to the Red Guards and the active rebels of the Cultural Revolution, I feel that the children featured in *In the Heat of the Sun* are more true to their nature. They have not been tinted by ideology or any thought system. You can use the word "marginal" to describe them, but I myself don't like this word at all. As a matter of fact, I feel the world through the eyes of these children is more genuine and real, and there is more substance in their feelings and response to the world. It is through them that we can better understand the nature of humans as social animals. In other words, because they are less "contaminated" by society, instead of being "marginal", I feel these children are the "central" figures of society. Why? They are neither the Red Guards nor Mao nor Lin Biao, so why do I call them "central" figures? It is because their response to and acceptance of this historical event are more direct and more pure. It doesn't mean they are "primitive" because the word "primitive" refers to something far away from human civilization. No matter where they grow up, I feel these sixteen- and seventeen-year-olds share many common features. These features do not change because of the change of culture, education, place, and social system. Among these are the attitude of rebellion and the longing for the opposite sex, idealism, and heroism. Many of these are actually related to the growth of their body. It is because these features are more thoroughly reified in these sixteen-to-seventeen-year-olds that I think they are the "central" figures of society. To me, the so-called "marginal" figures refer to those who are deeply tinted by ideology and who do not know how distant it is between their mouths and hearts and minds. I despise those people. Actually, the voice-over of Ma Xiaojun is spoken by the grown-up Ma. The voice-over, therefore, doesn't completely match the images we see on the screen. To me, it is quite interesting to compare the two. There are actually conflicting moments between his narration or remembrance of the past and what really happened in the past. This clash is what shocked and inspired me most when I read Wang Shuo's original story.

As for the so-called "narcissism", I don't quite understand this word. I think this notion could easily lead to misunderstanding. Based on my humble opinion, I know human beings can't even sustain themselves without some kind of narcissism. Oftentimes I feel I can't go out every morning without some sort of self-encouragement. Or, every evening I would customarily examine myself as to whether I've done something inappropriate. This kind of self-reflection often bothers me. No one is forcing me to behave that way. My friends often remind me that I should treat myself better. Sometimes I am even filled with self-remorse. I am not so much in love with myself as some people might think. But I don't know if this is contradictory to the notion of "narcissism". To me, narcissism probably doesn't necessarily mean you are in love with yourself. On the other hand, I completely disagree with the notion that narcissism and autobiography are the two sides of the same coin. To me, every work of art carries some autobiographic traces, my *In the Heat of the Sun* included. But the characters featured in this film do not necessarily deserve your compassion and love. I don't think Ma Xiaojun is a role model. If in this semi-autobiographic work I made the Ma Xiaojun character quite reckless can you say I am narcissistic?

If the word "nostalgia" is used, I may agree that *In the Heat of the Sun* has certain "nostalgic" qualities. But I am not totally sure about this "nostalgic" remembering. There are many doubts in the film. In addition, I am very doubtful about the notion that nostalgia refers only to the positive feelings of what happened in the past. Recollections of the past are unavoidable in human life. In other words, as soon as something memorable has passed, we as human beings will at least feel some regret. This feeling of "regret" can be easily misunderstood as regret for the disappearance of something good. But I think it is not so simple. Sometimes regret doesn't mean one wants to go back to the past. For instance, you could be very nostalgic about your first love, but you won't probably reunite with her if given the opportunity. Therefore, I think not everything you feel nostalgic for is necessarily positive or good. The nostalgia you have is actually a regrettable feeling toward what no longer exists, can't be repeated, and is impossible to get back. The current of time can't flow backward, but even if it could, you probably wouldn't want it to. In this sense, *In the Heat of the Sun* is not a film about the nostalgic feeling of "how beautiful the past was".

Chapter Four

Jin Chen

I think depicting socially "marginalized" figures, or, figures ordinary people are not so familiar with, is one of the common characteristics of some of the "Sixth Generation" filmmakers. As a matter of fact, this is also the aspect of their films that most draws our attention. These "marginalized" characters are the ones whom ordinary people either don't pay attention to or don't like. It is through these characters that we are able to detect where the filmmaker's point of view lies. Like these characters, the filmmakers themselves also belong to a generation or a group of artists whom people seldom care about. But they are determined to let their voices be heard. The way to make this possible is to use these urban and "marginalized" fictional figures to voice their concerns. I myself don't particularly like some of the depicted characters because I think they are not true to life, and there are many subjective elements in these depictions.

In the early years of this generation's filmmaking, "marginality" was indeed an important feature of their works. In recent years, however, there has been a gradual change on this feature. Although still city-centered, their films start to show a tendency toward diversity in both subject matter and characters. This tendency can be seen in Wang Xiaoshuai's *Beijing Bicycle*. I think the protagonist in that film is no longer a "marginal" figure. He is a bicycle delivery boy, or one of the "little guys" in the city. The subject of my next film will also concern the lives of ordinary people in the city. I think audiences are more likely to identify with the notion of "ordinariness". Although this "ordinariness" involves things that we see almost everyday, we tend not to pay enough attention to it. After all, "marginal" figures, such as rock stars and thieves, are not so familiar to ordinary people. It is certainly a good thing that some filmmakers have shown a marked interest in their lives, but the films that are concerned about these "marginal" or "alternative" figures have had a hard time attracting the interest of the ordinary audience. First of all, they can't stand up to the pressure of the market. Second, the government hasn't given this type of films enough space for further exploration.

As for the notion of narcissism, I think it's actually a good thing to make your films in a narcissistic way. However, you have to be financially secure to be "narcissistic". If you have a large investment in your film and don't worry about the box-office, then it's perfectly all right to make a personal film. It would be even better if such a film were applauded by your friends and admirers. In other words, it's desirable to be "narcissistic" if you can afford the potential financial loss. To young filmmakers such as us, however, it's almost impossible to be completely "narcissistic". To put it in another way, we don't have the qualifications and money to be indifferent to both the market and the government. To be only concerned about one's own feelings and self-expression is actually a director's utmost joy. Some of the world-class filmmakers might be able to make a few films of this nature in their whole career but would often find themselves paying a high price for this "self-indulgence". While most of these works are critically acclaimed, they are rejected by the box-office, which often leads to a career low tide. Certainly every master has his/her way of dealing with this dilemma, which is to compromise with and score high points in the market after returning from the low tide. I think both Francis Coppola and Martin Scorsese have had this kind of experience. As young filmmakers, however, I don't think we are ready to take this risk. One day, if I see myself ready, I would be more than happy to make a film completely for myself. I envy the "narcissistic" way of filmmaking. It is similar to creative writing. Every writer longs for the opportunity of writing a novel for himself/herself, not for the publisher.

Li Xin

One of the characters in my feature debut, *Your Black Hair and My Hand*, might be a little "marginal", but most in my films are quite normal. They are the little guys, as ordinary as our daily life. There is a difference between "marginal" figures and little guys. The former may behave differently from most of us. I think some filmmakers are a little obsessed with these figures. If dealing with a barbershop, for instance, instead of featuring barbers, they often focus on the one who is grinding scissors in the back. I suspect such a choice has something to do with the fact that they view themselves as being different from others. Because of this preconception, they invent stories and attach them to those "marginal" figures. In doing so they also risk alienating a lot of audiences. If I feature such a "marginal" figure, I would do it differently. I think I would use my own ways to make him/her appeal to the general public.

As for narcissism, I think every director is to some extent "narcissistic", because he or she is usually inspired by the things that are familiar or close to him/her. In this respect, I feel *Dazzling* is more "narcissistic" than *Your Black Hair and My Hand*. Actually, it seems to me that I am more concerned about finding a voice that can speak for me than being simply "narcissistic". *Your Black Hair and My Hand* is more story-oriented, consisting of three different stories. The film is therefore less "narcissistic". *Dazzling*, on the other hand, has a lot to do with my intuitive thinking. To tell you the truth, originally I didn't mean to make a film like today's *Dazzling*. I had no idea that *Dazzling* would turn out this way. It took me 270 days to edit the filmed footage, and the voice-over was added only after the editing was done. No matter how "narcissistic" you are, however, one thing seems crucial to me: this group of

Chapter Four

young filmmakers, including myself, has to confront the issue of how to carve out a portion of the domestic and international film market for themselves.

Liu Binjian

What interests me are not the small circles of people surrounding me or the so-called "marginal" figures of society, but the exploration of the multiplicity of my characters from different angles. I think film ought to have a freer and broader space to maneuver. Certainly some people may argue that there is a variety of characters in my films, and some of them, including homosexuals, are quite "marginal". I feel being "marginal" or not is only a form of presentation. In essence, human beings share a lot of commonalities. The most important thing, I think, is to delve into the inner psyche of each individual. It really doesn't matter which social strata the character belongs to or what the character does for a living. As an art form, film should be open to all kinds of possibilities. For the time being, I think those little guys featured in my films are the only ones who can truthfully represent the life and reality of today's society. It is from these little guys that I am able to clearly see the true nature of the human race.

Lou Ye

It is not completely correct to say that the "Sixth Generation" filmmakers are interested only in cities. For example, although Jia Zhangke's *Xiao Wu* is about people on the fringe, it is not set in a city. In general, however, this observation is somewhat fitting. The key reason is that these filmmakers have little experience of China's countryside. I grew up in Shanghai and then went to Beijing for college. Therefore, I have little idea about what the countryside is like. I can do nothing about my background. To me, there is no alternative. People born before us are much more likely to be deeply connected with the Chinese countryside.

As for the claim that we are concerned only about so-called marginal figures in society, it really depends on how you define the word "marginal". Just now I mentioned that ten years in China are perhaps equivalent to forty years in Europe. Those who are considered "marginal" now will probably not be considered "marginal" ten years from now. They might even become part of the mainstream. It is impossible to define "marginal". You simply cannot rely on certain abstract concepts to make films or to judge certain things. This is especially true in the setting in which the concept or standard of judgment you have established today will likely become invalid in a week. This happens quite often in a rapidly developing country like China. This means that your standard of judgment must always shift, and your view of reality must be constantly renewed, because economically we try to use only ten years to achieve what other countries took thirty or forty years to achieve, which in turn makes our social experience highly compressed. To cite the example of the label "Sixth Generation", maybe two years from now no one will even mention this term. It is quite normal, because it will for sure become passé. Several years from now, therefore, when you reexamine the situation, you will find that most people at that time may live the same way as the so-called "marginal" figures today. Ten years ago, you would have considered people who hung out in cafés "marginal", but take a look at this café—it is crowded with people. In your imagination, cafés are supposed to be quiet, but look at this café. This is exactly what I mean.

There is probably a narcissistic tendency in me, but all artists are perhaps narcissistic. It is not a valid accusation. You cannot be an artist if you are not narcissistic. To take art as a profession you must be narcissistic. Otherwise it would be too hard for you to handle art. You would engage in another profession. Narcissism is deep-rooted in artists, and it is an integral part of artistic works.

You want to understand and express your view about human beings via the medium of film. This seems to be a non-narcissistic issue. But to delve into this non-narcissistic theme you must begin with an understanding of yourself. To try to come to terms with yourself is itself narcissistic. It is very hard, therefore, to say what is narcissistic and what is not. I believe narcissism is an integral part of my work. Sometimes I might spend a lot of time exploring myself. In this sense, to say somebody is narcissistic is not always derogatory. Besides, it is not always easy to reveal one's true self to another person. Film as an art form demands public attention. If, after acquiring a clear understanding of myself, I tell you who I really am via the medium of the film, it is actually quite risky. So, to some extent, it seems to me that "pure" narcissism rarely happens in film.

As for the accusation that we have limited experience of life, that is even more problematic. What does "limited" in experience mean? How can your experience become "unlimited?" How extensive can one get in terms of life experience? Or, more simply, how many people would you be able to become acquainted with in your life? Human experience, therefore, is always limited. If you claim to be a person with extensive life experience, I believe you are short of self-knowledge. How many people do you know? How many people have you talked to? It would not be too hard for you to figure out the number, right? Just scan through your address book. You only know a limited number of people in this world. Moreover, probably you have already lost contact with many of the names recorded in that address book.

Chapter Four

Lu Chuan

I probably feature "marginal" figures in my films, but the "marginal" figures I like are not those who hang out in nightclubs and bars. I like to feature either mental patients or those who are psychologically traumatized or repressed. I don't like rock stars and the like. They can't win my sympathy and love. My deep sympathy is with those mental patients, or with those whose life is divided into black and white and therefore is an unreal or fantasized world. One might be able to get hold of a cola can this time, but would fail the next time. I've had some firsthand experience with the lives of this particular group of people. In addition, I always feel everybody is to some extent a mental patient, and the only difference lies in the degree of seriousness. Based on this observation, I don't think the term "marginal" connotes anything meaningful or concrete.

Lu Xuechang

I think that in the early years of the "Sixth Generation" "marginality" did play a role in their films. As a matter of fact, when *The Making of the Steel* was finished, I had to face this accusation, too. Since that film is not about ordinary workers or peasants but depicts the life of a college graduate who knows how to play guitar and always hangs out with long-haired rock musicians, it was categorized by some as a film featuring "marginal" figures. To be frank, I don't necessarily agree with this kind of criticism. Even if a film is really about socially marginalized people, why does it deserve harsh criticism? Since there is nothing wrong with films featuring workers, peasants, intellectuals, and other ordinary people, why can't someone make a film about hooligans? If it's true that depicting "marginal" figures is a common feature of our generation, I don't see anything wrong with it.

In addition, the notion of "marginality" is also relative. It really depends on your point of view. To us, a film about the life of the Americans is rather "marginal", because we don't know their life very well. There is also a possible link between this notion and the broader environment of China. For a long time, Chinese cinema has been dominated by the formula that the main character must be a model or a fine example to be followed. Looked at from this angle, therefore, I think young filmmakers have at least made some breakthroughs in this respect, despite the fact that their insistence on only dealing with what interests them may not be readily accepted by the majority.

As for the allegation that we are "narcissistic", I take it as a complement rather than some kind of criticism. Film should be divided into a variety of categories. If you are making a commercial film backed by Hollywood money, then there is nothing to be proud of if you are accused of being "narcissistic". But if you are making a film with limited or little interest in commercial success, then being a little "narcissistic" is not a bad thing at all. "Narcissism" can be easily understood as a mark of one's individuality.

Ma Liwen

There has been discussion about the differences between the "Sixth Generation" and the younger filmmakers like me. What concerns the "Sixth Generation" most are individual-centered marginal themes, such as drug addiction and prostitution. In contrast, we as a group are not primarily interested in making "underground" films (cynical critics might say that we don't even have opportunities to make "underground" films). We want to make "legal" films, the films that will pass the official censorship and be screened domestically. Because of this general attitude, we are sometimes labeled as the "Sunshine Generation". As a matter of fact, some older filmmakers are quite like us. Directors like Huang Jianxin and Huo Jianqi are very smart and talented, but they are not obsessed with the subjects they favor most. Instead, they are making films most of us feel comfortable watching. Certainly I don't mean that I can be grouped together with Huang and Huo. At best, I am only a lonely tent set up by the side of a certain generation.

Meng Qi

I think there is a difference between college graduates and those who do not have a college background. College graduates tend to think they are somewhat special. I once visited the campus of the Shanghai Academy of Theater Art and got a real sense about how deep this feeling of being "special" was among the students there. I remember I saw many foreign films and plays there, especially German and French ones. Most students there are overwhelmed by these so-called "masterpieces". Even though a lot of them didn't quite understand such works, they are still overjoyed. To cite such an example is to say that, first of all, although they seem to know a lot, college graduates are in comparison weak in life and social experience. Second, their sense of crisis or anxiety is relatively weak, because college is ultimately a greenhouse for them. I've also had many college friends. Their sense of superiority is overwhelming when they are in college. After graduation, however, many of them become disillusioned and lose their goal in life.

Filmmaking is closely connected to one's life experience. Because of the aforementioned, I feel it's understandable that those filmmakers who were trained in college tend to be more interested in more radical subjects, such as those featuring drug addicts and homosexuals. Both their film education and their self-centered nature call out to them to explore the new and the novel.

Chapter Four

But as a filmmaker who lives his everyday life with common people, I naturally fall in love with things that are more ordinary and realistic. For instance, I became interested in the life of the characters in *What a Snowy Day* because it reminded me of my life with my friends prior to my joining the military. It is because of this resonance that I made the story into a film.

I don't think any one of the characters in *What a Snowy Day* can be called "marginal". All of them are quite normal. My film is only a truthful representation of their normal life. Certainly the film is sometimes socially satirical. I think the satirical moments mainly come from two directions. First, satire arises when the protagonist finds himself in an ironic situation. When he feels neglected and no one seems to take him seriously, the protagonist starts to question himself. Second, when the audience examines his ironic situation from the outside, the film becomes a little comical, and these comical elements are also meant to be socially satirical.

Shi Runjiu

If "marginal" figures mean those who don't do legal things for a living, then my characters, except for the underworld boss in *All the Way*, can't be labeled "marginal" at all. They are the common people, or at least the people living at the bottom of society. In other words, their status of living may be "marginal", but they are not "marginal" figures. In China, many young people are living this way.

I've had many contacts with the music people who seem to be outside the mainstream of music art. But I would rather use the word "alternative" to describe them. Just use the street musician character in *A Beautiful New World* as an example. This character is actually based on a real incident I encountered in Shanghai. One day, I was at a musical instrument shop on Shanghai's Jinling Middle Road. Suddenly, a young man walked into the store and said to the people inside: I'd like to sing a song for everybody. Then, he began to sing. After singing, he thanked each bewildered customer and waited. Some people gave him a few bucks and he walked out of the shop, satisfied. As a matter of fact, I've had many encounters with this kind of people. I don't think the label "marginal figure" suits them.

There is nothing "narcissistic" in my films. My focus is not on my own life, but on the life of ordinary people, the people who don't aim high or dream unrealistic dreams due to the heavy burden of life. Unlike filmmakers like Lou Ye and Wang Xiaoshuai, I am more concerned about the everyday reality of life as well as the people who are living through this everyday-ness.

Tang Danian

I think featuring "marginal" figures is a conscious choice of the "Sixth

Generation" as well as a natural response to the changing environment of China. To tell you the truth, after the "Sixth Generation" filmmakers graduated, most of them turned into "marginal" figures themselves. Against the social environment of China and the studio system of the time, this group of people suddenly found themselves as well as their understanding of filmmaking marginalized. To some extent, therefore, their interest in "marginal" figures has been a form of self-expression. In addition, if purely out of the consideration of artistic creation, "marginal" figures are more interesting because they embody more elements of humanity. This is one of the reasons why they've attracted the attention of the "Sixth Generation". Since "normal" people tend to conceal their true selves, it is not always easy to find strong emotional conflict and struggle in them. Another reason has something to do with the system. This system does not allow you to fully express the inner repression, predicament, and depression of "mainstream" people. The only choice for the "Sixth Generation", therefore, are the so-called "marginal" figures.

Of course, at the time of our graduation, the word "commercialization" was almost unheard of in Chinese cinema. Nowadays, however, the injection of commercial elements into Chinese cinema has transformed the nature of this generation's filmmaking. It seems to me that there are much more directions being taken, and the once "unified" voice has turned into a diversified polyphony. With the increase of opportunities and outside influences, it has become almost impossible to draw a general picture of these filmmakers as a group, because every individual director seems to have his/her own agenda.

In *City Paradise*, I indeed intended to make so-called "marginal" figures my central characters. The film is actually about a country boy's feelings of rootlessness and marginality after he comes to the city. To me, the notion of "marginality" is sociological, and *City Paradise* is meant to depict this kind of "marginality". Of course there is a sub-narrative in the film, the narrative of the countryside. The categorization of Chinese cinema has been quite rigid: urban film, youth film, country film, et cetera. By adding this sub-narrative, I intended to break this rigid division and build a link between the city and the country. Although city life looks quite prosperous, it is so only against the background of a collapsed country life. The huge gap between the city and the country makes it almost impossible for country folks to find their place in the city. In *City Paradise*, the collapse of country life can be felt throughout the film. For instance, the mother comes to the city hoping to find her lost son. But she immediately loses her sense of direction in the labyrinth of the city. Her daughter-in-law also locks up their house in the country and comes to the city looking for her husband. This is to say that the life in the country has actually collapsed.

Chapter Four

As for so-called "narcissism", I think this is actually an issue about the contradiction between artistic creation and social responsibility. Generally speaking, I feel literature and art shouldn't be burdened by the heaviness of social responsibility. To say this doesn't mean that young filmmakers don't have a sense of social responsibility, however. I feel their sense of social responsibility can easily match that of the previous generations. Their involvement in featuring those disadvantaged or "marginal" people itself is a reflection of their sense of social responsibility.

Wang Chao

Words like "narcissism" are not particularly accurate in discussing the so-called "Sixth Generation" filmmakers. Narcissism is actually an ideal state of art. I even feel the "Sixth Generation" hasn't reached that ideal state. Nothing is more "narcissistic" than the aestheticism of Marquis de Sade or Oscar Wilde. Compared to these two great authors, the "Sixth Generation" is far away from that ideal state in both philosophical and aesthetic terms. Indulging the self doesn't mean one has reached the ideal state of narcissism. One also needs to go beyond that and explore the ontology of narcissism. I don't think any one of the "Sixth Generation" directors has achieved that goal.

To me, therefore, narcissism is not a negative thing at all. Most world-renowned filmmakers are quite narcissistic. Isn't it true that Pedro Almodovar is narcissistic? Many great works of Almodovar are utterly narcissistic. Narcissism is a two-edged sword, one pointing at the self, the other at the human race. In this sense, we are actually not narcissistic enough. This is particularly true in China. First of all, we don't love ourselves. We don't know how to treat ourselves as independent human beings. China lacks this tradition. Most Chinese critics also don't quite understand the true meaning of narcissism. They think that narcissism is at the least a derogatory term. Actually, reaching the state of narcissism is a sign of maturity in literature, art, and philosophy. I really hope China can produce a few extremely narcissistic filmmakers. So far, however, I haven't seen any of them. Moreover, I think China is in urgent need of this kind of filmmakers. You love yourself as an independent subject to the extent that you could transcend all values and norms. Is there anyone like this in China? I hope so.

Of course the "Sixth Generation" can be further divided into the former and latter periods. Purely from the point of view of art, I think in the latter period the "Sixth Generation" has already begun to overcome some of their limits. For instance, Xiaoshuai's *Beijing Bicycle* has successfully emerged from the constraint of the self. I think they will continue to work toward that direction and eventually form their own characteristics. This is especially true for Lou Ye. Although Lou's *Weekend Lover* is a little self-indulgent, it shows his extraordinary filmmaking talent. This self-indulgence, however, is extended beyond a single individual in *Suzhou River*. We can sense that the feeling of predicament expressed in *Suzhou River* is no longer limited to oneself. It seems Lou Ye is aware that this predicament also extends to the culture of a whole generation. There is a sense of fatalism about this predicament. The film forces the audience to confront the issues of fate and death. It is because of this concern over fate and death that Lou's narcissism becomes attractive and intoxicating. Furthermore, it is also because of this concern that Lou Ye's seemingly fatal exquisiteness manifests its irresistible nature.

As for the so-called "marginality", I can't speak for other filmmakers of my generation, but the characters featured in *The Orphan of Anyang* are not "marginal" figures. They were probably "marginal" in the later 1980s and early 1990s, but definitely not so at the turn of the century. In the early 1990s, if you said to people, "There are prostitutes in China" or "that person is an unemployed worker", they would be startled. But time has changed. Even the top officials in the central government are openly talking about the issues of unemployment and peasant hardship. In other words, we are actually witnessing the emergence of another "mainstream" group of people: the unemployed and underprivileged.

To a certain extent, my film is about this newly emerged group. I would have been very happy if my film had come out before May or June 2001, since that was the time when the Central Committee of the Communist Party openly called for solicitude toward the underprivileged. I am pleased that the term "underprivileged" has been eventually written into the official document of the central government. After I converted to Christianity in 1995, with the compassion of an engaged intellectual, I really felt there was an urgent need to speak out for this underprivileged group of people. In no more than half a year, this concern was echoed in the official document. That's why I am overjoyed. Although it remains to be seen whether the official edict is only rhetorical, it is at least a proof that China is making progress in this respect. Just think about the sheer number of the laid-off workers of those state-owned companies. Sometimes several thousands become unemployed in an instant. Then take a look at the issue of the troubled peasants. Millions of them are being forced to leave their fields and come to the city for jobs.

We Beijingers tend to think everybody is a white collar worker and the society belongs to no one but us. This is only a narrow view of the city's residents, however. China is a huge country. There are fewer than twenty cities that are as big as Beijing. The vast region of China is mainly composed

Chapter Four

of thousands of counties and small towns. There are so many people living in poverty. With this in mind, how can you label the characters in *The Orphan of Anyang* "marginal"?

Wang Guangli

One of the reasons I don't view myself as a member of the "Sixth Generation" lies in our different attitudes toward the self. My impression is that the "Sixth Generation" is too narcissistic. One time I went a little too far, claiming that they resemble those amateur karaoke "singers" who love to indulge in self-entertainment, sometimes bordering on masturbation. This is what I feel about the so-called "one's own feeling and perception". Isn't it analogous to masturbation? As long as I've reached climax, nothing else matters. If one or two people are masturbating under a quilt, it is quite all right. But if a number of people masturbate together under the quilt, then something must be wrong. To critique somebody is actually an action of self-criticism. I feel that, as a group, we all shared this narcissistic complex at the beginning of our careers. It was probably a reaction against the Fifth Generation because they tended to show off their sense of social and historical responsibilities, we wanted to reverse that trend by shifting away from that moral burden to the self. But this can't be an excuse for narcissism. Narcissism should belong to adolescence, and it should only last for a short period of time. After all, an artist or a film should broaden his or its scope to go beyond the limited concern for the self.

I think neither *I've Graduated* nor *The Maiden Work* can be called narcissistic. On the contrary, both films contain a sense of irony and a spirit of self-criticism. Indeed, comparatively speaking, narcissism is more obviously reflected in the works of the "Sixth Generation". Because many of their works couldn't be officially released in China, I've only had a passing knowledge of them. Sometimes I only watched segments of their films, and sometimes my knowledge of them was only based on non-visual descriptions or movie posters. Therefore, I might be biased. In any case, I don't think their works will remain narcissistic in the future. As a matter of fact, they've already changed. You can sense that they have made efforts in their recent works to consciously reflect upon their earlier works. Besides, with good intentions, many critics have also pointed out the danger of narcissism.

Wang Quanan

First of all, I think the theory that young filmmakers are obsessed with the so-called "marginal figures" isn't even worth refuting. It is simply ridiculous. Why? Because in nature art is by and about individual. When we are focusing on every individual, each of them will naturally turn into a "marginal" figure, because everyone's inner self is distinct. When you really delve into the inner psychology of each individual, you will find each of them actually thinks differently. The notion of "marginality", therefore, doesn't hold water at all and must be expunged from our critical language.

Looking at this issue from a broader point of view, I think that morally we should learn how to respect and understand people who are different from us. Also, we need to understand that the world is made up of various kinds of different individuals. To be frank, we are not very good at respecting others. In the past, we thought "others" were nothing but our enemies. Our education was simplified to the extent that all those who were different from our perceived norms must be eradicated. When this view is applied to art, you see the emergence of the term "marginal figures". To label someone "marginal" actually means to sentence him/her to death, because he/she is no longer perceived as a "normal" person. According to this theory, not only are homosexuals, homeless people, or drug addicts "abnormal", but all adolescents belong to this category as well, because their youthful restlessness and discontent are often channeled through social norms. The notion of "marginal figures", therefore, is nothing but nonsense.

As a matter of fact, the often mentioned term "masses" is also a reflection of our self-deceit. It is only a fantasized form of political power, and doesn't exist at all. If you look into the inner psychology of people, each one is distinctive, or, if using their term, "marginal". Actually, if you are able to delve into Jiang Zemin's inner self, you will probably find that he is also a "marginal figure" because I think the inner psychology of any mature and intelligent person must be quite complicated, not as flat as the image shown on television. Facing the disorder of the world, what does he really feel? In his inner heart, he must have an array of different standards in judging the behavior of different nations, particularly that of the United States and Russia. If you were able to dig out what he really feels, or if he himself revealed what he really thinks, then I am afraid that China and the whole world would be in great shock.

I think the protagonist of *Lunar Eclipse* actually represents the top portion of the social strata of today's China, or what we usually call the "social elites". Certainly I didn't directly write about the "social elites" but use a woman to refract the feelings of this group of people. Women are the reification of social values. I have no negative feelings about them. They are the products of this changing society. In *Lunar Eclipse*, there is a good-looking, well educated, and cultivated woman. I wanted to explore how she really feels in her pursuit of a better life and what she has gained and lost in this process. This exploration was further expanded in my second film, *The Story of Ermei*, through which we are able to get a glimpse of how those who are not as well-off as the protagonist of *Lunar Eclipse* feel about the changing China. I wanted to explore how she adjusts to this system, this changing economy, and the moral principles imposed on her. I think this process is actually quite hair-raising and brutal. Yes, psychologically this is a brutal experience. When she comes home, her inner self could be shattered, never to be put back together again. My work, however, is not to reveal the brutality of this experience but to search for the shining moments from these shattered pieces. This is what I've been pondering after *Lunar Eclipse*. I didn't want to express this through an alienated character, such as an unemployed wanderer or a thief. Instead, I focused on a relatively traditional and simple figure. Although somewhat rebellious, she is still confined to her traditional role in society.

Wang Xiaoshuai

I don't think a single human being can be labeled "marginal". How can such a label be applied to human beings? On the basis of equality, a janitor is the same in status as the rest of us. The notion that we are at the center and he is at the margin is absolutely false. He can be called so only in the sense that, in relation to the power of the dominant discourse, he is marginalized. Unlike those who are affiliated with government and party institutions, he is absolutely powerless in the face of the dominant ideology of the nation. As a matter of fact, the word "marginal" goes together with the notion "central". If you don't have a strong sense of the "center", then you'll have little conception of the "margin". Because most of us in China believe there is an absolute center, from which the mainstream ideology and moral judgment of the Central Committee of the Party radiate, the corresponding conception of the "marginal" and "non-mainstream" is also crystal-clear. I think the distinction between the city and the country, the "marginal" and "mainstream" in the West is not as remarkable as that in China. Actually, being "marginal" or not really depends on your point of view. If you judge people with the ideology and morality promoted by the state apparatus, then some people would naturally turn "marginal". But if you give up this practice, then no one can be possibly labeled "marginal".

As for narcissism, I feel it is meaningless to debunk the accusation that we are "narcissistic". I am always startled by the fact that after so many years of political upheavals in this country many people still haven't realized that our filmmaking should remind people of their rights in voicing their individual concerns. It is a voice of individualism, not narcissism. In the past, we failed to treat ourselves as independent individuals. We submerged ourselves into the deep ocean of the collective and followed every word of our great leader. In so doing we actually denied our own subjectivity. At this historical moment, however, the age of individualism has arrived in China. The most remarkable feature of this group of young filmmakers, therefore, is the articulation of an awakened self-consciousness.

Xu Jinglei

I don't think my film is narcissistic. One sign of maturity, I believe, is the ability to look at things from another person's point of view, not purely from one's own. In the meantime, I think none of the characters in the film *Me and My Dad* is "marginal". Is the daughter "marginal?" I don't think so. If it is true that such a character is rarely seen in Chinese cinema, it's because it has so far failed to confront some of the changing aspects of China. In fact, I feel there are many women in real life who live in a way similar to that of the daughter in my film.

I also don't think characters with flaws are necessarily "gray". We should realize that humans are flawed creatures. Only with this realization can we face life with a correct attitude, that is, to show our tolerance toward others. This is not the tolerance that results from one's condescending attitude but from an objective point of view. Our sympathy, forgiveness, and tolerance should be based on this understanding. It is because of this understanding that I let the daughter bury her parents together in the end of the film.

Zhang Ming

I don't think my films are about the so-called "marginal" figures. The characters in my films are actually real human beings. When many outsiders go visit Wushan [Zhang Ming's hometown in Sichuan], they probably want to see the county chief or the richest entrepreneur in the local area. But are they the main figures in Wushan? To me, they are the top official or the richest person there, but not the most important ones. Some people may be eager to have their pictures taken with them, but I'd rather focus on the overlooked motel attendants. In the past, most filmmakers shut their camera eyes to them. I feel my camera can no longer disregard these people, because I think they are not "marginal" people, but the most important ones of this society.

Zhang Yang

I don't agree with the conception of the so-called "marginal figures". To me, every human being is the same. It is my belief that regardless of their difference in profession, value, or religion human beings share some essential similarities. My interest is not on my characters' profession, but on the very base of their inner self. For instance, from my point of view, the Jia

Chapter Four

Hongsheng character in *Quitting* is only an ordinary human being. His struggle in the ordinary space of the family is the emphasis of my portrayal of his character. He is only "marginal" in the sense that his lifestyle differs from that of the majority, but what's troubling him is, in essence, the same as it is for most of us. Drug addiction is actually only on the outer edges of this film. What concerned me most was the exploration of this character as a human being and his spiritual world. I can't speak for the others, but in the future I will continue to focus on those universal themes in my films or stories. No matter who the character might be, I'll always treat him/her as an ordinary human being.

Zhang Yuan

My films have nothing to do with so-called "narcissism". So far I haven't made a single film that is really related to my life experience or memories of the past. I am sometimes narcissistic, but this sentiment hasn't been sufficiently explored in my creative works. I hope I'll be able to do something more autobiographical in the near future.

I don't like the term "marginal figures", but I agree that my characters, as many people have already pointed out, are somewhat extreme in both emotion and behavior. I remember some people used to ask me: why can't you feature the lives of "normal" people? But what kind of life can be called "normal"? Is it necessarily "normal" if a person goes to work at eight in the morning and comes back at five in the evening, who does not smoke, drink, and overeat? Maybe 99 percent of the people live that way, but my main interest is on the remaining one percent. I feel only those who are quite extreme in temperament, get crazy after a few drinks, and dare to love and hate can arouse my interest. In face of these people, I often feel I am quite ignorant and unimaginative. It is they who constantly inspire me.

CHAPTER FIVE

ON THE OTHER SIDE OF THE CAMERA: MALE DIRECTORS AND REPRESENTATION OF WOMAN

With the exception of Xu Jinglei and Ma Liwen, whose takes on female characters call for a more sophisticated reading, all the interviewed filmmakers are male. Yet, in most of their works, female characters are always as important as, if not more important than, male characters. In films like Lunar Eclipse *and* Eyes of a Beauty, *the woman's point of view is privileged, seeing and understanding the changing world. This poses a classical feminist question: What happens when a male director attempts to locate a woman's point of view and convey the "discourse of a woman", including women's desire and fantasy? Is it a valid claim that the visual presence of a woman in a man's work is no more than a projection of a male's fantasized female "other"? The interviewers recognized the unsettling nature of the questions but presented them to the filmmakers by asserting the changing directions of feminism in the West.*

* * *

Guan Hu

Those who know me thought *Eyes of a Beauty* was a great departure from my previous works. But I know it's not a departure, but a result of the cumulative changes in me in recent years. Now I feel a good film should be first and foremost tranquil, calm, and composed. This was unimaginable to me just a few years ago. Back then, my goal was to make my films feel provocative, *avant-garde*, and forceful. I think this change or transformation is out of my natural growth, not because of the teaching I got from any outside force.

With an understanding of this change, you would probably agree with me that, despite the fact that *Eyes of a Beauty* features three women, gender is no longer an important issue in my creative process. What I did was to only realistically and calmly record how they reacted to the environment. There is nothing allegorical in the film. I used some amateur actors and asked them to speak the local language, which gave the film a documentary look. The film consists of three stories, the first about a sixteen-year-old country girl, the second about a twenty-six-year-old female high school teacher, and the third about a thirty-six-year-old out-of-fashion actress of the Yue opera. They were all born in the birthplace of the legendary Chinese beauty, Xishi.[xxvii] As the women living in the place where beauty worship is deeply rooted in local history and culture, they are actually under tremendous pressure not to "embarrass" the fame of the place. So, what I wanted to do was to examine how they reacted to this environment as well as how they struggled to live up to the expectations of the outside world. It is a film about dreams and life. The sixteen-year-old girl always dreams of going to Shanghai but doesn't have enough money. When she finally manages to save up enough, she is betrayed by the boy she falls for. The boy takes her money to Shanghai, leaving her behind. As for that female teacher, when she is about to get married, the arrival of a Shanghai student rekindles her dream. Her future husband is a local government official, not bad based on the local standard. But the sudden arrival of this tall Shanghai student steals her heart. Nothing dramatic happens in the end, however. She eventually returns to the town and gets married. The third woman always dreams of playing the lead role in the local opera troupe. She can't stand being replaced by a younger actress in the role. It is unbearable for her to be assigned to play a supporting role. One day, the younger actress is suddenly transferred to a provincial-level troupe, which makes it possible for her to play the lead role again. Life has simply played a joke on her.

The stories of these three women unfold calmly. Therefore, the issue as to how gender politics plays a role in the film is not particularly important. I view them first as ordinary human beings, second as women. I feel I don't have to necessarily understand them as women. If you make a film about the war between China and Japan, is there a need for you to understand how the Japanese really feel? Even if you feel there is such a need, you won't be able to really understand them, simply because you've never lived through what they've experienced. Besides, different people look at a thing in different ways. The meaning of "understanding" really depends on your point of view. Similarly, as a male director, I don't think I can possibly enter the deep psyche of the female subject. But what I am able to do is to study and research their lives and search for the inner beauty in them from a man's point of view. This is analogous to the fact that, although a northerner, I was the one who went to the south and made *Eyes of a Beauty*. I didn't have the ambition to really understand or create something. What I did was to only explore things with an observing eye. That's enough.

Jia Zhangke

The issue of female consciousness is not emphasized in *Xiao Wu*. Female characters in that film are actually introduced from a man's point of view. I think the main female character in *Xiao Wu* is more or less the embodiment of social problems. But when it comes to *Platform*, you can sense the emergence of this consciousness. For instance, there are actually two groups of women in *Platform*. The first group is represented by Yin Lijuan, the tax collector who dances in the office. The second is represented by Zhong Ping, the one who leaves the town in the end and we have no idea where she has gone. Zhong Ping and Yin Lijuan actually represent two types of women and two ways of life. Yin is the one whom no one can easily hurt, because she is able to be happy with and make the best of the life that she lives, no matter how insignificant it might be. I think most girls in China are quite like her. What I mean by "make the best of" is that their expectation for life is actually quite low. These girls have various ways to stay immune to the wounds of life, and the most important one is not to invest emotion too easily so that they can withdraw or advance at will. Yes, Yin is a girl not easily carried away by emotion. She is in command of her own fate, can calmly say goodbye to her boyfriend and, when she feels like it, is capable of coming back to him with ease. To a certain extent, it is she who makes him come back to her. I know many girls have this kind of strength. To see her from another angle, we can say Yin is a woman who is very protective of herself. Because of her self-centered nature, she will never get hurt.

In contrast, Zhong Ping, the one who does the bullfight dance, is a woman who is willing to sacrifice herself for the benefit of others. Because of this, she is the one who continuously gets hurt. For instance, she is hurt by both her lover and the police. As a matter of fact, she is the one upon whom I placed my hope. I think the bravest thing she does is to leave the town in the end. She is the only one who decides not to return to her old life. I even shot an ending sequence with the focus on her: on the day of another Chinese New Year, this group of small-town friends gathers at a restaurant to sing karaoke. When one song starts, they are stunned to see that the beach girl on TV is their old friend, Zhong Ping! But I eventually decided not to use this concluding sequence, because I thought it was too "clever". One of the principles I uphold in my narratives is to refuse overt "cleverness". Many people thought this ending was a knockout, including some of the crew members. They felt overwhelmed and were reluctant to edit it out. But I felt I'd rather replace this "powerful" ending with a more ambiguous one, because I thought overt "cleverness" would weaken the power of ambiguity of my films.

When depicting women, therefore, I am actually focused on the rise of their self-consciousness, or a consciousness of power. In *Platform*, this consciousness of power begins to emerge when the two girls light their cigarettes by the window. During that scene many forms of consciousness emerges, including the consciousness of the self, the consciousness of freedom, the consciousness of democracy, and the consciousness of opening-up. The burgeoning female consciousness is only one of them. This consciousness is not the one that resembles the political slogan of "women can hold up half of the sky". Instead, it is a female consciousness that permeates the details of daily life, such as the conviction that I can also light a cigarette, that I can wear a skirt and wander about the streets, and that I can openly ask my boyfriend to accompany me to get an abortion. This consciousness is externalized not through theories and slogans but through the daily details of a woman's life as well as the changes of the female body. As a filmmaker, however, I don't want to exaggerate the intensity of this consciousness or to de-contextualize it. I want to give my female characters a lovelier look than that of the male characters. Maybe this is a result of my personal experience. In my life, I've seen too many irresponsible men. Compared to them, women seem to be more committed to assuming the responsibility of life. Some of them could even risk their life and reputation for what they desire. This is power.

I think male directors probably can't free themselves completely from their subjective point of view in depicting women. But what we can do is to jump out of our familiar framework and reflect upon our male-centered position. I view myself both as a filmmaker and as a man of self-reflection. Film means a lot to me, including its function in expressing one's view of the world. I often think I have too many shortcomings. Some of which, I believe, are the result of the lingering influence of traditional Chinese culture. Nowadays I often get on the Internet to read young people's comments on my films. I feel some of these young people are not only critical of my films but also critical of themselves. I think this shows their merits. What do I mean by self-reflection? Let me use the omniscient point of view as an example. In film and literature, self-reflection means that, you begin to question the use of this point of view: can you, as an omniscient narrator, explain all the secrets of life? Can you, like God, determine and control everything, including the development of the narrative and the fate of your characters? When you start to raise these questions, I think your narrative will undergo a great transformation.

Self-reflection also makes me think about the nature of my career. I think reflecting on your position in society will always bring positive things to your work. To me, filmmaking is only a profession. I once wrote an article, "I Don't Poeticize My Life Experience", in which I argued that even when we are surrounded by fame and limelight we should not forget we are as ordinary as the folks in the streets. In other words, when we are working in a profession that has more media exposure and therefore makes us easily stand out in a crowd, are we capable of going back to ordinariness and mingling with the general crowd? I think this is a very important question, and this is also one of the major reasons why many Chinese filmmakers have a short career. It is quite regrettable that some of them, after a short period of success, can no longer go back to the crowd and life itself. Take a look at (Federico) Fellini. The reason why he was able to make so many films but still remain so creative and keenly observant is because he was deeply embedded in his culture and people. As a matter of fact, he had never left them. Compared to Fellini, I think it is too easy for many Chinese filmmakers to forget where they came from. Therefore, I feel it is necessary for us to demystify the whole profession of filmmaking or to erase the "aura" that surrounds this profession. If there is a difference between the Fifth Generation and the "Sixth Generation" filmmakers, I think this is the most remarkable difference, not the difference between their individual works.

Jiang Wen

I think the question as to whether male directors can express the soul of the female subject is rather simplistic and contrived. To me, how to handle the female characters is never an issue. I simply view them as human beings. Having said this, I don't want to deny that there are indeed differences between men and women. But every man is different, too. Certainly this difference is not the same as that between men and women. I guess what I really want to say is that you have to analyze your characters according to specific circumstances. Without an analysis of the given circumstance, it is almost meaningless to raise such issues as "how to represent women, how to represent men, how to depict the Chinese, and how to depict the Japanese". In my eyes, they are first and foremost human beings. Then, if put in certain special circumstances, they will act or react according to their understanding of the world. To me, this is more interesting.

You might have noticed that women do not play a significant roll in my films. This is not intentional, however. My previous films were conceived in a way that is hard to rationally explain. If you reach your conclusion based on the finished films, then it is true that there aren't many women characters in my works. I personally have no idea as to why this is the case. But one thing is clear: I don't take it as a personal duty to represent women, and I also don't intentionally search for a subject that is focused on women. If I encounter such a subject by accident, however, I will pursue it.

Jin Chen

The screen writer of *Love in the Internet Age* is a woman. Her name is Guo Xiaolu. As a matter of fact, in writing the original screenplay, Guo adopted a man's point of view. It was me who changed it to a woman's. In other words, there was a double switch of gender roles in the creative process. My second

Chapter Five

film, *Chrysanthemum Tea*, also adopted a woman's point of view. The difference in point of view will certainly result in different responses to the world. My feeling is that women are more willing to observe the world from a man's perspective and vice versa. Here I am of course talking about artists. For example, suppose you are a southerner, having southerner's habits and characteristics. When you move to the north, your lifestyle will change. Actually, this is when you are in a better position to represent northerners and northern characteristics, simply because you would be able to bring your southern background into the representation. As a man, I may have a better understanding of the male sex, but if I look at things from a woman's point of view, I think a new sensibility will be formed, a combination of both female and male elements. To answer your question, despite being a male director, I think I am able to assume a woman's point of view.

Actually, if men and women can switch their roles, they would become more comprehensive in looking at issues. If you are only able to explore the world from your gender-defined perspective, you are apt to go to extremes. To me, many feminist ideas have gone too far, and some male-centered views have further radicalized those ideas. If we can switch roles and adopt a different perspective, I think we will be able to see the emergence of many interesting works. When we consider an issue with the spirit of equality and tolerance, we will have a more objective view of the world and the human race. So far I've been consistent with the use of the woman's perspective. I remember that Li Hong, in making her first feature, *Flying High with You*, favored a man's point of view. Her second feature, *Homicide in the Black & White Apartment*, an action film that features cops and gangsters, looks quite masculine. I find her works quite interesting.

Certainly I don't plan always to stick with the same perspective. My next film, for instance, will be structured around a man's point of view. I think it's quite normal for an artist to switch his or her perspective or point of view. From an old man's to a child's perspectives, there are many options available to an artist. My third film, *Three Doors*, which was just finished, is entirely based on the perception of a middle school student. Sometimes I feel switching roles is just like changing camera angles. If you want to take a picture from the perspective of a toddler, you ought to lower your camera's position. Furthermore, if you adopt a toddler's point of view, you will be overwhelmed by new discoveries, because he or she can only see adults' thighs.

It should be noted that compared to the Fifth Generation or previous generations of directors, the directors in our group are more flexible. In response to the diversification of the world, our views have also become diversified. Besides, I don't think there has been a set pattern for my works.

When I gather together with fellow screenwriters and directors, every one of us often speaks about the necessity of not falling into a set pattern, simply because there are so many different things we want to try. For example, I always dream of making a martial arts film. I also want to make a horror film or an animated film. There are simply so many different things I am eager to try. I don't think it's a good thing to form a settled pattern or style at our age. We don't want to follow the rigid steps of Neo-Confucianism, do we? It is certainly true that Neo-Confucianism is a great achievement of Chinese thought, but it is also no denying that this school of thought has greatly limited people's imagination and development. Changes in styles, genres, perspectives, and other artistic forms, therefore, should be encouraged. Personally, I would like to try as many subjects and perspectives as possible. Today I may have a special interest in the women's point of view, but tomorrow I will probably switch to other angles.

Chrysanthemum Tea was not meant to be a women's film, but it turned out that women responded more positively than men. I figured this is because many male audiences, who tend to be more rational, and women with masculine tendencies, would question the "truthfulness" of the story. They probably think the film is too sentimental and illusory. In contrast, most women tend to be moved by stories with a softened edge. In addition, compared to the lackluster response from the young audience, old people are especially drawn to the film. Maybe this is because women and old people are the two groups in our society who still have dreams. The former still live in their dreams, while the latter are especially nostalgic for the dreams they had when they were young. For those young men who are burdened by the daily struggles of life, this film is probably too illusory. What they need are the things that are down-to-earth or confrontational. To be frank, I am quite satisfied with my film's reception. No film is able to appeal to all the people.

Li Xin

Unlike the past when many jobs required physical strength, nowadays a single push of a button can destroy a whole army. So, the boundary between men and women is increasingly blurred. Men and women differed drastically in their social roles in the past, but nowadays men seem to have become more feminized, and women more masculinized. Therefore, it is hard for me to clearly state whether my point of departure is based on men's or women's point of view. One thing is for sure, however. No matter what subject is featured, be it a children's story or a story about a house, everything presented on the screen is seen through my eyes. Of course, my point of view is also constantly affected or influenced by other people, and mine is not necessarily as reliable and interesting as children's. Sometimes I do feel

Chapter Five

children have an advantage in point of view. They have the ability of looking through things. I'd like to occasionally mimic their point of view. I think things will be completely different if this point of view is privileged.

Liu Binjian

I am often confronted with the question as to how I, as a male director, can know how a woman reacts to certain things. To tell you the truth, I've never thought of approaching the issue from the angle of gender or sexual politics. I only feel as a filmmaker or artist it is a basic requirement to have at least a general grasp of your characters' psychologies. It is simply a natural and necessary requirement. Certainly as a male director I might be susceptible to the so-called "male bias", but I do feel it shouldn't be too hard for a male filmmaker to switch his gender position.

In addition, I also think most people haven't realized that there are many possibilities in human life. The issue of gender and sexuality always involves the notions of changeability and complexity. There are also many unresolved mysteries surrounding this issue. To have a better grasp of what I am not familiar with, I always rely on open discussions and exchanges of ideas with other people. For instance, the process of making *Men and Women* is actually the one that involved constant debates between me and Cui Zien. As you know, Cui is the first one who openly acknowledged he is a gay. Like the characters in the film, we were constantly searching and exploring, trying to find the best way to develop the narrative. Sometimes we quarreled, sometimes we clashed, and sometimes I was blamed for being unable to understand certain things. It was through these brainstorming sessions that *Men and Women* came out. To me, it was also a great learning process, a process in which I, as an individual, mingled with the group and gained mutual understandings.

Lou Ye

I rely on my own point of observation to approach female characters, not on a woman's point of view. When selecting actresses, you always tend to focus on those who have certain traits you feel are right. You have to find something in her that speaks to you or you give her the freedom to act. At least she should have a pleasant disposition. Otherwise, you would be aggravated to death [laugh]. Just imagine: how could you handle the situation if you let an actress you disliked play the lead, considering the fact that you would see her face thousands of times before the film is done? For this reason alone, you would want to find a lead actress you feel comfortable with and who is pleasant.

As a matter of fact, the line between masculine and feminine is not always so clear-cut. Inside a lot of men, there are many feminine elements and vice versa. These elements are often mixed together. It is my personal belief that gender can hardly be the only category that divides all things. Besides, if you are one hundred percent female, it serves you better to make films about men, because this profession is nothing more than focusing the camera on objects. Male directors, therefore, are the most suited to make films about women, because filmmaking is actually about looking. In this profession of looking, it is more interesting to look at the opposite sex than to examine the same sex. Since men and women are different creatures, there is an interesting tension between them.

Actually, it has become more evident nowadays that many of our preconceptions were wrong. For example, in the past, we thought tables had to be made of wood. This is in fact false. There are tables made of stone and steel, and there are even tables made of paper. Anything is possible. So, if you say, "man has such and such a nature", it too must be false. In other words, by saying so, you have excluded many other possibilities. Your premise is already questionable. It is all right for you to say "*I think* man is such and such", because that is what *you* think. But if you state, "man *is* such and such", I am sorry, you are wrong because there are many kinds of men. The same logic also applies to women. There are many kinds of women. In addition, there are also transsexuals. The general trend of the last century or earlier was to divide and distinguish: divide territories and distinguish things into classes. But as this practice reaches the point where there is little space for further division and distinction, the line that sets things apart begins to fade. So, we are actually heading back, trying to efface this line. What we are doing nowadays is in fact to erase or cross the lines we set before, including the lines demarcating categories and the line between the sexes. To draw lines is to have a better understanding of things, but now these lines are precisely the ones that obstruct our understanding. Thus, it is inevitable that we are heading back. The world is rich and colorful. You can't simply claim that the world is either red or black. Certainly there is also a "soft" part in my point of view.

Lu Chuan

Although *The Missing Gun* centers on a policeman, in my original screenplay, the two women characters were of equal importance. But in the film version, many scenes that involved the policeman's wife, played by Wu Yujuan, were taken out—not only the lovemaking scenes but also the ones that highlighted her and her relationship with her son. Originally, I wanted to portray a middle-aged woman who, like many women of her age, lived in her self-constructed fantasy and imagination. She fantasized about having a solid

Chapter Five

family, a filial son, and a husband who is able to shoulder the sky. Living in her fantasy, she was never psychologically prepared to confront the reality that her husband used to have a mistress of whom she was not aware. But one day, when exposed to the reality, she completely collapsed. She wanted to mobilize all the means possible to grab what no longer belonged to her. One might be sickened by her desperation, but her action was quite understandable, because she had nothing left. All these scenes that were meant to bring forth this female character, however, were edited out in the final film.

The same is also true for the character Li Xiaomeng, the policeman's longtime mistress. In the original story, this woman was depicted as an outrageous slut. But I toned down the moralistic rhetoric and changed her into a more ambiguous character in the screenplay. I don't think a so-called "slut" is necessarily evil. Such a woman might be quite beautiful, and a beautiful woman can at least remind one of the beauties of life. Most importantly, you can often find a certain power of transgression and revolt in this type of women. Regrettably, however, these elements were largely pushed to the background in the film. A potential multi-layered woman was reduced to a simple character. On the surface, this reduction seemed to have helped foreground the main storyline, but to me the result is the opposite.

As for switching one's point of view to that of the opposite sex, I think it is both necessary and possible. If one can't observe things from a point of view other than one's own, then he or she won't be a good filmmaker. I am not saying that filmmakers or filmmaking can transcend sexual differences. But I do think that if you are compassionate toward your characters and really immerse yourself in the exploration of their souls you will be able to overcome your gender limits. I think I have a good understanding of and perspective on women.

Lu Xuechang

When my first feature *The Making of the Steel* was shown abroad, some audiences also raised the question as to why male bonding is so pervasive in the film. To be frank, I was dumfounded, simply because I had never thought of the issue. I remember an elderly American woman was a little upset by the film, labeling me a male "chauvinist". I didn't want to defend myself and only acknowledged: "I am guilty, I am guilty."

Actually, the part about the relationship between Zhu Helai and Li Qiang, the two male characters in *The Making of the Steel*, was later added when I was revising the script. My understanding of Zhu Helai is that he is not so much an idol as a symbol that makes a deep impression and evokes recollection of that particular historical period. My original intent was to portray a righteous character that is always generous in aiding people in distress, including fighting. Because of this quality, when the teenager Li Qiang can't find paternal love at home, he turns to Zhu Helai to fill the void. As a matter of fact, Zhu is modeled after a prototype I encountered when I was a child. In my memory, that man was also a boiler house worker who, although quite righteous, received disciplinary punishment from his employer. I remember I was quite puzzled at that time: how could such a good man be disliked and punished? Because of him, I began to understand that the distinction between "good" and "bad" men is not always so clearcut. Unfortunately, to this day, this distinction is still clearly drawn and sometimes even reinforced in many Chinese films.

I don't have any prejudice against women. When I was a child, I had a passion for painting, but my family was very poor at that time. My parents couldn't even afford to buy paints for me. I was actually taken care of by a girl much older than I. We became acquainted by chance. She was studying foreign languages at a college-affiliated school, and I often went there to sketch. Then we became friends. I've actually written an article describing our friendship. She was the one who later introduced me to some painters. She even came to my home and cooked for me every day. You see, I was in fact looked after by a nice girl. After I was admitted to the art school affiliated with the Central Academy of Fine Arts, she stopped seeing me. Because of this, I felt she was quite a remarkable person, as if she was saying to me: I've helped you open the door, and you're on your own now. To be frank, I've learned a great deal from this childhood experience. But I have no idea why my works always give the impression that I am "rough" on women characters. In actual life, I treat my wife with respect and care. I am quite tender and considerate toward her.

I used to say to myself that I must write a script that features a female protagonist. But this wish has never materialized. Often as the writing progresses the intended female lead is gradually pushed to the background and only plays a supporting role. The focus is again shifted to men. I think this is probably due to my way of thinking. Or, this might have something to do with the fact that I always see things from my own point of view and am unable to jump out of my own framework. For instance, personally speaking, I don't like those films that make you feel "sweet" and "tender". I favor the things that are powerful and full of vigor. Although *Cala, My Dog* doesn't look so "hard" on surface, you can feel the inner strength of the film.

I don't think it should be hard for men to switch their perspective to that of women. As a mature director, one must be able to represent different subjects and portray different characters from multiple points of view. As for me, I haven't tried these multiple possibilities. It is partly because the stories I

Chapter Five

want to tell haven't been exhausted. Maybe I will try something different after these stories are told. Actually, I am very intrigued by the female characters in Su Tong's novels. I feel ultimately these women are quite foolish, but all of them are simply not aware of their stupidity. Unlike Xiang Lin's wife in Lu Xun's "New Year's Sacrifice", who doesn't know she is babbling on asking the same question, these women understand and enjoy what they are doing, but this doesn't mean they are smarter than Xiang Lin's wife.

Ma Liwen

I never thought of the issue of gender politics when making *Gone Is the One Who Held Me the Dearest*. But after the film came out, many audiences reacted to the husband with distaste. My friends said to me: why didn't you just have the female protagonist widowed? When the final cut was submitted to the censors, they also said to me: what an asshole the man is! Does Zhang Jie's [author of the original novel] husband also behave like that? Actually, it was not my intention to demonize the husband. The female protagonist, for instance, is not particularly favored, either. I didn't want to pass moral judgment on her. She is simply what she is.

The husband plays a more visible role in the film version, however. The original novel, written in diary form, emphasizes the relationship between mother and daughter. The husband exists only as a minor character. Now the husband is more visible. In fact, there are more details I could have added to the description of this character. For instance, in the novel, the husband develops a bizarre habit of carrying a bunch of coins in his pocket. Whenever the wife talks to him, he noisily jiggles the coins. I think the husband's indifference is a realistic reflection of the relationship between Zhang Jie and her husband in real life. Zhang Jie's husband is twenty-four years older than Zhang, and this marriage is the second for both of them. The emotional detachment between them, therefore, is quite natural. I didn't try to change or distort the general situation of their marriage. I lived at Zhang's home for half a month and believe I understand Zhang quite well. When Zhang's mother was about to die, her husband actually traveled for fun at the expense of the taxpayer. He is a bureaucrat. What do you expect him to do? Therefore, I don't think I've been particularly harsh on him. What I did is only to give this character a realistic treatment. He is not a bad person.

Meng Qi

To tell you the truth, it would be hard for me to look at things from a woman's point of view. But I do think the two sexes always have something in common. No matter how hard it is, I believe there is always a common ground based on which we can establish some sort of communication.

Besides, anyone is entitled to reflect upon the things he or she may have never directly experienced. Although somewhat subjective, I am often willing to shift my position to another's. For instance, whenever I witness a car accident, I am always sympathetic with the driver. Despite being an onlooker, I find myself quite ready to suspend my perspective and assume the driver's position. The same is also true when I deal with the issues related to women and children. I used to be a child myself, and this gives me an inkling as to how children view the world. I also have a girlfriend, from whom I've at least acquired some limited knowledge of women. My general understanding of women is that they are relatively unstable in disposition. They treat people with extreme warmth when joyful, but can suddenly lose their temper for no reason. I think this is somehow realistically reflected in my film *What a Snowy Day*.

Shi Runjiu

Psychologically, I have more trust in the female sex, largely because I was brought up by my grandmother. I think my grandma has had a tremendous influence on me. She was a person of integrity and honesty. Hardworking and with an amazing capacity to endure, she was the one who brought up the ten children in the family. I remember spending most of my childhood with grandma, and she taught me the meaning of love and kindness.

But my trust in the female sex is also conditional. Some women are not so pleasant and trustworthy. I remember when I was in my second year of elementary school, a girl in the same classroom secretly passed a "love" note to me. I was quite ignorant back then about this kind of thing and therefore decided to keep my distance from her and remain silent. Later on, however, this incident became the talk of the whole class. I was furious, because no one was in on the incident except the two of us. My suspicion was confirmed later when I overheard her gossiping with other classmates. Although nothing happened between us, my parents were notified by the school authorities. Fortunately, my parents were quite open-minded, and I was only warned not to let this kind of thing happen again. After the fuss subsided, I approached the girl and tried to figure out why she revealed the "secret". I got no direct answer. This incident, I think, has led to my prolonged sense of estrangement toward the female sex, which still lingers today.

To be more precise, this sense of estrangement does not affect my daily life at all. I can hang out and make friends with girls without the evocation of this feeling. But there is a limit: whenever I'm about to become intimate with a girl is also when I say goodbye to her. I think this is largely due to my pessimistic view about the man-woman relationship. When a man and a woman live together, friction, fights, quarrels, and mutual intolerance are almost unavoidable. I shudder to think about these scenarios. I often ask myself: if we've already foreseen the result, why is there a need for us to repeat this experience over and over again? The Spanish film *Lovers* [d. Vicente Aranda, 1990] ends with the couple committing suicide. I was deeply touched by this film. It really saddens me that the relationship between a man and a woman could reach to such a conclusion. But I identify with the film. Nowadays most films have a happy ending. I don't think it's a healthy tendency. There ought to be more films with a tragic ending.

Tang Danian

I think it is possible for male directors and scriptwriters to shake off their male-centered point of view and enter the female subject. Denying this possibility actually means the negation of many other possibilities in life. As a matter of fact, human life is full of possibilities. For instance, homosexuals' attitudes toward life, including the ones about love and family, open up many possibilities. I think extreme views often run the risk of negating many other things. It is my belief that lots of gender differences actually result from economic pressures. Once these pressures are alleviated, cross-gender communication and switching will in turn become possible. After people are free from economic struggle, they will find there are abundant choices and freedom in life and human relationships. A one-on-one relation often causes pain in life.

I am not sure I understand feminist theory very well, but I am personally more inclined to the feminists' view of men. Sometimes I feel human nature can be seen more clearly from a women's point of view. Men are more inclined to put on a bluff and disguise their real selves. It is in women that men's ugliness is especially highlighted. On the other hand, homosexuality, due to its potential to open up a variety of possibilities in life, can sometimes close the gap between the two sexes. I personally believe it is a status that is more suited for the natural development of human beings. Ultra masculinity is a deviation and flaw brought about by civilization.

As for the films I've directed or written, they are much related to sexual politics. In those works, women usually play traditional roles, such as that of wife and girlfriend. So far I haven't made a film that deals exclusively with the issue of sexuality. *City Paradise* is more concerned with social instead of sexual issues. In *Beijing Bicycle*, sexuality is not the central concern, either. You might be able to find some sexual meanings in the scene where the female maid attracts the gaze of two men, but I don't think Chinese artists and audiences are especially conscious of such meanings. Chinese film audiences are usually not so aware as to relate smoking with sex or something like that.

Wang Chao

Subconsciously, I think I cherish a deeper hope for the female character in *The Orphan of Anyang*. Like many male artists, I find myself hopelessly entangled with the maternal fantasy. My original plan was to make both male characters die in the end, and the only survivor would be the prostitute. At the end of the film, she was to be sent back to where she originally came from. On her way home, she would dream that her newly found child was entrusted to a resurrected Yu Dagang. In this version, you can see that the mother figure was to play a more important role.

As it turns out, however, the male characters, especially Yu Dagang, are more prominent. When attending various film festivals abroad, I noticed that mature women in their forties or fifties had a particular fondness for Yu. I think this is largely due to Yu's unconditional acceptance of Feng Yanli. When they lie together on the bed, Yu says to Feng: don't be a prostitute anymore, to which Feng replies: I am not working for myself. Then, Yu suggests: why don't you just work here, and I will take care of the kid. Young women or those who have had little life experience would probably have a hard time understanding this scenario, but women over in their forties would instantly understand what a remarkable man Yu is. No matter what his original motive, either out of the pressures of life or his low social status, Yu is a tolerant man, making a decision that wouldn't even occur to most men. To some extent, Yu is the one who makes us rethink the very notion of manhood. Since the turn of the century, people, especially those in the West, have started to really raise questions about what a man can do and how gender consciousness gets constructed through history and culture. I think *The Orphan of Anyang* provides a few clues regarding these questions.

I remember a French film critic once said to me at a film festival that *The Orphan of Anyang* is "subversive" in almost every way. If this is true, I think the most "subversive" part is the portrayal of Yu Dagang. He is not manly according to our "normal" conception of or the Hollywood construction of a man. The development of this character also does not follow the "normal" path of a bad man turning into a good man. He can do almost anything that is deemed "unmanly". He can buy a nursing bottle for the baby and feed him syrup. When the prostitute insists on continuing to sell her body, he even suggests she work at his place while he takes care of her baby. In this sense, one might say that there are certain maternal qualities in him. Between Yu and Liu Side, who is the baby's biological father and seems to be manly, Feng in the end chooses Yu, because she realizes that the so-called "man" is actually quite fragile and selfish.

Chapter Five

Wang Guangli

I think it shouldn't be hard for men to depict women characters. Being a man doesn't mean that I don't have any understanding of women. I've always dreamed of making a film about sexual relations in China. After *The Maiden Work* was finished, I thought about making it into a trilogy. Since *The Maiden Work* is about a director, I decided to focus the second one on a scriptwriter and the third on an actress. Eventually, however, I was only able to write the outlines of these two projects.

Certainly it is not an easy thing for men to really enter the world seen from a woman's point of view. Although this is the case and the difference between the two sexes is dramatic, sometimes even essential, I think it is still possible for men to get close to this world. One of the many possible ways is so-called "psychological substitution". Just use the Internet chat room as an example. As a man, I can enter the chat room pretending I am a woman. Once your gender role is reversed, you will be able to see how men typically respond to certain issues. If your purpose is only to kill some time, then entering the chat room probably won't help you understand the opposite sex. But if you enter the room as a careful observer, you can definitely get hold of something about women and figure out how women respond differently than men in certain circumstances. Therefore, I feel it is not impossible to cross the gender line. Of course it sometimes depends on your education and cultivation. If you are a male chauvinist, your point of view will be entirely different from that of a feminist. What you need to do, I think, is to balance the two opposite positions.

If purely based on the point of view of the West, I probably can't call myself a male feminist. But based on the Chinese standard, I think I am at least a man siding with the cause and independence of women. Determined by my education and cultural cultivation, I am totally at odds with those male chauvinists. But I also have the feeling that Western feminism is somewhat dogmatic, for example, the insistence on women wearing jeans instead of skirts, women behaving like men, et cetera. I think it has gone too far.

Wang Quanan

I don't think gender plays a role in representing the male or female sex. Whether one is able to represent men or women doesn't depend on one's gender. A peasant might not be the perfect one to represent the peasant class, right? It usually takes an artist to do so. The same is also true for the representation of the female sex. It is quite odd to claim that only women are capable of understanding and representing women. Women might have their unique way or point of view when approaching the same sex, but my feeling is that the male, because he tends to be more rational, is closer to reality itself in his representation of women. Ultimately, however, it matters less as to which sex is capable of doing what, because what concerns us most is society.

If my previous works have shown a marked interest in women's issues, it is because I personally respect women and have a genuine fondness of women in general. There are indeed great differences between the two sexes. To a certain extent, the female is lovelier than the male. As an object of attention, the female is not quite as pretentious as the male, which makes it easier for her to reveal her true feelings. In contrast, the male tends to hide his true feelings, and his role in society is more or less caricatured. Although both *Lunar Eclipse* and *The Story of Ermei* are focused on women's issues, it doesn't mean I don't have an interest in men. My next film, for example, will probably give men a more prominent role. Sometimes I feel I should try something different after having made two films about women. I always think there is more than one area in an artist's spiritual world that is worth exploring. After these two films, therefore, I may shift my focus to men. Maybe I'll write something about myself, and there is another area I am obsessed with—history. The subject that particularly interests me is the Cultural Revolution.

It goes without saying that I always try my best to suspend my male perspective when representing women. Layer by layer, you must peel off your familiar frame of reference, which is conditioned by your gender, and approach women from a more neutral angle. When writing *Lunar Eclipse*, for example, I kept reminding myself to look at things from the female protagonist's point of view. I am certainly aware that one can't completely sideline one's subject in artistic creation, but it seems to me that depicting women is ultimately a means of expression, a method to achieve your final goal. In the final analysis, I am not expressing my views about women, but commenting on the changing society through the depiction of women's responses to certain things. Let me give you an example. A few days ago I drove by a red Buick Sail made by Shanghai General Motors.[xxviii] When the door opened, a woman in her forties, who wore a pair of exaggerated glasses, emerged. In no time, however, this red Buick Sail suddenly changed to blue, and, to my surprise, there was also a woman of the similar age with the similar pair of glasses sitting in the car. You see, how similar this car's targeted consumers are! In other words, it is almost pre-determined that, because of its price, look, and function, cars like the Buick Sail are innately connected to women of that age group. You can make a film about them, and the title can be simply "The Clan of the Buick Sail". Writing about them is actually writing about the changing values of Chinese society. To this group of women, youth has already slipped away. They can't afford to buy

Chapter Five

expensive cars, but they still want to catch the tail of youth. That's why they end up with the Buick Sail. As for the cars like Mercedes, their owners are the girls in their twenties who are as beautiful and youthful as the students of BFA's acting department.

I often feel regret for the passing beauty of women. Life to them is both beautiful and cruel. It is always intriguing to me how the passing of youth can change a woman. After several years of separation, for example, you would often find your long ago female friend totally transformed. She has probably turned into another kind of woman due to the passing of youth. Now she never stops complaining and gossiping. To tell you the truth, I am really saddened by this change, a change that is largely caused by the fading of her youthful looks. As a filmmaker, I always feel it is impossible not to carry this feeling of sadness into my works. If there is certain beauty in my films, it is largely due to the presence of these qualities. *Lunar Eclipse* is an exemplary case. The woman character finds herself being gradually trapped in the mundane-ness of life but can't do anything about it. She used to be full of youthful vigor, and she used to be able to do whatever she dreamed, but to a large extent the most colorful days in her life have now come to an end. Maturity comes at a high price, and with the choice of one road comes the impossibility of other alternatives. This is also how the female protagonist feels in *Lunar Eclipse* when she witnesses the death of her other self.

Wang Xiaoshuai

I think whether a male director is able to enter the female subject depends on his nature. Many male directors who specialize in women's films, such as (Pedro) Almodova, possess certain female qualities in their nature. They are attentive and detail-oriented. If you asked them to make a film that is potentially male chauvinistic, they would certainly object to the idea. Based on this understanding, I think it is hard to come up with a generalized answer. Some filmmakers are male-centered by nature, and it is impossible for them to alter the male-oriented position of the camera. But some male filmmakers, because of their natural orientation, psychologically tend to be more intimate toward the female sex. To them, entering the female subject is quite a natural thing. Conversely, some women directors are not so "feminine" in the traditional sense. Films by women directors are not always pro-feminist. Some of them could be quite neutral or even violent.

Personally, I am not confident of my ability in looking at things from a purely female point of view. In both scriptwriting and actual shooting, I tend to naturally follow my male instinct. For example, some people would instantaneously think of laid-off female workers if had the opportunity to make a film, but I can't. I am perfectly aware that women's subjects are where my weakness lies, but so far I haven't been able to come up with a remedy. The key issue, however, is to find the subject that best suits you. If this were solved, I would be more than happy to devote my whole life to exploring this subject.

I've also thought about adapting some women writers' novels to remedy my weakness, but there are a few obstacles. First, if I decide to adapt a novel, this novel must have a strong appeal to me, but so far I haven't come across any that do. Second, I am not as talented as Zhang Yimou, who is capable of extracting only one or two spectacular elements from a novel and disregarding the rest. I used to try to do this but was never satisfied with the results. To me, an adaptable novel must first and foremost fascinate me from beginning to the end. I lose interest if a novel has only a few bright spots.

Xu Jinglei

First of all, I often feel there is certain inferiority complex in feminism. I think ability, not gender, is the decisive factor that divides human beings. As for my film *Me and My Dad*, I am not sure if I approached things from a woman's point of view. Certainly I would think so, simply because I am a woman. One thing is for sure: it is impossible for me to approach things from another person's point of view. I may be able to understand the surface of other people, but will be never able to unravel the inner truth of them. This being the case, I think *Me and My Dad* is a film that more or less reflects some female sensibilities. But what is the so-called "female sensibility"? Is it the ability to handle minute details? I am not sure. Everyone is different. Although a woman, I am not quite detail-oriented.

I think I very much rely on my own experiences when depicting male characters. For example, it seems to me that the father figure in *Me and My Dad* is quite understandable. When I was a teenager, my father was quite hostile to my male friends. If a male friend of mine called me, he would become rather irritated: I don't care if he is just your classmate. Instead of annoying you with phone calls, why can't he speak to you face-to-face? In his eyes, those male friends of mine were all little kids who thought they knew quite a bit but in actuality knew nothing at all. In my film, the father is actually contemptuous of his daughter's boyfriend. It is not because the boyfriend has low upbringing, but because he instinctively feels there must be something wrong with a man who, having read some books, thinks he's had truth on his side. In the film, the daughter finally returns home and lives with her father. The father treats her more like a companion than a daughter, because it is she who helps him rediscover the feeling of family.

Zhang Ming

Some people may like to theorize the issue of gender, but I am not so fond of doing this. I think for the most part I am not as conscious as one might think with regard to the issue of gender difference or politics. To be more reflexive, I think male directors are often unaware of the fact that women are usually depicted as the object of punishment, of fantasy, or of desire in their films. In the eyes of most male directors, women are either consciously or unconsciously objectified. I think this is partly a reflection of our social reality. Since women are somewhat objectified in life, it is also reflected in cinema.

Speaking of fantasy, I think *Weekend Plot* has much to do with it. The whole film can be viewed as a fantasy of the male protagonist, or as his seventeen-hour-long dream. Actually, the whole of China is preoccupied with fantasy now. On a personally level, I find myself often struggling for reconciliation in this environment. My personal dream may encounter obstacles and I'll be never able to find a way out. Broadly speaking, the old fantasy embraced by the nation as a whole has already evaporated. Nowadays a new fantasy is on the rise, but no one knows for sure what this fantasy is about. In the past, people identified with the ideas promoted by the government, but nowadays it is no longer possible for authority to reach that kind of consensus. Despite the fact that the general populace do not identify with the government-sponsored fantasy, they still dream dreams. They long for something beyond their mundane lives. But no one is certain about what exactly constitutes this "something beyond". I think the original intent of *Weekend Plot* was to convey this feeling of uncertainty.

Zhang Yang

Personally speaking, I think it is not difficult for me to free myself from a male-centered view and look at things from a woman's point of view. Not everybody can achieve this goal, however. It really depends on who you are and how you view the female sex. Are you a self-centered person or a person who always tries to understand others? Relatively, I think I am quite objective in viewing things. I often look at things from the perspective of the opposite and am always ready to explore what people really think. Only by doing so can we free ourselves and examine things from a position other than yours. Without such a shift, your depiction and representation of women would be solely based on the male perspective or a pseudo female point of view.

So far I haven't made a conscious effort to especially foreground the female role. My debut feature *Love Spicy Soup* has a prominent female role, but the film is concerned mainly with love. The next two films center on men. For obvious reasons, it's impossible for me to use a female bathhouse as *Shower*'s setting. In actuality, men's and women's bathhouses are always next to each other, and there must be many good stories happening in women's bathhouses. In fact, we also discussed the possibility of setting the story in a female bathhouse. Foreseeing the difficulty in actual shooting, however, we gave up the idea. Because it would be quite hard to depict a woman in a predominantly male environment, I decided to focus exclusively on men. I've seen some foreign films that only feature male characters, but they are still great works. By focusing on a group of men bound by the public bathhouse, therefore, I wanted to foreground the friendship between men, especially the relation between father and son. As for the third film, *Quitting*, I originally hoped to have a female lead but was compelled to give up this attempt for a variety of reasons. *Quitting* is actually a film about Jia Hongsheng's life and his family. Jia's sister should have played an important role in the film, but she didn't want to have anything to do with the filming. So, we had to hire a professional actress to play his sister. With the exception of this character, the rest are all played by real life figures. Another difficulty of giving a female a more prominent role in this film lies in the fact that it turned out to be a headache to direct Jia's former girlfriend. Actually, we were all worried that she would bluntly reject an offer to play Jia's girlfriend again.

Therefore, there are various reasons that determined the lack of female roles in *Shower* and *Quitting*. It doesn't mean that I am against women playing dominant roles in my films. My next film, for instance, will feature a female lead. My usual point of departure is to first come up with a story idea I feel passionate about. Then, I will gather a few friends of mine to develop this idea. After that, I will position myself as the center of the storyline, and it will radiate out to the people surrounding this center. In the future, however, I will probably give up this center and construct the story based on a woman's point of view. If this is the case, I think the result will look quite different. I may even try two different points of view in a single film, one a man's, the other a woman's. The result must be quite interesting if this idea is realized.

Zhang Yuan

My first film, *Mama*, features a woman, and my remake of *Sister Jiang* also focuses on a female hero. As a male director, I guess my point of departure is to have a compassion for women and women's causes, nothing grand or complicated. Being a man, however, I do hold certain idealistic views about women. I remember when *Mama* came out, a French women's film festival insisted on having the film. The female director of that festival said to me that *Mama* is more female-oriented than that by most female filmmakers. Ironically, however, after *Beijing Bastards* came out, I came across this woman again at a film festival, but she refused to speak to me. I guess it was because there is a scene in *Beijing Bastards* she thought offensive to women. What can you say? I guess my answer is to continue making films.

CHAPTER SIX

UNDER THE SHADOW OF COMMERCIALIZATION: THE BOX OFFICE AND INDIVIDUAL EXPRESSION

The first group of films made by the Fifth Generation filmmakers—including One and Eight, Yellow Earth, The Horse Thief, King of Children, *and* Red Sorghum*— were all financed by the state-owned studios. The old studio system, like all state-owned institutions in China, promised filmmakers an "iron rice bowl", a Chinese phrase that refers to life-long job security, a fixed salary, government-subsidized housing, and free medical care. Working within the system, filmmakers had limited freedom. To a large extent, they were ideologically constrained, artistically restricted, yet, ironically, commercially free. During the time the "Sixth Generation" filmmakers emerged with their first group of films, however, this "iron rice bowl" had been already smashed to pieces. Young filmmakers found themselves facing an environment far more adverse than that which the Fifth Generation confronted: They have to deal with the pressures coming from both government censors and the market. As a matter of fact, with the gradual relaxation and liberalization of government policies on cinema, it becomes increasingly clear that a film's "success" will be measured predominantly by the box-office returns. Under the "shadow" of the commercialization of Chinese cinema, how will young filmmakers manage to maintain their individual voice, a trademark of this generation? Can they find a balance between individual expression and the mass market?*

* * *

Guan Hu

I became involved in filmmaking because there was a soaring enthusiasm in me. Driven by an innate desire to express myself, I've never paid attention to what other people thought about my films or how the market would respond to my work. This being the case, I feel really strange that I've survived for so long and am still in the filmmaking business today. Logically, I should've died as a filmmaker in today's commercialized society. I've never had a good relation with my producers, and my films usually do not make money at all. As strange as it seems, I am still walking on this path. Looking back, I figured there must have some reason in my "longevity". Maybe as long as you are still around, there is something meaningful in your existence. The very fact that there are people still interested in supporting my filmmaking testifies that the current environment needs the kind of people like me.

Jia Zhangke

In general, I don't consider the issue of the audience or market during the creative process. But after completing my work, I use the most commercial and market-oriented method to promote my film. Once the work is done, I never reject the idea of marketing and promotion. At the same time, I feel the "commercial" value of my films, if any, comes from the method of my filmmaking and the issues I most care about. I think this is why my films possess so-called "commercial" value. If not for this, people wouldn't bother to pay to see my films because they are not designed for the mass market.

I aim to construct a world of its own in my films. I think there is no miracle as far as my films' mass market is concerned. But there is indeed a stable niche market for my films, and it is also steadily gaining strength. For instance, suppose *Xiao Wu* was sold to ten countries, then this number would increase to fifteen for *Platform*. When it comes to *Unknown Pleasure*, because of the Cannes effect, it might be able to reach thirty countries. So, although my films would never win the Super Lotto as the blockbuster *Titanic* did, they are slowly but steadily building an audience base. It's impossible for me to create a *Titanic*-like miracle, and I've never asked myself to do so, but I am not pessimistic at all about my films' "commercial" value, because now it is perfectly clear to me that if I don't exceed a certain amount in investment, I won't lose money. You can say I have a basic calculation in my mind.

So far I've been quite lucky in dealing with my investors. They've never put any pressure on my filmmaking. It seems they are quite open minded, and they consider their investment in my projects a long-term one instead of a one-time gamble. As long as my films earn what they've put in, they consider it a success. In addition, even at the time of deciding whether to invest in me, they seem to care less about the market and the issue of commercial success.

Jiang Wen

I don't think about the audience, because I am clueless about where to start on this issue. Just tell me who the audiences are. Audiences differ from one another greatly. Besides, the basic relationship between human beings and works of art also defies any speculation about a homogenized audience. For instance, we may think today that [the book] *Dream of the Red Chamber* is a great work, but this might not have been the case when we were ten or twenty. In the 1970s, Mao called for a re-appreciation of *Dream of the Red Chamber*. But this appreciation of the novel differed greatly from that he experienced when he was twenty, thirty, or even forty. Looking back further, can we claim that Cao Xueqin, author of *Dream of the Red Chamber*, had us in mind when he wrote the novel? He never cared about how we would react to his writing. Actually, even if he wanted to, he wouldn't be able to foresee the response from an audience several generations removed from his lifetime.

I think the more important question is this: did he write for other people, or write for himself? I am asking this question because I believe to a great extent Cao wrote the novel for his own fulfillment. It is for this very reason that *Dream of the Red Chamber* is still considered by us today as one of the greatest novels ever written. Even so, when it comes to the appreciation of this novel, each reader will probably come up with his/her own reasons as to why it stands out in Chinese literature. Does this sound a little pessimistic? I don't think so. I think this is precisely the normal relationship between readers and artistic works. In other words, when people watch a film, they often react to the scenes or story elements that speak for themselves. What he/she sees is him/her self. For example, suppose I was a second grade elementary school student, what I could get from reading *Dream of the Red Chamber* would be limited to who I was and what I was capable of. You can't say my reading was wrong. This is actually not an issue of right or wrong. It goes back to what I just said: all audiences are actually trying to express or find themselves through watching a film or reading a novel. If we acknowledge this fact, then it would be completely unrealistic for me as a director to even think about how each audience will react to my film.

I think Mao was a genius in dialectic thinking. But it seems to me that this thinking is often absent in our daily life. What I mean by "dialectic thinking" is this: it is highly possible that, when your only concern is how to express yourself, not how to please the audience, your creative work will be more appealing. Often you will find your work is less appealing when you think too much about the audience. So, I am not saying that I have no concern about the audience at all. What concerns me most is this: in order to make more people like my work, what should I do? My answer to this question is that to achieve this goal I must first like the work myself. I don't know whether I've made myself clear, but it is to some extent like the working principle of a lever. With a supporting point in the middle, a lever can be divided into two parts. In order to lift the other side, you must first push this side down. The same principle is applicable to the relationship between the artist and audience. In order to make your work appealing to the audience, you must first neglect them. This is what I call "dialectical thinking".

Jin Chen

My debut film was *Love in the Internet Age*. Actually, before this film came out, the label the "Sixth Generation" of filmmakers had not been widely circulated because of official sanctions. Those were the darkest years for young Chinese filmmakers. During that time, almost all films by young filmmakers were suppressed and banned from theaters. One exception was Lou Ye's *Weekend Lover*, which was shown in some insignificant places and quickly disappeared. At that time, therefore, most people had only heard the names of the so-called "Sixth Generation" filmmakers but never seen their films. As young graduates of BFA and CATA, however, we were able to see some of their films. Frankly, I didn't like the way they portrayed our life. Furthermore, I was very curious about why, after so many years of hard work, their films weren't allowed to enter the market.

Therefore, you can say young filmmakers like me had some reflections on our fellow senior apprentices' works and came to the conclusion that under this system and in this country the first question you must ask is why you want to make a film in the first place. The answer is quite clear to me: the primary goal of our filmmaking is to satisfy the Chinese audience. If your films are inaccessible to Chinese audiences, and if your primary goal is to satisfy the needs of a foreign-language audience, then your way of thinking will gradually change. Truth will also evaporate in your intentional efforts to cater to the taste of foreign audiences.

When I started my first film, therefore, I decided to make it a marketable one. To make it accessible to the market meant some compromises had to be made. In order to let your film be seen by a large number of people, sometimes you need to make certain compromises with the government. In other words, you must try your best not to step on the so-called "mine field". At that time, it seemed to me that the only "mine-free" subject was love, because love is something our Party doesn't frown upon. There is the promotion of "revolutionary love", for instance. After deciding on the subject, I calculated that my experience of growth in a transitional China—from beepers to cellular phones, from computers to the Internet, and from high school to college student—could be utilized to reflect the transformation of Chinese cities and culture. This is where the story of *Love in the Internet Age* came from. The story was structured around the theme of "love lost" and "love regained". Later on, however, I added a fashionable word: Internet. At that time, I had absolutely no clue about the rapid growth and popularity of the Internet in the following one or two years. My only idea was to use a catchy title to differentiate my film from others. It should be noted that *Love in the Internet Age* was made under special circumstances and supported by a state-owned studio. I was able to make this film because it was not concerned about sensitive issues and marginal figures. Despite the fact that there were no political slogans in the film, it passed the censors because China's social transformation and urbanization were treated as a bright backdrop for the unfolding love between the young people. Almost everything in the film was painted in warm colors.

Chapter Six

After the release of *Love in the Internet Age*, I think the government began to have second thoughts about young filmmakers: "Hey, these unruly kids can be also used!" Thus, it quickly lifted the ban on several films. In other words, *Love in the Internet Age* was a barometer because of which many previously banned films were able to reemerge from below the horizon. It was also because of this film, I believe, that a semi-official symposium was held in Beijing, during which a group of young filmmakers "emerged" from the unknown.[xxix] One after another, Zhang Yuan's *Seventeen Years*, Wang Xiaoshuai's *So Close to Paradise*, and Lu Xuechang's *A Lingering Face* were green-lighted for public showings. It is not to say that *Love in the Internet Age* is a historical work. But I do feel that after this film the authorities discovered that young filmmakers had begun to show a less confrontational attitude toward the rules and regulations of filmmaking in China. Ultimately, I think this subtle change was also a response to the rapid development of commercialism throughout Chinese society. I think both sides since that time have realized that the survival of Chinese cinema depends very much on the market.

However, my second film, *Chrysanthemum Tea*, was less concerned about the market and commercial success because I found paying too much attention to the market inevitably weakens the true meaning of filmmaking. *Chrysanthemum Tea* tells of a painful love story in which the man and woman must overcome their psychological and physical obstacles to embrace each other. You can see it is not a subject as pleasing as that of *Love in the Internet Age*. But this is also the exact reason why I personally like this film more than *Love in the Internet Age*. My view was also shared by film critics. Whereas *Love in the Internet Age* received an award at a small film festival in Belgium, *Chrysanthemum Tea* received a major award at the Moscow International Film Festival. It is always a hard thing, therefore, to strike a balance between commercial success and individual expression in filmmaking.

Li Xin

Between popular appeal and self-expression there ought to be a way to balance the two extremes. To me, it is just like finding a beautiful coat to wear. In film, this coat could mean a very attractive storyline, or what we usually call Hollywood-style filmmaking. It is perfectly OK to have a strong personal voice in your film, but in order to make a large number of people identify with your self-expression, you must always search for and wear this coat. I feel this is the path we should take. When one was a film school student, it might have been excusable to make a film that was both narcissistic and marginal. But this kind of film won't survive the test of the market. As professional filmmakers, we should avoid this path.

Having said this, sometimes I also feel bewildered about what exactly the phrase "popular appeal" means. For example, it is not a surprise that many young students liked *Dazzling*. But to my surprise, those who disliked the film most were also students. So, it is quite hard to generalize the "popular". Students at Shanghai University might love the film, but students at Fudan University might feel the opposite. You may love the film, but your friends might feel the opposite. So, I've learned not to care too much about what other people think of my works. One time I went online and had a virtual talk with my audience. To be frank, I had never done this before but was persuaded by my friends back then. I found *Dazzling* had divided them into two opposite camps, one for the film, the other against the film, cursing it with the dirtiest words in the world. As the online chat continued, the two camps started to fight against each other, and I became an onlooker. I chose to be silent because I found myself no longer so eager to know how other people responded to my works. Instead, I should just continue to do what I like to do.

Liu Binjian

To me, it is not an issue at all as to whether I want to be a commercial filmmaker or an art house filmmaker. First of all, as an individual, I can't control how my films will be received by the general audience. After the films are finished, they tend to develop a life of their own and no longer have a special relationship to me. As for how well they do in the market, it is a complicated issue. There is no such thing as a monolithic film market. Different countries have different markets. I've always insisted that my films are made for the worldwide audience, not exclusively for a domestic or foreign audience. Second, it is impossible for me to trade my principle for a wide theatrical audience. If the Chinese audience can't find my films in theaters, they can resort to pirated DVDs or VCDs. If catering to the taste of the market means weakening the artistic quality of my films, I'd rather sacrifice the market. I increasingly feel the audience also needs to be trained and educated in film appreciation. We can't simply give up or make concessions in what we believe for the purpose of the so-called audience and market. I am not suggesting my films are made for next century's audiences, but I do believe there are some films that can wait for ten or twenty years to be released, because they are made for a different kind of society and audience. You may think I am a little naïve, but I am not so concerned about losing some of the audience.

Despite the fact that the market or the audience is seldom my major concern, I did try to make certain adjustments and experiments in my films. For instance, I introduced some humor into my second film, *Men and Women*.

Chapter Six

When it came to *Cry Woman*, I was somewhat in a quest for a balancing point at which art and commerce would perfectly meet. However, these changes or adjustments were purely out of my own creative needs. My financiers weren't involved heavily in the creative process. Having read the scripts, they seemed to be very comfortable granting me the total freedom I desperately needed. They respected my judgment and tried quite hard to follow my way of doing things. At least 90 percent of the time I had the total control of my works.

On an operational level, because most of the production money came from abroad, I didn't have to worry too much about direct interference. My first two films, *Stone Bed* and *Men and Women*, were financed by American and French money. Because these two films did relatively well in the world market, some French and Korean distributors, along with some film foundations, approached me and expressed an interest in financing my third film. In our talks, they positioned my films as having a niche in the world market, but they hoped I could continue to raise the artistic quality of my work. It turned out that they were quite right. At Cannes, *Cry Woman* was sold to five major world markets. Certainly they also wanted it to make some money in the Chinese market, but they could do nothing but gave it up due to the current environment in China. I'm all for the international cooperation in Chinese cinema. In recent years, international cooperation and financing has been a catalyst for the development of Chinese cinema, particularly Chinese independent cinema.

Lou Ye

It is not the director's job to consider the market issue. A director ought to be entitled to make whatever suits him or her. It's as simple as that. Of course sometimes a director may be in a position of being forced to confront such an issue. But it must be made clear that the director should not have to play such a role. It is not the director's business. However, the situation has gradually changed since the 1960s. Since the emergence of independent producers, many have played the dual roles of director and producer. This is especially true in the case of "New Hollywood" directors, who quite often played this dual role. Coppola once claimed that all producers are good-for-nothings. They are clueless about what film is. His view is quite right. The director should be the one responsible for what kind of film should be made and should handle this matter alone. As a matter of fact, nowadays the director's workload has increased. Although in theory the director should not be concerned by the issue of whether or not the film sells, in practice he/she must. Therefore, it truly depends on what you really want: to make a film that sells well or to make something that is from your heart.

Speaking of the audience, you cannot accuse filmmakers of not having the audience in mind, because what I provide is only a reference point and a personal view of the world. The audience has total freedom to reject or accept it. In other words, I am only casting a stone into the ocean that is your mind. As for how big a splash the stone will make, that's up to you, not me. My job is to produce the stone. If you have seen the stone, that means I have passed it to you. What happens afterward is no longer my concern.

I have a bad reputation as a director. People often say I am an especially difficult director to work with because I always want what I want. I am afraid I will carry this "stubbornness" to my grave. I never give up on what I have envisioned for a film, including the right of making the final cut. Whenever I negotiate the contract, I always demand to have this right. The investor will say: "You want the final cut, right? Don't you know only a selected few enjoy this privilege?" So, it's quite tough to work with me. Of course it sometimes depends on what project I'm working on. If the film is of special importance to me, surely I would not make any compromises. If it is a work-for-hire project, which also interests me, then I would be a little more flexible. I wouldn't mind adapting a pre-existing work, either from film or fiction. So far, however, I haven't made a single film that is based on the work of someone else, The main reason is that I haven't found any novels that interest me. Ideally, the director is not supposed to write the screenplay. I wrote my screenplays because I had no choice. I couldn't find what I wanted from other sources. To be frank, playing the dual roles of writer and director is both time-consuming and tiresome. It lengthens the whole creative process of each film. For example, it usually takes me a year to write a script, and then I will spend another year to turn it into a film. The whole process therefore takes two years. It is certainly ideal to start with an already finished script, but finding a satisfying one is very difficult. Indeed, there are few good scripts or novels. If there were more, I would definitely quit writing my own scripts.

Although I sound like a "fascist" director, the *Suzhou River* team really had a pleasant experience. I was the chief editor of the film, but there were four other editors. In Beijing alone, I had three editors. The film was shot in 16mm, and one of the initial editors, Xiao Quan, is now working for the Chinese Central Television Station. He is very good at AVI editing. The beginning sequence of *Suzhou River* was actually first edited by him in Beijing, and I lent a hand. It is quite strange that this sequence remains intact despite repeated editing. Maybe it ought to be that way. In Germany, I had another editor. He is a "tongzhi" [homosexual], but especially good-natured. We worked together for three months and had an exceptionally good working relationship. After I came back from Germany, somebody joked, "Have you also become a 'tongzhi?'" This was the first time he had worked as a film editor. The composer was also German, and this was also the first time he composed for film. Actually, *Suzhou River* was a first for many people: It was a first not only for the German editor and the composer but also for Zhou Xun as a leading actress and Wang Yu as a director of photography. All of us were passionate. It is because of *Suzhou River* that Zhou Xun's name became known outside of China. Her previous films did not have worldwide release.

Lu Chuan

I am very much against elitism in filmmaking, especially against this tendency in Chinese cinema. This attitude is a reaction to the specifics of Chinese history. I once said to an American friend of mine that it is absolutely harmful for China to promote "art film" at this historical moment. Instead, China should encourage the production of commercial and entertainment films. Why? In the overpowering structure of the American film industry, you will probably be regarded as a hero if you can survive outside the system doing independent filmmaking. But in the Chinese system, making an "art film" has little to do with your artistic talent because many self-proclaimed "art film" makers have nothing to offer except for the crude reality of China.

This is not to say that *The Missing Gun* is a purely commercial film, however. If you know how difficult it is to make a film in China, you would understand that the concept of the market was almost nonexistent in my mind when I started the film. It is absolutely beyond my imagination that *The Missing Gun* did so well in the market. It is almost like rolling a snowball. It keeps rolling and rolling, until you find one day that it is no longer what you want. To put it simply, I had never cared about the "commercial-ness" of my films. I felt the same when making *Keke Xili*. I didn't cast famous actors in that film.

Lu Xuechang

I've signed a director's contract with the Huayi Brothers Company. I like this contract because it can liberate me from the mind-boggling issue of the market. Just use *Cala, My Dog* as an example. I was drawn to the story and wanted to make a film about it. Thus, I submitted the script to my producer. Having read the script, the producer came to me with a budget that detailed the amount of investment and sales. This careful calculation made him believe that if I could make the film with a budget of 5 million RMB then the company would give me the green light. But if it came in over that budget, say 6 million RMB, the company wouldn't let me do it. Why? He laid out his reasons one by one. Speaking for myself, I feel this filmmaking model fits me quite well. It would be too demanding for me to get involved in both artistic creation and business issues. I have only one brain. Just let the producer worry about the market. As a director, I should focus on filmmaking itself. To me, the logic is quite simple: if you feel the story is investment-worthy, then pursue it with your money; if you feel it isn't, let's change to another script. Luckily, up to now I have never worked on something that doesn't interest me.

Certainly the audience is always in my mind. Since the beginning of my filmmaking career, I have always felt it is most important to work within the system and make my films accessible to ordinary audiences. But I failed to do so on some occasions. Such failures made me rethink why I want to be a filmmaker in the first place. If you don't care about whether the audience sees your film, why do you pursue this career? Filmmaking is not painting. In painting, if you paint something you don't like, you can simply throw it under your bed. It really doesn't matter too much as to whether it has an audience. Later on, you may even throw it into the garbage can when cleaning the room. This is also the case with writing. You can write a novel for your own sake, because writing is by and large an individual art. But filmmaking is an entirely different matter. For one thing, it involves so much money and so many people. For another thing, how can you call yourself a "director" if your work can't be even seen by a single audience? Interaction with the audience is an integral part of filmmaking. I often feel it's not a good thing for young filmmakers not to share their works with the Chinese audience. I hope I can somehow change this situation.

Ma Liwen

The total investment of *Gone Is the One Who Held Me the Dearest* was around 1.9 million RMB, including the payment for Siqin Gaowa and the acquisition of the copyright of Zhang Jie's novel. Four investors were involved in financing the film. They were brought together just like an assorted dish. It was distributed by the Forbidden City Company and the China Film Group. Because the investment was quite modest, I thought it wouldn't be hard for the investors to get their money back. I heard Hong Kong-based HBO alone has decided to pay nearly 900 thousand RMB to purchase the film's broadcasting rights. But the issue of how well the film sells in the market is not my concern at all. As an inexperienced director, I am only entitled to a salary.

I don't know how to comment on the relationship between self-expression and the market, but I do know filmmaking is a quite agonizing experience. This is especially true when a first-time filmmaker like me deals with his/her financiers. My investors were quite stingy with their money. We were not insured, were paid monthly salaries, and were not entitled to anything even if the film made money. Although I feel I've done something

Chapter Six

that is definitely worthwhile, the whole filmmaking process, from pre- to post-production, is nearly unbearable. Considering the fact that four investors shared the responsibility of such a small budget, what could they lose even if the film didn't make money? Therefore, I think we need to create a favorite environment for young filmmakers, especially for the newcomers. What do the newcomers need most? They need talent scouts with acute judgment, the judgment that tells whether the proposed project is worthy of investment.

Meng Qi

Because I just made my debut feature, so far I haven't come up with a clear vision about my future direction: purely commercial or working toward the perfection of an art film? But my basic understanding of film is that a good film must both appeal to the audience and stand the test of time. I think a classic should possess these qualities. A crowd-pleasing commercial film must be equally good in artistic qualities and vice versa. If a commercial film contains no thoughtful ideas, I don't think it is worth mentioning. After all, providing some kind of intellectual stimulation is better than offering nothing but pure entertainment. Sometimes I also go see those purely commercial films, but I am not passionate about them. As a filmmaker, I admire those films that combine both commercial appeal and art. It is just like a man rich in both material possessions and in taste. If a man is only rich in money and understands nothing but money, he must be quite dull.

My next project is centered on a hero in turbulent times. It crosses several periods, from the late Qing dynasty to the founding of the People's Republic of China. I hope the finished product will come close to my conception of a good film, namely, combining commercial elements with individuality and artistic quality. On the one hand, it will showcase the richness of Chinese culture, a theme that fulfills my personal longing. On the other hand, because the hero is connected to a variety of social classes, including political circles and gangsters, it will appeal to ordinary audiences. I chose this project because these two aspects can potentially merge into one.

Shi Runjiu

I think the best lesson I've learned from my CATA education is that unlike painting, which is an individual art form, drama and film are both collective forms of art. Despite the fact that the director plays a pivotal role in these art forms, he/she is ultimately a member of a collective team. In this collective, each one plays his/her proper role and works toward the goal of a finished product. Therefore, I don't necessarily agree with the saying that a certain film or play is authored by a certain director. I always believe it is the result of a collective effort that involves every individual's wisdom and labor. I don't deny the fact that there are many cinematic *auteurs* in film history, but their ideas would not materialize without the contribution of the entire crew.

Because of this belief, I always have other people in mind during the creative process. Films are made for the audience. On location, I am always open to suggestions from all sides, including from the actors. Take *All the Way* as an example. The original idea was to make a road movie. It was inspired by films like *Lock, Stock, and Two Smoking Barrels* and *Pulp Fiction*. Having seen those films, I thought I might be able to find a way to make a similar kind of film in China, mixing a contemporary subject and characters with a sophisticated plot and structure that would attract the young audience. Certainly the film itself was not something I can be proud of. The fact was that we were probably too concerned about the market and in return underestimated the importance of human emotion in film appreciation. We spent a lot of time debating whether such and such a scene would cause such and such a result in cinema, and such and such a story twist would produce such and such an effect on the audience. So, we weighed plot more heavily than emotion in affecting the audience. In reality, people come to cinema with the expectation of emotional involvement, not so much for a sophisticated plot. Plot may have some influence on the audience, but it is more a factor that makes the audience sit through a film. When the light is on, the audience will probably forget many details of the plot, but the emotional impact will linger. I don't know the audience in the United States, but at least I believe the Chinese audience is close to what I've described, not so much Hollywood-oriented. Chinese audiences expect to be intellectually inspired and emotionally touched through the cinema-going experience. Looking from this angle, I think *All the Way* deviated from that direction. Instead of making the film emotionally appeal to the audience, we were focused on style and technique.

We also had problems with the actors in that film. Jiang Wu was not my first choice to play the lead role, but the producer insisted in having him. Having built a good relationship with the producer from my first film, I agreed. To be frank, however, Jiang Wu was not the best choice for the role of the driver. Having said this, I also understand the difficulties the producer has to face. Peter Loehr was the producer of my first two films. I feel he is a man of vision and talent. At least in China, such a man is rare. Although an American, he understands the Chinese film market and is good at marketing on an operational level. He used to be a law student, but is quite professional in the filmmaking business. As a producer, his position was quite different from that of the director. I think his job was more tedious and tiresome. Not only must he worry about film financing, but he was heavily involved in shooting and promotion as well. He was actually playing the role of a businessman. I know being a film businessman is quite rough, because such a person is not simply managing a product, but a sophisticated cultural product. With this understanding, I worked hard to accommodate Peter's judgment and suggestions. Of course businessmen are, after all, businessmen. As the saying goes, every businessman desires profit. There is nothing wrong with that. Although we disagreed on many issues, in most cases those were healthy discussions. We were able to eventually reach some kind of consensus and move forward. In principle, we listened to each other and would carry out the ideas that were deemed more reasonable. As far as the ideas guiding the creative process are concerned, if I insisted on something, he would usually let me have the say. So, you can say that we had a great working relationship. Seldom did he interfere in my creative process.

I think BFA-educated filmmakers are quite distinct in the sense that they are mostly individual-centered and therefore less concerned about the market and audience. The education they received emphasizes the power and importance of film *auteurs*, and the films they were exposed to at BFA tend to be the ones that have strong individual characteristics. When they set foot in real society, however, they often find there is a dramatic difference between their understanding and ordinary audiences' conception of film. They will find their understanding of film has little relation with the reality itself. I guess this is quite a painful experience. I am not saying that there is anything wrong with BFA's education. A few outstanding filmmakers, especially some from the Class of 1985, did emerge. But there are also many of them who are still struggling to get their first film made.

Increasingly, I find making TV programs is a good way to balance market demand and individual satisfaction. I am now making TV documentaries for CCTV's program "Eastern Landscape" (Dongfang shikong). I feel making documentaries is quite an interesting endeavor. You build relationships with your subjects in a gradual manner, and the final product of this process is something fictional film cannot compete with. There are usually only two or three people in the crew, and oftentimes I am in charge of the camera myself. I gain a strong sense of freedom in this process, because I no longer feel the pressure from the financier, don't need to worry about how the producer feels and how well the actors perform, and have no concern about whether the finished product makes money. Without these pressures, I suddenly feel that my spirit is liberated. In making a film you must confront many thorny issues, such as censorship, distribution, and marketing. I am not saying that there is no censorship in CCTV, but censorship in TV, at least based on my relation with the "Eastern Landscape" program, is much more relaxed than that of film. Most censors in the Film

Bureau are simply bureaucrats. They instinctively want to show their power of control.

Tang Danian

It all depends on whether you are able to strike a balance between the market and self-expression. As a matter of fact, since commercialization has already taken roots in China, it is almost impossible for one to have the luxury of pure self-expression, especially in the business of filmmaking. Filmmaking involves a lot of money. How can you completely disregard the market? This being said, however, every filmmaker has his/her own principle. How far can you go in commercializing your film? Which one is more important to your film, individuality or commercial success? Of course it also depends on one's ability. You have to figure out whether you are capable of making a commercial film. Maybe you are only capable of making films that are individualistic and true to yourself. Therefore, it is hard to generalize.

In filmmaking, you can't do whatever you would like to do. For instance, suppose you have ten projects, among which there is one you like less than the others. But if it happens to be the case that someone is willing to invest in that one, you might go for it without hesitation. It seems that poetry and novel writing is a little simpler, but you also need to consider other factors, such as the sales volume of your book. Actually, I am not against commercial filmmaking. This is especially true in today's China, because my current understanding of film has changed a great deal. I think the most important function of film is to entertain the public, and filmmaking is by and large a business enterprise. In addition, many artistic ideas can be also effectively conveyed through commercial films, such as technologies, techniques, visual preferences, and story elements. Self-expression is something that should be encouraged, but it doesn't necessarily require an expensive medium like film. You can also achieve this goal through writing or through private conversations with your close friends. Why do you need several million RMB to express yourself? By the same token, I am also against the current blockbuster-style filmmaking, including those big budget films enthusiastically pursued by Chinese directors. It is just too wasteful to spend 30 or 40 million Chinese yuan on a film whose main function is only to entertain the general public. Maybe the same goal can be easily achieved through a mere investment of 5 million.

Wang Chao

To make a film that is either commercially successful or artistically satisfying is ultimately a question that concerns one's conception of film. Take *The Orphan of Anyang* for example. The story itself is full of dramatic elements.

Chapter Six

But I didn't indulge in the drama of the story. I was quite reluctant to settle down with a scripted plot and later record it with the camera, a process that ordinary films usually follow. Instead, I wanted to use the film medium to re-experience and deepen my understanding of what I've witnessed and heard. So, it boils down to the question about the purpose of the film medium: using the film medium to duplicate a scripted drama or using it to intellectually explore what you've experienced in your life? The answer to this question determines the nature of one's filmmaking. Without a doubt my choice was the latter. Despite the fact that it has many dramatic moments, *The Orphan of Anyang* is not meant to feast the audience on drama. It is actually an externalization of my inner emotion and psychology.

It is my belief that if you make a film that appeals to the popular taste, you inevitably end up making some compromises in matters of your personal value and principle. By doing so you are actually telling a story that would emotionally resonate more with the general audience than your own. This is indeed a matter of choice. I don't know if the best film is the one that combines commercial value with your own individuality, maybe the result of which would produce a more mediocre work. This is an issue I really need to think through in the future, especially in the case of a big-budget production. As my first feature, however, *The Orphan of Anyang* was designed to make a most telling case that showcases my individuality as well as what I care about most. Maybe in the future I will need to work on the transition from an individual-focused cinema to an audience-centered one. I can imagine this is not an easy process. This is also why I respect the Fifth Generation filmmakers. Directors like Chen Kaige were making very personal films—such as *Yellow Earth, King of Children*, and *Life on a String*—at the beginning of their careers, but they were able to reinvent themselves by incorporating commercialism in their personal vision. This is another testament to their cinematic genius. They are well grounded in all aspects of filmmaking. I used to be an assistant of Chen Kaige, so I know directors like Chen are well grounded. I think young filmmakers have a lot to learn from them.

On the other hand, I think I am not optimistic, not optimistic at all. I do have these issues on my mind, and I think about them quite often these days. For example, can China afford to cultivate a small audience dedicated to art house films? Will we enable this audience to have access to China's own art house films? How to build such a venue? This I consider quite important. As for the box office, I will be happy if my films do well, but if not, I will still think it is a worthwhile effort. I feel confident I will be able to cultivate a garden of my own.

Wang Guangli

If you are able to express yourself with charm and skill, the work that comes out of it will surely bear commercial value. But if you have no charm and skill in self-expression, even when you try hard to create a commercial sensation, you would fail miserably. I am somewhat against the blind critique of Hollywood. I think there is a big hole in BFA's education, in which the students are taught that as long as they are against Hollywood they are in tune with art. This is at best a misconception. There are many artistic elements in Hollywood products. A single film can make tens of millions dollars at the box-office. You tell me what this is, art or commodity? It must be both an art work and a commodity. So, I would say that the most artistic work is at the same time the most commercial one. I don't feel there is an internal contradiction between art and commerce. It is absolutely beyond my comprehension when one claims that his/her film is an artistic treasure because no one wants to see it. Let me ask you this question: is it easier for a beautiful girl or an ugly girl to find her lover? The answer is quite clear to me. In some cases, the beautiful girl might have a hard time finding a suitable companion, but it is merely due to the fact that few men can afford her. In the case of the ugly girl, you can't claim that she is beautiful because no one wants her. But sadly this is the logic of the film circle in China: "This is a great piece of art because no one wants to buy it." How strange this logic sounds! In my opinion, a great piece of art also possesses high commercial value. Van Gogh is a great example. We should get rid of the slogan "I am an artist, therefore I am against commerce" and replace it with the one "I am an artist, therefore I am also commercial."

Wang Quanan

First of all, I am willing to change myself. We have to realize that the survival of both director and art depend very much on adaptation. In this respect, Mozart is the best example. His attitude toward music was never as serious as some of us have claimed. He could compose for whatever reasons, but what he came up with is absolutely music. No matter whether it is because of politics or of business, therefore, I am willing to make compromises. I think the status of art can be achieved through different means, and each individual has his/her unique way of expression. Ultimately, it is an issue of talent. Why did I use Mozart as an example? Let's suppose a noble lady gave some wine money to Mozart and asked him to come up with a melody using her name. I think Mozart would have done it without hesitation. Then, the lady played his melody in front of an audience and won both popular and critical acclaim. It turned out that the melody composed in this situation could survive the test of time and also become a classical work.

Therefore, I think Chinese artists shouldn't think highly of themselves and deny the connection between art and commercial success. If Mozart could create art under the above circumstance, then I don't think any adverse situation could prevent the emergence of art. Unless society is as reactionary as that of the medieval Europe or of the Cultural Revolution in China, we shouldn't exaggerate the so-called "oppressiveness" of the system. As a matter of fact, filmmakers in the United States also need to fight for their freedom of expression. For instance, some directors even have no say in editing. As far as I know, some of them are very smart and tactical in dealing with all kinds of problems. Just take a look at the relationship between director and producer in the States. I was told that a producer usually dislikes nude scenes, because nudity customarily leads to the film being rated "R", which in turn affects the film's performance at the box office. But what would the director do if he/she wants to have nude scenes in the film? On the set, there are normally two monitors, one for producer, and the other for director. Why does the producer need a monitor? That's because he/she wants to have firm control over the filmmaking process. To fight this excessive control, the director sometimes disables the producer's monitor and inserts the nude scenes without the producer noticing it. Then, the director dismantles the set, making re-shooting impossible. When the film is test-screened, the producer certainly notices the difference. But the director tells the producer: since the set has been dismantled it would require additional funding to re-shoot the sequence. Saving money is producer's ultimate concern. Under this circumstance, therefore, the producer usually gives in, a situation that often confronts the Chinese Film Bureau.

The reason why I cite the above Hollywood example is to remind our Chinese filmmakers of the importance of intellectual maturity. If confronting the above situation, the Chinese director would normally try to change the mentality of the producer or simply condemn him/her for not being brave enough to sacrifice commercial success for art. But why does the producer have to make such a sacrifice? We must understand that making money, or at least not losing money, is a producer's ultimate concern. Being intellectually mature means that we Chinese filmmakers should no longer feel complacent about the little maneuvers and small successes we've had in the past. What we must do is to learn how to create great works in a normal but interconnected environment. It is one thing to feel happy about being able to shot down a bird in someone else's garden, but it is another thing to be consumed and controlled by this "ability". I feel it's becoming less and less popular for Chinese filmmakers to play the role of persecuted artist or dissident outside of China. Even some festival organizers have begun to realize the "fakeness" of such self-proclaimed "persecution". To tell you the truth, these self-proclaimed "dissidents" are no better than the emperor in the "Emperor's New Clothes".

I felt gratified when attending the 2002 Berlin International Film Festival. Why? I had the feeling that finally the situation had returned to near normal. People gathered in Berlin to experience a great film event, not for other purposes. At the festival, Chinese artists were no different from the artists from other parts of the world. What they provided was the pleasure and enjoyment of cinema, not a small "window" through which non-Chinese people, especially Westerners, got to know the supposedly "prison-like" China.

After Berlin, I went to Harvard University. I felt my talk was warmly received there because there were many questions from the audience after the screening of my *Lunar Eclipse*. I still remember one of the questions, which was phrased like this: although studying in a place like Harvard, I must say I still can't quite understand your film. My answer was: don't blame Harvard. Instead, what needs to be reexamined is our understanding of the nature of Chinese filmmaking. When I am abroad, I find myself always confronted with political issues, sometimes being forced to play the role of a political commentator. I simply refuse to play this role. My standard answer is: anybody can speak about Chinese politics, but if you are really serious about this issue, you should discuss it with Jiang Zemin or Hu Jintao. I am only a Chinese director, and what I care about most is my film. If you are interested in my film, then we can sit down and use this opportunity to talk. As for politics, I am sorry but my knowledge is quite limited. What I understand about politics is simply this: despite the fact that there are many problems in China, the same is true in the United States. This debate has been around for quite some time and will continue to be so in the foreseeable future. I think what I want to let them know is this: I don't want to step in that trap anymore, and I refuse to play that "traditional" role. This role is both a temptation and a trap. When you are really lured into it, you will find it's hard to escape. In other words, when you begin to talk about art or filmmaking itself, they feel quite puzzled.

Compared to Chinese cinema, Korean cinema is healthier and has returned to its rightful place. On the one hand, we've witnessed the renaissance of its commercial film industry. This is quite important, because film needs to generate profits, to help shape social fashion, and to bring pleasure and excitement to people's mundane life in order to survive. On the other hand, art film in Korea has also benefited from the growth of commercial cinema. Rather than being overshadowed, it is moving upward alongside commercial cinema. This is what I call "healthy". Art film is one kind of cinema. It of course has its own commercial requirement. But the development of art film depends absolutely on the solid base of commercial cinema. When a Korean director won the top award at Cannes, the president immediately called and congratulated him. This is

Chapter Six

what I call "normal" and "healthy".

I guess what I want to really promote is the feeling of relaxation. We should return to film as an art form in and of itself. It is very easy for filmmakers to be tempted by power and fame. Talented filmmakers must learn self-discipline and refuse to fall into this trap. When there is space for artistic creation, I think what we should do is to engage in construction and to make the environment more conducive to filmmaking. I really hope China can achieve a great new period of development. Actually, I've already sensed the coming of this transformation. This is based on my recent observation of Chinese society as a whole. I've always felt that compared to the glorious times of Chinese history, Chinese tradition is at its low point in the current period. Our culture used to be magnificent and full of wisdom. But I've always felt that we contemporary Chinese are not able to understand the spirit of the past, the tradition that has been distorted or misinterpreted for a long time. However, recently I begin to feel the resurgence of this seemingly lost tradition. It is not something that can be found in a textbook, but is a kind of spirit that is hard to describe verbally. To convey it in simple terms, I would say Chinese people have begun to pick up the confidence in their own tradition. Some of them have started to wear traditional Chinese clothes, appreciate Chinese architecture, and decorate their apartments with Chinese furniture. In the past, many of us were ashamed of these traditional things because they were considered ugly. This is what I call "awakening". It is not some sort of meaningless intellectual argument, but a feeling deeply embedded in everybody's heart and mind. This is where the real power lies. You can sense the gradual recovery and resurgence of classical sensibility in many places, particularly in restaurants. In the past, many of us, myself included, felt that kind of elegance and beauty belonged to the Japanese tradition. Now I've realized it is actually an integral part of Chinese culture that was "appropriated" by the Japanese. This sense of confidence is based on the rediscovery of the richness of Chinese culture. It is also based on this recovery that I think Chinese art has entered a period of active creation.

With the above realization, I think we should follow the trend of our time and come to terms with the rapid development of our country. This necessarily requires us to abandon the attitude we upheld in the past decade, the feeling of self-indulgence and self-pity, even including the tendency of "inventing" a repressive environment in order to win sympathy from the outside. In the past, you might have been able to live an easy life by pretending to be a street beggar, but times have changed and you have plenty of opportunities to support yourself through normal work. Why don't you just throw away the begging bowl and go find a normal job? I have the feeling that many Chinese artists used to behave just like a street beggar.

Although by no means poor, they liked to play the role of a beggar thirsty for sympathy, particularly from the West.

When attending the "Chinese urban cinema" screenings at Lincoln Center [in New York City] and in Washington, D.C., in 2001, I had good discussions with some of the young film scholars and critics in the States. They also felt that the things expressed in *Lunar Eclipse* are universal and pertain also to the United States, such as the issue of women in the city. I think this is only a reflection of the emerging ambition of Chinese artists. Chinese artists shouldn't be merely content with the expression of their own characteristics. We ought to address those issues or feelings that pertain to the entire human race. What needs to be exchanged [through film] is nothing but our view of the world. We've learned life lessons from watching Western films, and our life has changed because of this. [Now] we also want to change their life.

Wang Xiaoshuai

The issue that concerns individual expression and the market is probably the most difficult to talk about and the hardest to figure out. Except for Hollywood, this issue is bothering every producer in the world. The reason why Hollywood is not as troubled as others is because Hollywood is an industrial apparatus, a gigantic machine, which only needs fuel to continue running. The only concern it has is to make films as eye-pleasing as possible, to expand its market to every corner of the planet, and to make as much money as possible. It denies one's individuality. Of course if you were Steven Spielberg or James Cameron you would probably be allowed to show some individuality. But this must be framed and contained in the structural model of commercial cinema. This model is an imposed combination of producers, screenwriters, cinematographers, and stars. The director certainly plays a role in this model, but he or she often needs to follow certain rules and instructions. You have to do what you are asked to do, such as where to have a close-up and where to have a shot/reverse shot. You also can't change scripted dialogues at will. When filming is done, you leave it to the editors to handle the rest.

So, unless you have an apparatus like Hollywood, all of the existing filmmaking systems in the world can't escape these dilemmas: The director or the producer: which one is more important? The market and film art: which has priority? It is always difficult to come up with a satisfying answer. I still think that there are two kinds of film: Hollywood-style commercial cinema and individual-focused art cinema. Commercial cinema is also not as homogenous as we might think. There is no shortage of mediocre directors in Hollywood. If you are a mediocre director with no special talent, you will

Chapter Six

be only entitled to make Hollywood B-movies. Mediocrity in filmmaking is rejected in many parts of the world. We all know that many of us are obsessed with the pirated copies of good art films, but we won't buy bad and self-proclaimed "art films". The same is true for commercial films. Pirated copies of a well-made commercial film are hot commodities. To me, therefore, the key issue here is to make good films. As long as the quality is assured, I am also willing to make commercial films.

In addition, I also think that the conception of the audience and the market in China is quite outdated. We need to further differentiate between the audience and the market. Audiences differ from each other, and there are also different kinds of markets. For a long time, the idea that a film must "appeal to the young and old" has dominated our thinking. In today's diversified market and society, this goal seems increasingly impossible.

Nowadays, Chinese directors are saying we need to learn from Hollywood, and making movies is all about making money. They seem to have forgotten that films can also be art. Today, in China, most directors are completely focused on the box office, and people will laugh if you don't make lots of money from your films. I realize that I should concentrate on making kung fu and action movies if I just want to make lots of money. But if the Chinese film industry that used to be completely controlled by the Chinese government now just wants to copy Hollywood, we will have lost again. Give us ten years, and we still won't be able to compete with Hollywood-style movies. So I want to tell people, let's not forget that in China we have our own culture and own history. Someday I hope China will have small cinemas like the art-house theaters I have seen in the United States and Europe. That would give us a place to show our less commercial films, too. I made underground films for twelve years before I was allowed into theaters. Now we might have to wait another twelve years before China can have a strong independent film industry.

Xu Jinglei

As a matter of fact, I didn't care too much about the market issue when making my debut *Me and My Dad*. The only thing I gave much thought to was making a low-budget film because there are several stable sources from which one can get money back from a low-budget film, such as the CCTV Movie Channel. At least you won't lose a lot of money making such a film. In other words, from the beginning, I had no intention of making it a commercial film. Although I was able to cast a few famous directors, such as Jiang Wen, the commercial aspect was the least I cared about. If commercial success were my goal, I wouldn't even bother to direct a film, let alone a film with such a subject. I chose a father-daughter relationship because it is something that can easily touch my heart. Besides, there aren't many good films about the father in China. In a few of them, the father figure is morally constructed, either good or bad. Although not really a woman with patience, I am quite stubborn about what I like to do. Right after finishing the first film, without any hesitation I decided to make my second.

Certainly I do hope my film can attract some audiences, and this is why I keep sending it to various film festivals abroad. It is after all not a bad thing to have a wide spectrum of audiences. As for getting money back, I've done some calculations. I've sold the rights to the CCTV Movie Channel for about 600,000 RMB, and I figure the film's VCD and DVD rights will at least worth 500,000 to 600,000 RMB. These two figures alone will pass the one million mark, and it only cost me a little more than one million RMB to make the film. If my film can gross two million RMB in domestic box office, I will even make a profit. But even if the figure is less than that, say one million, it is perfectly fine with me. I haven't counted the foreign market. Maybe I can also get extra money from selling my film's foreign rights. Therefore, because this is a small budget film, I don't worry too much about the market and the possibility of losing money.

When I was making *Letters from an Unknown Woman*, however, I thought more about its commercial success. After all, film is not purely a personal medium. It is meant to be seen by a large number of people. As a matter of fact, throughout my career as an actress I've never stopped thinking of the issue of whether I want to act in a film I like most or a film the audience likes most. From the point of view of an actress, I certainly think I can benefit more from acting in a film that appeals to a large number of people. I am officially affiliated with the Beijing Film Studio. Han Sanping, the studio's head, and I had a talk after my first film was finished. While supportive of the film in general, he also said to me that I can't always make this kind of film because I need a solid audience base to make my filmmaking career a sustainable one. It is only through the broad support of the audience that I can accumulate sufficient capital to make films I'd like to make. In other words, he wants me to walk with two legs: one is to make commercially successful films, the other to use the money earned from those films to make personal films. It's just like what I am doing now: perceived by young people in China as an idol, I've acted in many popular films and TV dramas, which made it possible for me to finance my own film. Han's words, therefore, are very inspiring to me. This is why I say I paid more attention to the market and commercial success when making my second film.

Chapter Six

Zhang Ming

I don't see myself as an obstacle to commercial film. As a matter of fact, my next project will be a so-called "commercial film". I think there is some truth in the following saying: the first film one makes is for oneself, the second for both oneself and the investors, and the third purely for the investors. This is especially true in the case of contemporary China. I think the strongest political statement today in Chinese cinema is to make the films that do well at the box office, that can draw a large crowd, and that can replace those state-sponsored "main melody" films. Perhaps the kind of film you make is apolitical, but the result itself is very political, because you've opened up a new space that a lot of people can identify with. As far as I know, few directors in China are capable of doing this. I do think, however, we must first push toward that direction in order to create some space for the things we really want to do. Only after enough space has been created can we indulge in the "luxury" of pure art. Right now I don't think there are many outlets in China for "art cinema". Just think about the amount of money one needs to make a film. How can you persuade a financier to invest in your project if he/she sees no possibility of making money or breaking even?

In my two previous films, I rejected any attempt to build a moral or ethical relationship with the characters. Otherwise, people could easily tell who the "bad" guy is and who the "good" guy is. They could also see where my sympathy lies. But I didn't give them any clue in those two films. I feel film is a medium to carry one's imagination, and imagination has nothing to do with morality.

I understand the above stand involves great risk. To a great extent, rejecting moral judgment means rejecting audiences' fundamental way of seeing things. Most audiences come to cinema with some kind of moral expectations. They are accustomed to appreciating a film with a clear sense of right and wrong as well as of conflict and some kind of conclusion in the end. When you break this expectation and refuse to take a moral stand, you are taking the risk of alienating a large number of people. On the other hand, however, one can also ask this question: who is the audience anyway? I actually don't have any direct relations with the audience. The person I am most familiar with is my investor. The idea of "audience" has always been an abstract concept. Who can really represent the audience?

Zhang Yang

First and foremost, I don't reject the commercial aspect of filmmaking. I also don't agree with the idea that art cinema necessarily means the films that are hard to understand and few people want to see them. I think when a film is projected on the screen, no matter what kind of audiences are sitting in the theater, even including intellectuals, if the film makes them sleepy, it is definitely not a good film. Although some may say this kind of film has its unique features, I think one of the key elements of cinema lies in its ability to communicate with the audience. A film must first get the audience involved and, in return, the audience will respond to what the filmmaker tries to offer. In other words, your film must first affect the audience in order to fulfill the purpose of communication and psychological exchange. If a film makes the audience feel bored or simply leave the theater, I think this film is at most a mediocre work. I always stress the point that it is a basic requirement for a film to grab the audience's attention in two hours. If this requirement is met, no matter what message you want to convey, the audience will gradually relate to you.

Good art films do not exclude commercial elements. Artistic quality itself is a part of commerce. Because an art film is refined in taste, it can appeal to the audience and arouse their sympathy. This is how art films gain their commercial-ness. When I spoke to my producer, both of us agreed that the most important distinction we can make is between a good film or a bad film, not between an art film or a commercial film. Even in the category of commercial film, there is also the distinction between good and bad commercial films. The commercial success of a film must first be based on the film's good quality. If a film is no good, no matter how "artistic" it might be, it will never achieve commercial success.

I also don't see that there is a conflict between self-expression and commercial success. I am a strong advocate of self-expression. I am engaged in filmmaking not because I want to cater to your taste, or because I want to address the needs of the audience, or because I want to make a lot of quick money, but because I have a strong urge for self-expression. The good thing about my relationship with the producer is that he never puts a limit on what I want to make. Except for the earlier film *Love Spicy Soup*, which was pre-arranged and carefully planned, all of my films were made when the producer came to me and asked what I wanted to do and what interested me most. Then, I would brief him on the storyline and both of us would sit and have a discussion. He was quite supportive of my ideas. Just use *Quitting* as an example. As soon as he got a sense of the project, he felt it would be a hard sell. Nevertheless, he supported the project wholeheartedly because he saw value in the story. It was only with his backing that I had the courage to take the risk. To our satisfaction, because the film is based on a good storyline and solid characters, most audiences sit through the entire screening and enjoy the film.

Chapter Six

Zhang Yuan

To me, the first step is to finish my film. This goal easily tops other factors in my filmmaking. Certainly I also hope my films can produce good commercial results, which will definitely increase my investors' confidence in me and subsequently give me more opportunities to make more films. Actually, some of my films were quite profitable. For example, although made on a small budget, *East Palace, West Palace* was sold to nearly forty countries worldwide. The film was mainly financed by such non-profit-driven institutions as the French government and the Rotterdam Film Festival. I was a little surprised that it turned out to be a commercial success. On the other hand, despite the fact that some people, including my close friends, were really crazy about films such as *Sons*, these films didn't sell very well. *Sons* was sent to hundreds of film festivals worldwide, but it did poorly in the market. I figured not too many people wanted to see a drunk's life. In general, therefore, an excellent film may very often earn little money at the box office. Only a few can achieve the balance between artistic value and the box-office. I think I will never make a commercial film like Zhang Yimou's *Hero*.

Ultimately, I think the issue of the market and the audience is what the investor needs to consider, not the filmmaker. I'll never make a film based on an offered script. I always choose the subject that interests me most. It is up to the investor to make the judgment as to whether he or she wants to finance my project. On the other hand, I myself also have my own judgment about whether the project will lose money. Since my early films, such as *Seventeen Years* and *Crazy English*, didn't cost too much to make, I think the chances were slim for them to lose money. With such a good record, I don't think my investors will walk away from me.

CHAPTER SEVEN

FILMS THAT MATTER:
DIALOGUE BETWEEN THE "SIXTH GENERATION"
AND WORLD CINEMA

Like the Fifth Generation filmmakers, the core members of the "Sixth Generation" were able to watch a variety of Western (European and Hollywood) films at BFA, an enviable privilege when even VHS, let alone VCD and DVD, was considered a household luxury,. In the late 1980s and early 1990s, BFA and the China Film Archive, the latter being the most prestigious film research institution in China, were the two major venues frequented by the privileged few. Not by coincidence, both venues featured European art cinema, particularly films by Truffaut, Godard, Bergman, Bertolucci, Fellini, and Antonioni. No wonder that when the interviewers raised the issue of cinematic influence, i.e., "how do you view your relationship with the cinematic tradition of the world, including that of China", these names constantly popped up. However, for the directors born in the late 1960s and 1970s, particularly for those not trained at BFA, Hollywood seems to have played a larger role in their cinematic endeavor. Enjoying these Western films in film history some of them were more surprised by the Shanghai films of the pre-Communist era such as Fei Mu's Spring in a Small Town. *It is also interesting to see what these filmmakers have to say about the Fifth Generation.*

* * *

Guan Hu

As a Chinese and growing up in China, I don't think I can deny the defining influence of Chinese culture. Just use Taiwan cinema as an example. No matter how *avant-garde* Taiwan films appear to be, we can easily distinguish them from films of other countries. They are the cultural byproducts of that small island. It's the same with mainland Chinese films. Sometimes Chinese culture only exerts an imperceptible influence, but you can't simply walk away from it. Some Chinese filmmakers want to break away from Chinese tradition and rebel against the cinematic tradition of China. I would say their films won't last very long. Sailing against the stream exacts a price.

To me, the single most important influence comes from the Chinese classics. I've been a fan of classical novels and poetry since childhood. There are simply so many valuable things you can inherit or learn from the rich tradition of China, and I don't think these resources could be possibly

Chapter Seven

exhausted in my lifetime. It is true that there are many great filmmakers in the history of world cinema, French and Italian in particular, but I think what I've learned from them is only limited to film language and technique. They don't leave traces in my inner self. I still remember it was many years ago that, thanks to the guidance of the Fifth Generation, I felt I got close to the true spirit of cinema. When I was with Chen Kaige, I always felt I was encircled by the depth and heaviness of Chinese culture and history. I don't think I can easily cast away his influence and start something anew.

Jia Zhangke

Among the Chinese classics, I particularly like Yuan Muzhi's films, especially his *Street Angel*. I admire him from the bottom of my heart. I think he started a tradition that has been largely abandoned by later Chinese filmmakers, the tradition of the vernacular and mundane. There are a few exceptions, such as Zhang Zeming's *Swan Song* and *Foreign Moon*. In Hong Kong commercial cinema, you can also find some traces of this tradition, such as in *C'est la Vie, Mon Chérie*. It is true that the film is quite commercial, but you can still feel the everyday-ness of the human-to-human relations as well as the charming aspect of the vernacular in the film. I guess it's largely due to the fact that Hong Kong is historically connected to Shanghai, and the tradition is therefore kept alive in Hong Kong cinema better than anywhere else. What surprises me most in Yuan Muzhi's films is the director's keen observation of the ordinariness of city life as well as his respect for this ordinariness. I think this feeling of respect is of vital importance. What are the reasons behind the fact that many Chinese filmmakers are obsessed with grand narratives and historical allegories? I think it is mainly because they despise this ordinariness and view it as a negative aspect of life. Regrettably, therefore, the tradition exemplified in Yuan Muzhi's films has vanished in Chinese cinema.

I remember seeing *Street Angel* when I was only a child. I was able to see it because the film is considered "leftist" and therefore "revolutionary". However, it was not until the BFA years that I discovered the real value of the film. I was quite overwhelmed when I saw the film again in my Chinese film history class. I think *Street Angel* has a stronger impact on me than Fei Mu's *Spring in a Small Town*. Although from an aesthetic point of view, the latter is superior, I feel *Street Angel* is a cultural landmark to me. It taught me what I should respect and what I should avoid in filmmaking.

On the other hand, Taiwan cinema, especially the films of Hou Hsiao-Hsien, has had a great impact on me. People often mention the use of long take in my films as evidence of Hou's influence. But I feel it's not the most important thing Hou taught me. The most valuable lesson I learned from his films is his affirmation of his own life experience, his tireless pursuit and search for meanings in life. It is through Hou's films that I began to value my own life experience, especially my small-town childhood. I particularly like Hou's *The Boys from Fengkuei*, from which I was able to relive my own life in the Fengyang County in Shanxi Province.

Jiang Wen

Before *In the Heat of the Sun*, there was a period when I was very attracted to the music and songs of the Cultural Revolution. Several friends of mine brought me a sampling of Cultural Revolution music, and we were all enthralled. Strangely enough, what ignited our passion for the music of the Cultural Revolution was Martin Scorsese's *Goodfellas*. The film opens with three gangsters opening a car trunk and shooting dead the man inside. Then, they slam the trunk shut, which is followed by a piece of pop music. When I heard the music, I said to myself: Wow, this sounds a lot like Cultural Revolution music! Actually, it is a piece of 1950s' American music, but for some reason it reminded me of my childhood during the Cultural Revolution. This is how my first film was initially conceived. Certainly, it was not until I read Wang Shuo's novel that the idea developed further.

Martin Scorsese has had an enduring impact on me, as does Chinese cinema. I grew up watching films like *The Child Soldier Named Zhang Ga*, *The Shang Gan Mountain*, *Heroic Sons and Daughters*, and *Guerrilla Forces on the Flatland*. Despite the fact that I still have no idea who directed those films, I must say they are deeply rooted in my memory. Oh, I forgot to mention the influence of Soviet cinema. During my childhood and adolescent years, Soviet films, such as *Lenin in October* and *Lenin in 1918*, were of monumental significance. Why did I choose to make *Devils on the Doorstep* a back-and-white film? It had something to do with my early experience of cinema. More than 90 percent of the films I watched during those years are black and white. Until today, I still think black-and-white films are more cinematic than color ones.

I don't think films by the Fifth Generation have had a special influence on me. We tend to forget that the most remarkable achievements of the Fifth Generation, be it *Yellow Earth* or *One and Eight*, lies in their composition and color. The rebel spirit of the generation is most evident in these two aspects. Their technical innovation in film composition and color, however, has been interpreted by some Western critics as "thoughtful reflection" on Chinese culture and history. Actually, as the Fifth Generation directors continue to make their presence known to the audience, you will see their films lack intellectual depth. They are quite skillful and confident when it comes to film form and technique. Once independent thinking is involved, they tend to run short of ways to deal with the situation. When they find themselves not so sure about what they are doing, therefore, they always go back to what they are good at: composition and color. This is why I say the Fifth Generation has never earthshakingly inspired me.

Jin Chen

Among the foreign filmmakers I like most, David Lean tops the list. I admire his works, particularly his *Great Expectations*, *A Passage to India*, and *Lawrence of Arabia*. His films are marked by a poetic quality, not in the sense of a small poem, but something that resembles an epic. In his early work *Great Expectations*, Lean had already showed his adeptness in film language as well as calmness in depiction and narration. As for his *Lawrence of Arabia*, words alone are not enough to describe my admiration. Since Lean started his filmmaking career as an editor, I regard him as the one who had a true understanding of cinema. Reading his biography I learned that his conception of cinema was quite different from that of other commercial filmmakers. There are many smart filmmakers out there, but David Lean was both smart and gentlemanly. He never compromised on his own ways of filmmaking. In order not to repeat certain mistakes in his early films, he stopped making films for a long period: seventeen years. It was only after he found the right rhythm and mode of representation that he sat on the director's chair again with his last film. In other words, he regarded filmmaking not as a means to make a living, but as something that spoke to his spirituality. Because there are few directors like David Lean, I admire him wholeheartedly. Looking at myself, I must say that for me filmmaking is more or less a means of making living. I rely on this job to survive. I don't know if I am capable of other jobs. But to David Lean, film was pure and spiritual. For him, nothing was more disrespectful than regarding filmmaking only as a means to make a living.

Although you can find some traces of Lean's influence in my first two films, I don't think his poetic style and humanistic concerns can be easily imitated. As ordinary filmmakers, we can never match his metaphysical weight. His thinking was truly international and all-encompassing. My films, particularly the first one, are limited to China in both thematic and stylistic terms. Some issues are only relevant to peoples of my age. Despite the fact that I view David Lean as my model, therefore, there is no comparison between my works and David Lean's.

Speaking of Chinese influences, it is undeniable that I, or we as a group, have benefited from the works of the Fifth Generation filmmakers. But it is exactly because they've had too much influence on us that we want to overthrow them. Otherwise, they would enslave us and make it impossible for us to achieve breakthroughs. As a matter of fact, times have changed. Gone are the days when the Fifth Generation's aesthetics were heroically celebrated. From a historical point of view, I think it was quite noble at that time that the Fifth Generation used film to convey their sense of crisis and duty for the nation as well as their outcry against the "backwardness" of Chinese culture. But from today's point of view, this kind of heavy-hearted view of both cinema and Chinese culture appears to be at best narrow-minded, even running the risk of becoming an obstacle to today's cultural pluralism. As the society is becoming increasingly diversified, people have generally lost their interest in the typical works of the Fifth Generation. Their films are mostly remembered as historical documents, a reminder of the great contributions made by a specific group of filmmakers in bygone days. If they continue to make these kinds of films, I don't think they could create another great sensation for their audience. The Fifth Generation emerged at a time when there was no such concept as pluralism in Chinese culture. In addition, China's door was just opening to the world when they started to make films. Standing between old and new, the Fifth Generation filmmakers were able to create a new cinema by injecting fresh cinematic language and new ideas from the outside world into Chinese culture. They were *avant-gardists* in the 1980s, but are old in the twenty-first century. As a matter of fact, they themselves are also eager to walk away from their past. None of the Fifth Generation filmmakers still stick to their original principles, and some of them are even more willing to cater to the popular taste than the "Sixth Generation" filmmakers.

Li Xin

I can always find something inspirational from Chinese films. Despite the fact that the Fifth Generation to me seems to have lost its direction, for example, I still think their films, *Farewell My Concubine* in particular, are great sources of inspiration. Shanghai cinema of the 1930s and 40s is also worth mentioning. Unfortunately, the only thing left that makes us proud of Shanghai cinema is history. Shanghai is the place that gave birth to a glamorous and glorious cinema. Some of the works produced during that period are second to none in quality and subject matter. However, those days are long gone. There are many reasons for this decline, and one of them has to do with the place itself. I am always puzzled by the fact that, although far away from the political center of Beijing, Shanghai is much more restricted in terms of creative freedom. Talented artists and filmmakers are lured to Shanghai by its fame and cosmopolitanism, but they will soon find they face two options: either leaving Shanghai or being assimilated into its overwhelming consumerism. This is the other side of the coin: money. Shanghai's economy is developing so fast that almost everybody is drawn into the game of moneymaking. You can easily fill your pockets working on TV commercials, Why bother sticking

Chapter Seven

to filmmaking, which is economically quite risky?

In terms of outside influences, I think the list is quite long. I find myself quite drawn to David Lynch-style filmmakers. As a matter of fact, my BFA graduation thesis is on David Lynch. Full of imagination, Lynch has an obsession for things dirty, dark, and bloody, which I don't particularly like, but he always ends his film with brightness. This is what I like about him. Many critics also claim my film *Dazzling* is largely influenced by Wim Wenders' *Wings of Desire*; I don't totally agree. I showed some respect for Wenders in my film, but *Dazzling* is in essence based on my own observation of young people's life in China. It is true that there are also angels in Wenders' film, but the angels in *Dazzling* differ greatly from the ones in Berlin, and there is also a difference in how angels are cinematically represented between the two films. I am a Christian. I believe angels are a universal symbol that can be found in any culture.

Liu Bingjian

Actually, when I begin shooting a film, I always try not to be bothered by all the great works I've seen. Otherwise they would become obstacles rather than inspiration. As for my favorite filmmakers or films, Pedro Almodovar tops my list. In his films, I can find exactly what I would like to achieve. Despite this affinity, I think my inspiration comes from different sources. Rather than a one-to-one link, it's a complicated mix. I don't know whether it's because of my nature or of outside influences, but I am always obsessed with painful experiences in life.

In terms of Chinese cinema, I think history has taught me that there is no difference between classical and modern traditions. Sometimes I can find avant-garde elements in classical films that are still refreshing and shocking from today's point of view. Cinema cannot be simply divided into old and new. Works by the Fifth Generation, such as *Yellow Earth*, *One and Eight*, and *Red Sorghum*, will stand the test of time. Politics and the subject matter may no longer be relevant, but their cinematic qualities remain inspirational.

Lou Ye

I am said to be influenced by [Krzysztof] Kieslowski in Europe, [Alfred] Hitchcock in the United States, and Wong Kar-wai in Hong Kong. Fortunately, all these three are cinematic *auteurs*. Otherwise, I would be insulted [laugh].

To be serious, speaking of the directors I like, the list is quite long. For example, I like those 1960s' directors, particularly of the French New Wave and Japanese New Wave. As a matter of fact, there is something special about the 1960s. Quite a few New Wave films emerged across the globe during that period. I also like the so-called "New Hollywood" directors, from Coppola and Scorsese to [George] Lucas and Spielberg. The list also includes some Hollywood B-movie directors, such as John Cassavetes. We saw many B-movies at BFA, because the A-list was quickly exhausted. Only later did we learn that they are also Hollywood B-movie directors. As for Hitchcock, he did not have a big influence on me. I wrote the script of *Suzhou River* myself. I divided the narrative into several sections, and then built each section on the basis of individual characters: "The Story of Meimei", "My Story", and so on. Although I roughly followed this structure, the shooting started even before the script was finished. The story was in fact finalized on the editing table. The production process, therefore, was a bit like that of Wong Kar-wai: shooting without a finished script. If you compare my films with Hitchcock's, first of all you will see they are quite different in appearance. Hitchcock's films look quite artificial, which makes one very uneasy. It is almost unbearable to watch Hitchcock's films after you've been exposed to films by the French New Wave directors. His films are simply too melodramatic and artificial. If not for the need to complete a homework assignment in order to earn a passing grade, I would never even have watched his films. They are always brightly lit and look quite unnatural, far behind [François] Truffaut's films of the 1960s in qualities of honesty, passion, and cinematic-ness.

As to the Chinese influence, if talking to a foreigner, I would answer "Yes", but to a Chinese, I would say "No". The same question is often posed to me when I am abroad. With a positive "Yes", I would cite the names of many old Chinese films that have influenced me. In reality, we all know that these old films are not up to the mark. I happened to see *Street Angel* and several other old Chinese films at the festivals that featured "Retrospectives of Chinese Cinema". These are excellent films, but all of them are fatally flawed. I couldn't breathe when watching *Street Angel*. Many scenes are masterfully shot, but the ending is simply ridiculous. It is quite regrettable that a masterpiece is ruined by only one or two fatal flaws. So, I say *Springtime in a Small Town* is an exceptional work, because it is held together from the beginning to the end, no fatal flaws. Most Chinese films of the 1930s lack such consistency. For example, parts of *A Spring River Floats Eastward* and *Goddess* far surpass Western films in artistic achievements. But regrettably, the quality of each film as a whole deteriorates because of a few fatal flaws. Certainly we cannot talk about the artistic quality of those films without considering the historical context of that period.

If somebody asked me which Italian director I like most, I would mention [Federico] Fellini or [Michelangelo] Antonioni without hesitation. But in the case of China, it is quite hard to come up with the names right

Chapter Seven

away. After much hesitation, I would say Fei Mu, or even Xie Jin, who has at least made such excellent films as *Stage Sisters* and *Hibiscus Town*. If still not enough, maybe I can even mention Chen Kaige. As a Chinese, I am obligated to mention some Chinese names. But to tell you the truth, the number is quite small.

Films of the Fifth Generation directors have not inspired me, but I personally enjoy them quite a bit, especially the earlier works. I feel moved by these films, particularly by their raw energy. Films like *Red Sorghum, Yellow Earth*, and *One and Eight* are both daring and powerful. It is as simple as this: one may be in disagreement with their views, styles, and artistic visions, but still appreciate of their films. There is one problem, however. I used to say to Xie Fei:[xxx] it is easy for us to understand the Fourth and Fifth Generation filmmakers, but not vice-versa. This shows the great difference between the two groups of filmmakers. I may not be homosexual, but I don't feel there is anything alien about a gay man; he is perfectly acceptable to me. I can still be moved by those old films, including those of the Fourth Generation, such as Professor Zheng Dongtian's *Mandarin Duck Apartment* [Yuanyang lou, 1987]. Although we are making totally different films today, I understand what this film is meant to communicate, I understand Zheng's vision, and I can immerse myself into the story with appreciation. I think most young filmmakers also share this feeling. However, although we don't think the Fourth and Fifth Generation filmmakers are of a different race, we feel they nonetheless view us as aliens. This was crystal-clear at the beginning of our careers. Sometimes this gut feeling can't be rationally analyzed. You just feel it. Of course, the situation is probably getting better now.

Another especially important difference between us is more philosophical. The Fifth Generation is adamant about its absolute correctness: the world must be such and such. But we as a group would say: We *believe* the world is such and such. Just use this cigarette lighter as an example.[xxxi] When I say this is a lighter, I also do not exclude the possibility that it is just a piece of blue plastic. But they would dismiss this possibility: how can it be just a piece of blue plastic? It *is* a lighter! They would make a fuss about that. Just take a look at their films. At the beginning, they didn't have this kind of attitude. Full of raw energy, their first films look exceptionally impressive. But gradually they become more and more adamant: how can it be just a piece of blue plastic? They are born with that attitude, which is impossible to change. Although I acknowledge the artistic value of these works and have no strong objection to this self-righteousness, I do think it is a terrible thing if we don't have other alternatives from which people can choose. In their conception, they are absolutely right, and you are absolutely wrong. But the truth is: it is impossible for you to be in an absolute position. You can only present your point of view for reference, and it's up to the audience to decide whether they will accept it.

Lu Chuan

I am not sure if Chinese cinema has any tradition that can make us proud. I've taken some classes in the history of Chinese cinema, but what really struck me were the films made under the direct instruction of Madam Jiang. It is a "red" tradition marked by strong characteristics in style. But can you draw on the experience from this tradition? I guess not. I've also seen some pre-1949 Chinese films, but those black and white flicks always make me feel unnatural. Even the characters played by Zhao Dan and Zhou Xuan, arguably the two most acclaimed actors in pre-1949 Chinese cinema, look quite unnatural and uncomfortable to me. I think no pre-1949 films, be it leftist or rightist or "neutral", can be regarded as the epitome of the times. In other words, it is to say that you can hardly see the features of the times through those films. I love history. I used to imagine myself as an anthropology or archeology student at Beijing University. My idea of film is that it must reflect the spirit of the times. A film made in 2002 ought to make the audience feel its characters are unique for that year.

I am not saying that there is nothing good about Chinese cinema. There are quite a few good ones, such as *Early Spring in February* and *New Year's Sacrifice*. Films of the 1950s, such as *The Child Soldier Named Zhang Ga*, often enchant me with their simplicity. But that enchanting simplicity cannot satisfy my desire for a more powerful display of human nature as well as an edgy anatomy of life. I was completely subdued when I saw [Ingmar] Bergman's *Cries and Whispers*. Only after seeing such a film did I began to really understand what cinema is, what cinema ought to look like, and how cinema should handle its subject matter. This is cinema in its true sense. Bergman's films opened the door of film art to me. They dare to directly confront the problems of life and reality. I simply love the power of Bergman's films. After I reach the age of forty or fifty, when I become more mature, intelligent, and richer in spirit, there might be a chance that I would be drawn to [Andrei] Tarkovsky. But what I really want today is something as sharp and direct as Bergman's films. I feel we are spiritually connected.

Besides Bergman, I also like [Pier Paolo] Pasolini and [Federico] Fellini. Their understanding of life and the human soul is what I aspire to. However, this does not mean that they've left marks in my films. I don't want to imitate other people, even though they are cinematic masters. They are my beacons from whom I've learned how to get close to the human heart. If I am able to overcome the feeling of regret in my future filmmaking, it will be because of the influence of film *auteurs* like Bergman, Pasolini, and Fellini. I worship these *auteurs*, but if you entirely followed their footsteps, you would never become a master yourself. To me, they only offered a perfect example about what cinema can truly achieve. When it comes to my own filmmaking, I hope to follow my gut feeling and step out of the footprints of "dinosaurs".

Lu Xuechang

Maybe I am a little radical, but I don't think I have inherited anything significant from the film tradition of China. There are a few truly outstanding films in history of Chinese cinema, but they all come from the neo-realist tradition. In the final analysis, they are the siblings of Italian Neo-Realism. The first Chinese films I saw were the ones like *Tunnel Warfare* and *Mine Warfare*. It was not until I saw [Michelangelo] Antonioni's films that I began to really understand what cinema can be. Speaking of influence, therefore, I think Italian Neo-Realism, particularly [Vittorio] De Sica's works, had a big impact on me. Later, at BFA, I also became obsessed with French New Wave films. Generally speaking, European cinema played a defining role in shaping my view of cinema. Hollywood was not in the spectrum, with the exception of Martin Scorsese. When I was a student at BFA, Martin was really big. But today he is no longer regarded as a cinematic genius. Many students think he is outdated.

Ma Liwen

I like stylistically simple films, such as the works of Edward Yang. He has the ability to tell stories in a simple and controlled manner. There are heartening moments in his films. I also like watching films with strong emotional appeal, such as Chen Kaige's *Farewell My Concubine* and *The Emperor and the Assassin*. But my personality determines that those films won't have an impact on my own filmmaking. As a filmmaker, I draw my inspiration from those works that are simple in both subject matter and style, such as Zhang Yimou's *The Road Home* and *The Story of Qiu Ju*. There is a long list of foreign films I like, among them *Titanic*, *Run Lola Run*, and Korea's *My Sassy Girl*. But I don't think they are as pure as [Roman] Polanski's *Bitter Moon* and Michael Haneke's *The Piano Teacher*. It's like the comparison between what is disposable and what is collectable. The former are the films you enjoy watching but have no intention to keep, while the latter are the ones you would like to watch time and again.

Although I draw inspiration from the films that are simple in style and sincere in storytelling, it does not mean that I am imitating them. I use the simplest and most natural way to tell my stories, and there is no need for me to learn any special tricks. If you drink water with a cup, I also drink water with a cup. To me, the most important issue in filmmaking lies not in style, but in story. For example, there are some long takes in my films. I am using them not because I want to mimic someone but because long takes should be used in filming those scenes.

Meng Qi

I am a big fan of Steven Spielberg. *The Color Purple* and *Schindler's List* are all-time favorites of mine. *The Godfather* series and Mel Gibson's *Braveheart* are also at the top of my list. I always find these films inspirational. I understand that at BFA students are encouraged to study the examples of cinematic *auteurs*, and commercial film is not particularly favored. I must say that intellectually I am also able to feel the depth of those experimental works. Unlike BFA students, however, I don't especially worship those filmmakers. To be frank, I don't like stylistically pronounced films. I never studied filmmaking in college, but I think film ought to appeal to the feelings of ordinary folks. This is what I've learned from watching Spielberg's films.

Shi Runjiu

Although there were occasional classes on Chinese drama when I was a student at CATA, "History of Chinese Drama" for example, like my classmates, I was mainly trained in the [Constantin] Stanislavski system. You can say we had more Western influences at school. It was not until I graduated from CATA that I started to gradually realize the value of Chinese classical films. At that time, it was really hard to get access to those old films. But I had an opportunity to work with the Beijing TV Station on a special program featuring the 100-year history of cinema, through which I was able to watch all the features at the China Film Archive. It was really an eye-opening experience for me. For the first time, I suddenly realized Chinese cinema also has a great tradition. Although those films were made some sixty years ago, they look just as good as today's films. Since then, therefore, I've switched my focus to Chinese cinema, both old and new. Of course occasionally I still watch foreign films, but I don't feel my life is connected with the lives depicted in those films.

Of all the filmmakers of the 1930s and 40s, I particularly admire Cai Chusheng, director of *New Woman* (1935). I am also a fan of Chen Liting, who made *Far Away Love* (1947) and *Three Women* (1949). Both films were well made. Of course, Fei Mu of *Spring in a Small Town* is the best of all Chinese filmmakers.

Tang Danian

In general, I think I have little relation with the cinematic tradition of China. As a matter of fact, I failed to pass the Chinese film history class when I was

Chapter Seven

a student at BFA. I don't like watching Chinese films. At one point I persuaded myself to go and see some Chinese films, including the ones that are called "classics", but I have to say they look quite naïve to me. If you compare those films with the ones produced elsewhere in the same period, such as the works of French Poetic Naturalism, particularly Jean Renoir's, and Italian Neo-Realism, you will see the latter are much more mature in both technology and storytelling. You can see I am a big fan of European cinema. I've seen many European films, including contemporary ones like *The Piano Teacher* and *The Son's Room*. American director Martin Scorsese also has an impact on me. I admired him so much when I was a BFA student.

Speaking of influence, I also like the works of Hou Hsiao-Hsien and Edward Yang. It seems to me the two Taiwan filmmakers are more sincere and truthful to their characters and stories. While I don't deny the achievement of mainland directors, particularly the early works of the Fifth Generation filmmakers, such as *Yellow Earth, One and Eight*, and *Horse Thief*, I do have the feeling that many of them are afraid of revealing their inner self, particularly their weakness as a human being. Behind the masculine look, strong visual impact, and grand history, which are the trademarks of the Fifth Generation, I don't see the true feelings of a real human being. I think this is the fatal weakness of the Fifth Generation as a whole.

Wang Chao

I've learned a great deal from working with Chen Kaige. Chen's dedication, professionalism, and willpower are deeply imprinted in my memory. He is a perfectionist, always striving to achieve the best. Some people may feel the works of the Fifth Generation are too heavy, but I even found their idealism quite attractive and powerful. I'd rather they keep this idealism alive. Certainly there is a great difference between me and Chen regarding the issue of art, but it's only secondary. The most important thing is that the Fifth Generation, particularly Chen Kaige, remains one of my inspirational sources.

As to the influence of foreign filmmakers, Ingmar Bergman and Robert Bresson are the two names, among others, that come to my mind. I like Bergman because to me there is always a psychological tension in his films, which in turn empowers his shots. You might find it hard to get involved in his stories, but you can't resist the cinematic power of Bergman's world: the composition, the cutting, the long take, and the pure power his cinema brings you. I also find other filmmakers inspirational, such as Yasujiro Ozu and [Michelangelo] Antonioni, but none of them gives me such a powerful feeling as Bergman does.

I only saw one or two Bresson films before making *The Orphan of Anyang*. I like Bresson's masterful use of cinematic space, a layered one that invites rich association. In a way I paid tribute to this in *The Orphan of Anyang*.

It was not until I finished the Anyang film that I started to watch all of Bresson's films. Some critics like to make connections between my films and Bresson's, claiming that I must have been greatly influenced by Bresson. While I acknowledge there is some connection between us, Bresson's direct influence has been largely exaggerated. I think the connection between us is more of an invisible affinity, which becomes possible because Bresson had a connection to Eastern culture.

Wang Guangli

I am a fan of classical films of China, particularly of films like *Street Angel* and *Crows and Sparrows*. I even think those films are superior to today's. There is certain kind of energy in those films that I rarely see in today's Chinese films. To me, cinema is not an issue of technology. Isn't it true that film technology back then was rather rudimentary? But I don't think today's Chinese cinema is better off. In fact, it has retrogressed. Telling the truth is the minimum requirement for a good film, but Chinese cinema today cannot even live up to this requirement. Many films are so out of touch with Chinese reality. I think veteran filmmakers must take more responsibility for this retrogression, because they are the ones who possess the power.

I've also been somewhat influenced by Iranian cinema. I always wonder why a country like Iran, which, because of religion, is ideologically more restrictive than China, can produce so many high-quality films. Despite the fact that Iran has been labeled "axis of evil" [by George W. Bush], through its cinema, I believe the country has a great future. The tenacity and upward spirit on display in Iranian films, particularly those themed around children, make me believe the country as a whole is optimistic about its future.

Wang Quanan

I think my inspiration comes mainly from foreign films. The education I received at BFA emphasized non-Chinese cinemas, especially European cinema. Personally I love Italian and Spanish cinemas. As for French cinema, [Jean-Luc] Godard is the one who influenced me most. What he taught me is the power of being oppositional. By this I mean you can do almost anything in film thanks to Godard's brave experimentalism. He is simply apocalyptical. His spirit of opposition is not toward the filmmakers of his time but toward any conventions in filmmaking. I hope Chinese filmmakers can also channel their passion toward cinema itself, not something else.

I also feel that magic realism has a great impact on me. To me, history is both attractive and absurd. My view of human beings is not to expect the arrival of some sort of idealized superheroes, but to treat them as they are in real life. This being said, I am especially impressed with the wit and dark humor shown in the former Yugoslavia's film *The Underground*. It seems to me that Cui Jian, the rock star and actor, is the only artist in China who can really express the similar kind of feeling that's shown in *The Underground*. It is a feeling in which love and hatred are no longer separable: your blood almost reaches the boiling point, but you really don't know what to do with this burning zeal. When I look at the recent history of China, this feeling also resonates. On the one hand, you may look at that special period of modern Chinese history with distaste. But on the other hand, we have to remember that it is only after so many years of soul-searching that we can comfortably judge the past. Ordinary folks like us don't have the power to transcend history. Didn't we all participate in our own ways in that part of modern Chinese history? Therefore, we can't simply pretend we have nothing to do with it, as if we were people of foresight. To a certain extent, reminiscences of the passionate days of the past, no matter how absurdly we behaved during those days, add certain nostalgic attractiveness to that part of history. This is what I call the feeling of both love and hatred.

Although Chinese cinema played a marginal role in inspiring my filmmaking, I value highly what Chinese filmmakers have so far achieved. It seems to me that the modern history of Chinese culture, including that of cinema, has been dominated by what I call the "chain of construction and destruction". By this I mean the emerging generation always tends to completely deny and destroy what has been achieved by the previous generation and, in turn, its own achievement is also rejected or destroyed by the generation that follows. As new comers, we must try not to repeat this seemingly ceaseless circle. I can't speak for others, but I myself respect my colleagues old and young, respect what they've done, and particularly respect the generations before me. Putting ourselves in the position of the Fifth Generation filmmakers, I think it is undeniable that they made historical progress in Chinese cinema. We can't separate what they achieved from the historical context and judge them from today's point of view. You might think their ritualized representation of Chinese culture is outdated, but at that time such a move was no doubt bold and earthshaking. I am not saying that their films are models for today's filmmakers, but as our predecessors, they did create something new and valuable for the history of Chinese cinema. Respecting them also means respecting ourselves and those who come after us.

Wang Xiaoshuai

When I was about to enter BFA, the Fifth Generation directors and films such as Chen Kaige's *Yellow Earth* and Zheng Junzhao's *One and Eight* were so different they were shocking. I also felt the same way. However, one day before the entrance examination, I went to the BFA campus and happened to see [Michelangelo] Antonioni's *Blow Up*. It was so exciting and completely different. It really showed me what a good film is. Later on, I leaned from director Yasujiro Ozu's works, particularly his *Tokyo Story*, that Chinese could also produce good films because *Tokyo Story* gave Asian filmmakers confidence.

In general, however, it is hard for me to come up with a list of names that has had an enduring influence on me. My sources of inspiration vary over time. The films that had a great impact on me when I was a student at BFA may not be what I like most today. We studied many "waves" of cinema at BFA, and I felt instantly connected to the French New Wave when I just entered BFA. Later on, however, Japanese cinema, particularly a couple of Akira Kurosawa's films, started to take the place of the French New Wave. As I grow older, I become more and more drawn to Chinese cinema. Films such as *Spring in a Small Town* really lead me to the realization that Chinese cinema does have something to offer to the world film community. As a matter of fact, it was only after I had been exposed to the French New Wave and Japanese cinema that I started to learn the value of Chinese cinema. As early as in the 1930s and 40s China had already made films that were ahead of their time in both aesthetics and subject matter. For the time being, I'd rather consider Chinese cinema as my inspirational source. This is just like learning how to paint. When young, you tend to reject traditional Chinese painting and fall in love with Western-style oil painting. But as you grow older, Chinese-style painting will come back to you as your favorite.

Xu Jinglei

I am a big fan of Zhang Yimou and Jiang Wen. I like Zhang's *To Live* and Jiang's *In the Heat of the Sun*. But what I like does not necessarily translate to what I would like to do. Furthermore, I am not the kind of person who likes to study a lot of other people's works before starting to create my own. Maybe this is partly due to the fact that I majored in acting at BFA and didn't have enough exposure to the histories of both foreign and Chinese cinemas. As a matter of fact, I consider myself quite ignorant of cinema. Maybe in the future I'll become more conscious of all the great works before me.

Zhang Ming

Nowadays it becomes almost fashionable for some to associate Chinese cinema with such films as *Goddess, Street Angel, Spring in a Small Town*, and *Crows and Sparrows*, as if they represented the core tradition of Chinese cinema. To me, however, the cinematic tradition of China is most evidently expressed in the works of early filmmakers like Zheng Zhenqiu and Zhang

Chapter Seven

Shichuan. You can easily find influences of Hollywood and Soviet Montage in Chinese the cinema of the 1930s and 40s, but in films like *Orphan Rescues Grandfather* (1923), Western influences are minimal. There is a close cultural connection between these early films and the opera tradition of China. Actually, it's not limited to pre-1930s' Chinese cinema. From the 1940s' *Spring River Flows East* to most of Xie Jin's films, cinema's connection to Chinese opera runs quite deep. One of the most important characteristics of Chinese opera lies in its moralization of the complicated world. In Chinese opera, almost everything is judged in moral terms, and characters are sharply divided into four types: evil, good, lewd, and virtuous. The complicated world and human emotions are simplified and transformed into a moral issue. This remarkable feature of Chinese opera is implanted in many films, and it actually appeals to the general audience.

When I got involved in filmmaking, my first wish was to break away from the opera-centered tradition of Chinese cinema, and give Chinese cinema a fresh look. I think dividing the world in terms of good vs. evil makes people intellectually lazy and prevents them from getting closer to the truth. When I first saw *Yellow Earth*, therefore, I was enthralled. It's not because this is my type of film, but because it gives me a fresh feeling that is entirely different from conventional Chinese films. To me, the freshness of a film is of vital importance.

Of course, I don't consider myself heavily influenced by the Fifth Generation. Since the very beginning of my film career, I've been thinking of the issue as to why the power of Chinese culture is seldom visible in today's reality, as well as in our films. I find myself in sharp disagreement with the Fifth Generation and their veiled adoption of a foreigner's viewpoint of China. When I was making my first film, therefore, I told myself to stick firmly to my own point of view and not rely on a perceived foreigner's viewpoint.

Zhang Yang

There are some great films in history of Chinese cinema. *Street Angel* of the 1930s, for example, is one of my favorites. When I first saw the film, I was quite surprised that China could make such an outstanding film back then. Those classical films, however, are not powerful enough to transform my view of cinema. Maybe I was too young to understand the significance of the film. I was only a film fan in my twenties when I first saw *Street Angel*.

Films by the Fifth Generation, on the other hand, really had an impact on me. At least those films, different in style and look, changed my view about what cinema is. My father is also involved in cinema, one of the so-called "Fourth Generation" filmmakers. But my father's generation left us few interesting works. Personally, I think there is nothing in their films, and they are even far inferior to the works of the early 1950s. Films of the early 1950s are worth seeing not because of their subject matter but because of the sincere revolutionary passion expressed in the films. You can tell from their films that the filmmakers really believed truth was on their side. In addition, filmmaking was a much longer process in the early 1950s. Directors had more time to "observe and learn from life" before production started. Therefore, even a film like *The Child Soldier Named Zhang Ga* has some great shots. My father's generation, on the other hand, lived in an age of confusion and chaos. They made absolutely no good films.

Despite the fact that the Fifth Generation taught me what cinema ought to be, individually none of them are my idols. I like Zhang Yimou's *The Story of Qiu Ju*, *To Live*, and Chen Kaige's *Farewell My Concubine*, but I've never considered these two as "masters" of cinema. Why? First of all, their films vary in quality. There is a great disparity in their output, some outstanding, some quite average. Second, it seems to me that they don't have consistent views of cinema and life. Between the beautiful imagery and their subjectivity there seems to be an impenetrable curtain in the middle. You can hardly get a glimpse of them as unique individuals. As a matter of fact, they are consciously imitating some of the classical works by foreign filmmakers. On the other hand, Hou Hsiao-Hsien and Edward Yang to me are the two real masters of cinema. It's not because their films are much better, but because they reveal the strong will and subjectivity of the two filmmakers. Just take a look at Hou's films. All of them actually bear strong personal marks of Hou. His views about the society and environment in which he lives bleed through the seemingly quiet surface.

Zhang Yuan

I was like someone who'd been starved for a long time on being admitted to BFA's cinematography department. I devoured the films of Martin Scorsese, watching *Taxi Driver*, *Mean Streets*, and others dozens of times. I also studied the works of Italian directors like [Michelangelo] Antonioni and [Federico] Fellini. But my biggest revelation was seeing Chinese films of the 1930s. To me, that was the time when Chinese cinema was at its liveliest, its most stylistic and passionate. Later on, Chen Kaige's *Yellow Earth* and Zhang Yimou's *Red Sorghum* also had a strong impact on me. Despite these influences, my films in no way resemble theirs.

CHAPTER EIGHT

Chinese Cinema in the Context of Globalization: Dilemmas and Opportunities

Viewed from a historical perspective, there is nothing new about Chinese cinema either benefiting from or being challenged by globalization. Immediately after the "birth" of cinema in Paris, the Lumiere brothers' and [Thomas] Edison's films were brought to Shanghai by Western showmen for public exhibitions. Starting from the 1920s, foreign film companies, especially those of the United States, began to build their distribution centers in Shanghai. By the mid-1930s, the eight Hollywood studios—MGM, Paramount, Warner's, Columbia, Twentieth Century Fox, Universal, RKO, and the United Artists—had succeeded in monopolizing the distribution and exhibition of first-run films in coastal cities of China. In 1933, for example, China made eighty-four feature films, but this achievement was dwarfed by the fact that, in the same year, a total of 431 foreign films were imported into China, out of which 353 were Hollywood products. There are many reasons why this wave of globalization is "new". First of all, when the first Hollywood film, The Fugitive, *was introduced into the Chinese film market after decades-long period of self-imposed policy of seclusion, Chinese cinema was at its low ebb. As a result, a few Hollywood blockbusters managed to dominate the Chinese film market with more than 60 percent of the market share. Second, the global trend toward media consolidation in recent years has concentrated power in a handful of transnational corporations, which has given these media giants an added advantage in dominating the global market. This is especially true after China joined the WTO club in 2002. As "wolves" are making their way into China, many Chinese critics and filmmakers argue that globalization or, more specifically, Hollywood dominance, will inevitably take its toll on the very existence of Chinese cinema. There are also some in the Chinese film community claiming that the lack of creativity as well as the censorship apparatus of China, not Hollywood, is to be blamed for Chinese cinema's lackluster performance. How does Chinese cinema face the challenge of globalization, and is it possible for Chinese cinema to rival Hollywood on a global scale in the near future? The interviewers posed these difficult questions to the filmmakers.*

* * *

Guan Hu

I don't consider globalization a grave threat to Chinese cinema. Since ancient times, China culture has shown a remarkable ability to assimilate foreign cultures. This cultural tenacity will remain strong despite increasing globalization. As for Chinese cinema rivaling or even replacing Hollywood's worldwide dominance, it's absolutely out of the question. Big problems aside, language itself is a factor that limits Chinese cinema. English-language cinema has its unparalleled advantage in the international film market. It's not an issue that can be easily solved through dubbing or subtitling. Rather than fantasizing about a utopian future for Chinese cinema, therefore, I think we should focus on making those films that are distinctive to our culture, such as Xiaoshuai's *Beijing Bicycle*. So long as we continue to make that kind of film, Chinese cinema will have an irreplaceable place in the world. Just take a look at Japanese cinema, Iranian cinema, and Korean cinema. All of them impress us with their distinct qualities. Although Chinese cinema used to be quite representative of its culture, it seems to me it has recently shown signs of departing from that direction.

However, I still feel good about Chinese cinema in general. At least each aspiring filmmaker is busy doing something. What concerns me most is the level of competence of Chinese filmmakers. I'm telling you the truth. Many of us don't want to recognize this problem, but instead name other things, such as the censorship system, as the major obstacle to the further development of Chinese cinema. In reality, no system is perfect. For example, most of us admire the achievements of Iranian cinema, but is the Iranian film system better than ours? If the censorship system is suffocating Chinese cinema, why are there always two or three excellent films emerging in China every year? Therefore, I think the most urgent thing is to foster and enhance our talent and level of competence in filmmaking.

Jia Zhangke

From a broader point of view, globalization has already taken place in almost all aspects of filmmaking. Just use the 2002 Cannes Film Festival as an example. Many films shown at the festival were co-productions that involved several countries. [Alexander] Sokurov's *Russian Ark* was jointly produced by Germany, France, and Russia. My *Unknown Pleasure* was co-financed by Japan, France, and Hong Kong. In response to this transnational trend of production, Cannes in 2002 began to use the director's home country to categorize the origin of the selected films. Prior to that, the producer's name was used for the purpose of categorization. I think this change reflects Cannes' recognition of the transnational nature of today's film production: a film can be produced by several countries, but the creator or the "author" of the film has his/her own individual styles and concerns.

As for whether transnational or global financing affects a director's work, it is difficult to generalize. Some directors may find it quite easy to handle, while others do not. Besides, the extent of producers' involvement in filmmaking varies. Here's what I think: suppose Hou Hsiao-hsien's next project was going to be financed by fifteen different countries across the globe, Hou would still turn out a Taiwanese film. Transnational financing wouldn't alter his way of doing things. To some filmmakers, however, certain compromises may be necessary. Just to give you one example: I love Edward Yang's *A One and A Two* and consider it a masterwork. But I don't particularly like the sequence where the protagonist meets with his girlfriend in Japan. I think this entire sequence could be edited out. My guess is that, because the film was chiefly financed by Japanese money, Yang might have had to keep this sequence in to attract the Japanese audience. As for me, I don't remember whether I've made any compromises simply because of the sources of money. Of course, it is another matter in terms of marketing and promotion. My producers frequently change the marketing strategies of my films. In Japan, for example, *Platform*'s poster features two women, because women account for a large percentage of film audiences in Japan. Japanese men are too busy. They have little spare time for films.

In my view, for Chinese cinema to compete in the global market, the formation of a market-driven film industry is of vital importance. Let me illustrate this with a fairy tale. Suppose I am suddenly empowered with the magic ability of cloning [Federico] Fellini and Spielberg. With the maximum of ten, I am allowed to either clone five Fellinis and five Spielbergs or simply make them all Fellinis or Spielbergs. What will I do? For the sake of Chinese cinema, I'd clone ten Spielbergs. Why? It's because the film industry in China is in serious trouble. China's commercial cinema is almost non-existent. This is quite worrisome. In the areas of art film and independent cinema, each year some new directors always emerge, and the production value of their works is maintained at a healthy level. But in the area of commercial cinema, it is almost impossible to pinpoint a real talent. Feng Xiaogang and Zhang Yimou might be two exceptions. But besides them, can you name someone else? Maybe Teng Wenji is one, but I think his films are neither artistic nor commercial.[xxxii] Even when a director is given the opportunity to make a commercial film, he or she usually shows little interest in craft and perfection. I saw Lu Chuan's *The Missing Gun* the other day. Although this film has many flaws, there is one thing I appreciate most: Lu Chuan's enterprising spirit. He knew this was a commercial film, but you can sense that he was determined to craft it with every possible means. Unfortunately, there are few directors like Lu Chuan in China. I hope Chinese cinema won't follow the footstep of Taiwan cinema. Besides Hou Hsiao-hsien, Edward Yang, and Tsai Ming-liang, who else is making films in Taiwan? In Taiwan, the commercial market is completely dominated by

Hollywood. Worst of all, the audience seems to have abandoned Chinese-language cinema in favor of English-language films. You can blame the audience, but ultimately it's because not a single locally made commercial film can attract that audience.

I still have hope for Chinese cinema, however. First of all, China has such a huge population, and its market potential is enormous. Second, I always believe every nation has a strong interest in its own experience and history. It is especially so for the Chinese people. History, both ancient and modern, has endowed us with so many collective memories and public topics that there are a lot of common areas yet to be explored. It is easier for a film to succeed if it tackles the uncharted areas in the public space. Private topics will inevitably alienate some audiences. Third, I also believe China has enough talent and financial resources. There is plenty of idle capital in our society. I was once approached by a pharmaceutical entrepreneur. He was very interested in financing a film. Since his company's annual profit was more than 100 million RMB, a budget of 3 million was not a big number at all. While his major concern was not to make money, he certainly expected certain tangible results from this investment. Because I couldn't guarantee that the film would pass the censors and shown in theaters, he finally decided to call it off. Once a film-friendly environment is created, therefore, I think Chinese cinema will eventually take off.

Jiang Wen

I don't quite understand what "national cinema" means. If the term "national cinema" means the whole body of a nation's films, then every single film we see today, including Hollywood movies, belongs to a certain "national cinema". I can easily distinguish a Hollywood movie by just having a glimpse of it. The joy and anger as well as the lifestyle of the Americans are entirely different from that of Europeans and Asians. Ethnically speaking, the United States is not a country as pure as Japan, India, or Uzbekistan. But even as mixed as the United States is, it also has its distinct cultures and regional characters. Looking from the perspective of reception, one can only say that it seems to be much easier for the audience around the world to appreciate American movies. But this doesn't mean that Hollywood is immune from regionalism. So, let's analyze this step by step. If Hollywood movies are also regionally based, why do we feel it is much easier to appreciate them? I think the answer is quite obvious. It is the overall influence of the United States as a country, not American movies alone, that makes this possible. As the old saying goes, when water rises, the boat floats higher. Hollywood is sailing on the big water of the United States, while other cinemas do not have the support of this rising water.

Chapter Eight

If you agree with me on the above, let's go back to the analysis of American society. As a society that is composed of immigrants from all over the world, America is characteristically open to all kinds of people and ideas. People of different national origins and racial backgrounds live together, creating a diverse mosaic that is rare in other societies. Walking down the streets of the United States, oftentimes you can't tell which ethnicity the person coming in the opposite direction belongs to. This is the reality of the American society. As a comparison, let's then take a look as the situation in Uzbekistan. With few people of the black or yellow race, the Uzbekistani society remains largely homogeneous in lifestyle and cultural tradition. On the other hand, compared to that of the United States, the overall strength of Uzbekistan as a nation is far less influential on the world stage. Thus, to understand Uzbekistani cinema, one also needs to spend a lot of time on the understanding of many previously unfamiliar things. In contrast, understanding American movies is a lot easier, because the United States as a country has already done the propaganda and paved the way for the easy appreciation of its movies. Since counties like Uzbekistan do not possess this kind of invisible capital, audiences have to ask a series of questions in order to fully appreciate their films. Even for a person who has never been to the United States, images of American cowboys, cops, and street gangs are not alien to him/her at all. Much of this familiarity, it appears to me, comes not from movie watching, but from the overwhelming amount of interest or concerns he/she has shown to the United States in general. Many questions would remain unanswered if we neglected the interconnection or mutual empowerment between a nation's cinema and its political and economic might. This is the reason why I also consider Hollywood a regionally based national cinema, a cinema that is as typical and distinctive as that of Russia and Uzbekistan, if one disregards political and economic factors.

Hollywood's "regional" characteristics can be further illustrated with the fact that its filmmaking is not something that is easy for China to mimic. First of all, we don't have that stage. It is only after [Arnold] Schwarzenegger left Europe and migrated to the United States that he was able to turn himself into today's Schwarzenegger. If he were still in Austria, he never would have become today's Schwarzenegger. Second, we don't have that kind of economic, political, and cultural network that can quickly turn a local or regional issue into a global event. For example, you don't feel too strange when Hollywood makes a fuss about a few GIs' death or anger in Vietnam, because the Vietnam War was widely covered by global media outlets. The whole world knew about the American involvement in Vietnam. Without such widespread news coverage, people in other parts of the world would have a hard time understanding such a film. From here you can see how the two forces, filmic and non-filmic, are interconnected.

I also don't see how transnational filmmaking affects the so-called "national cinema". As a matter of fact, transnational or multinational filmmaking is not as frequent as some of us might think in today's film production. In addition, the label "transnational" could be quite misleading because the "transnational" production between China and the United States is not the same as that among European countries. Connected by the European Union and their small size, European countries have a lot in common, including some degree of linguistic similarity. The interaction or cooperation among EU countries is very similar to provincial relations in China. In other words, it's quite natural, or even necessary, for EU countries to engage in all kinds of "transnational" activities. If every province of China were considered a foreign country, then the frequency of so-called "transnational" financing in filmmaking would certainly increase.

I think language plays a more important role than the state in determining filmmaking trends. For instance, when France markets its films, it probably first considers the French-speaking territories. Only then would the English, German, or Spanish-speaking territories be considered. Similarly, for Chinese cinema, language is increasingly becoming *the* factor that unites the markets of the Chinese-speaking countries or regions. In this sense, the term "transnational" only points to the interaction or integration of countries that have already shared common cultural and linguistic heritages.

As for the possibility of Chinese cinema rivaling Hollywood, let's suspend this fantasy all together and take a look at the film market and audience in general. As I've said earlier, the overall strength of a nation and its cinema is correlated. Because the United States is the only remaining superpower, many people in the world are dying to know or understand everything about that country. You can't deny that Hollywood benefits a great deal from this eagerness to understand the United States. If the whole world someday wanted desperately to know or understand everything about China, then the market for Chinese cinema would no doubt be greatly expanded. But in order for the people around the world to become intensely interested in you, what qualifications do you need to have? You must at least possess two things: national strength and the power of worldwide influence. Don't you agree? Let's make it clearer by giving this example: today you decide to interview me, not somebody else, not because I am the most authoritative voice on this issue, but because I've made a few films and established certain name in the area, right? Therefore, you can't deny the fact that the strength or influence of a nation is a big boost to the popularity of that nation's cinema. What on earth has made the fucking Coke-Cola, only a cheap soda, so popular throughout the world? Isn't it because the drink is

Chapter Eight

produced in America and therefore carries a certain aura of the United States? Isn't it because American GIs are taking it all over the world with their tanks and guns? To make it possible for the Chinese cinema to rival Hollywood, therefore, you need a lot of backups beyond cinema itself. When China as a nation trails behind the United States in capital, worldwide influence, and people's willingness to accept its values and culture, how can you expect Chinese cinema to rival Hollywood?

Jin Chen

I think Chinese cinema has already established itself around the globe. Why should it be afraid of globalization? Of course, becoming a dominant force like American cinema is still a long way off. First of all, it will take a long time for a purely market-driven film industry to develop. China's total annual box-office is almost negligible compared to its GDP figures. You can certainly list a number of factors that caused this sluggish development: the poor distribution system, the ill-equipped exhibition venues, and the lack of clear-cut laws and regulations concerning censorship, for example. But the ultimate cause, I believe, is the rigid system. If we still view cinema not as a form of culture, entertainment, or business, but as an ideological weapon, then a market-driven film industry would never take shape. Second, the growth of China's cinema relies very much on the general development of Chinese society and economy. If the outlook of the latter is rosy, then people, including the authorities, would look at certain cultural phenomena with a more tolerant attitude. When cinema is truly understood as a cultural phenomenon, as an enterprise that can boost the image of the country and other related industries, and as an integral part of Chinese culture, it will then undergo tremendous growth. Right now I don't see such a development coming. You can make one or two good films, but this can't change the overall situation.

If the rigid system persists, it is even unrealistic to expect a scenario in which Chinese cinema occupies a substantial market share in Asia. Right now the popularity of Korean and Japanese cinemas is on the rise. Chinese cinema used to be far more influential than that of Korea and Japan. This was especially true in the 1980s. At that time, Chinese cinema, particularly the cinema of the Fifth Generation, sent a shock wave through the international film community with its bold ideas and refreshing styles. That was probably the peak for Chinese cinema. With the exception of the commercial cinema of Hong Kong, Chinese cinema came to be understood as a symbol of Asian cinema. But the momentum has now shifted to Korea and Japan. After a number of years of reform and rebuilding, Japanese and Korean cinemas have really transformed themselves and established their strong foothold in world cinema. For the next decade at least, therefore, China won't be the center of Asian cinema.

Li Xin

I don't think globalization will threaten the development of national cinema. On the contrary, it will have a positive impact on national cinema. Films with strong national characteristics will no doubt survive the globalized circulation of commercial products of Hollywood. It is quite possible that an increasing number of Chinese films will be funded by foreign money, and some Chinese filmmakers will also aim to make more international market-oriented films, but this doesn't mean a Chinese director's film will look the same as that of a Hollywood director. It is the viewpoint, not the subject or financing, that determines the nature of a film. A film about the Great Wall does not necessarily qualify it to be a Chinese film.

In the past, China's door was tightly closed. People inside and outside didn't know each other very well. As the door opens wider and wider, and economic disparity between China and the West is gradually shrinking, I think people's objects of concern are also beginning to converge. Films like *Suzhou River* appeal to a transnational audience because the represented issues are also what the world must confront. However, common or similar subjects do not lead to an identical point of view. No matter how "international" a Chinese film might be, it is still embedded with elements of Chinese sensibility. In representing violence, for example, two cultures may approach it from entirely different points of view. The blood you see is not the blood I see. I see it from a Chinese point of view, but you see it from a non-Chinese angle. In addition, despite anti-traditionalism in recent history, we as a generation still take great pride in our nation's cultural heritage. I think globalization can't simply take away something already embedded in your mind.

Speaking of the possibility that one day Chinese cinema might be able to effectively compete with Hollywood on the world stage, I think this assumption itself is absurd. To be honest, it seems to me that asking this question is just like asking Chinese soccer fans when China's national soccer team will win World Cup. In theory, anything is possible. But I don't think this is a question we should raise, at least for now. How far the distance is between Hollywood and Chinese cinema in terms of international influence? You tell me. I am not saying that Hollywood is flawless and perfect, but as a whole, its business model is something that will take the Chinese film industry years to learn. To me, it's already a success if a few young Chinese filmmakers' works can make their way into major commercial theater chains and be seen by the mass audience.

Chapter Eight

Rather than wasting time on the empty talk about Chinese cinema rivaling Hollywood, therefore, I think we should focus our attention on clearing our own house. Every filmmaker in China needs to answer the question as to why there is such a genuine lack of creativity in Chinese cinema. You can't simply attribute this to the system or a lack of money. It seems to me that many filmmakers' creative energy is being paralyzed by a self-assumed sense of right and wrong. When a film is structured in such a clear-cut moral framework, it leaves no space for creative imagination and aesthetic ambiguity.

Liu Binjian

To me, the single most important factor that hinders the development of Chinese cinema is censorship, or more generally, the film system itself. Money is not a major issue of concern, because independent cinema abroad also faces financial difficulties. When I talk to foreign media and friends in filmmaking, they always complain about the lack of financial support for independent cinema in their own countries. Therefore, it seems to me that politics in China really puts Chinese cinema in an awkward position. Both censorship and the slowness of film-related legislation are a drag on Chinese cinema in this transitional period. Because of the close connection between cinema and politics in China, we can't simply blame those foreigners for their simplified interpretation of Chinese cinema from a purely political point of view, either intentionally or unintentionally. To a large extent, it is we who have provided them with the weapons to use against us. In other words, we ourselves are to be blamed for giving them such an easy topic to play with. The result of this is that many Chinese films are being discussed not as an aesthetic or in filmic terms, but as a political issue when they are shown abroad. I used to be quite puzzled by this over-politicization of Chinese cinema. But against the background of the current mechanism of censorship in China, isn't it normal for them to make such a connection? In addition, because their understanding of China is usually based on sporadic and somewhat distorted media coverage in the West, the non-Chinese audience tends to view our films as a way to approach the "reality" of China. Therefore, their responses to our films are often distilled through colored glasses or filters. It is also quite normal. Isn't it true that most of us in China also tend to mistake Hollywood representations for the reality of the United States?

As for the issue of globalization and national cinema, I don't think it's my concern. To me, the most important thing is to have my own voice heard through filmmaking. In spite of all the grandiose talk, Iranian, Korean, and Japanese cinemas have found their own ways to success in recent years. What concerns me, therefore, is to break a trail for Chinese cinema. Because of the global circulation of Hollywood blockbusters, we tend to forget the fact that there is no pre-fixed model in filmmaking. Everyone is entitled to imagine and even create his/her own ways of filmmaking. The creative space is unlimited, and there is no law to stipulate that you must follow the Hollywood model of filmmaking. *Russian Ark*, for example, consists of only one ninety-minute-long shot with more than 800 characters. Regrettably, you rarely see this kind of experiment in China. I am not saying that we should follow the model of *Russian Ark*, but my question is this: since it's possible for Iran and other countries to create their own styles of filmmaking, why can't Chinese break a trail of its own?

Lou Ye

Certainly globalization will have an impact on national cinema. But the issue of what Chinese cinema is needs itself to be re-examined. When *Suzhou River* was shown in some places, it was accused of being "un-Chinese". "How can China produce such a film?" Some asked. I was a little annoyed by this question. My answer was: if your image of China is still one of long gowns and mandarin jackets, then China today is not China at all. Take a look at China today. To what extent do you understand China? There is no denying that there are many poor places in China, but China also has many cosmopolitan places. I have to say sorry, but I was born in a very cosmopolitan city that looks "un-Chinese" by your standard. I can't make films about subjects I am unfamiliar with. It is not my job to focus on poverty just because you don't have poverty [in your country], or to show long gowns and mandarin jackets because you find them exotic. Do not first ask the question about whether it is a Chinese film. Just go see the film if you feel like it, or save a few dollars if you don't.

Once you are on an equal footing with them [the West], they will immediately raise their eyebrows. Questions like "How can you make films that we are supposed to make?" and claims like "the human predicament is our concern, not yours" will be heard. Yes, you'll get a different kind of attention if you are working in that milieu. As a matter of fact, *Suzhou River* has already achieved this goal. I felt especially proud of that. Not a Chinese film? It's impossible. You are in doubt because your conception of "Chinese cinema" itself is wrong. In a fast developing country like China, ten years is equivalent to thirty or forty of your years. If you don't catch on, you will forever be in a fog.

Of course there are some Chinese directors who might be eager to show what others like to see, but this is not what I want to do. Although I am not totally against this practice, because there are reasonable explanations behind it, I personally don't like such a practice. I want to film what interests me most. To me, it is quite ridiculous that some filmmakers in China, although born and bought up in China, are eager to jump from their position and look at China from a foreigner's point of view, namely, that I will film whatever interests you. Maybe this practice can be tolerated at the beginning of one's career, but it is absolutely absurd if it becomes a professional habit.

The most serious and obvious problem facing Chinese cinema is the system. It is far too early to discuss what kind of films a director is going to make, because making a film is already such a daunting task. For a director, it is already a remarkable thing to simply continue with this career in the current situation, let alone to choose what kind of films to make. Of course some people might have a different opinion about where the problem lies in Chinese cinema, but my view is that you must first reform the system. The concern for artistic style and creativity is secondary. In other words, if you don't reform the system, few films can be made. Even if a few films are eventually made, what use are they if they can't be released in China? The issue of the market can't be separated from this fundamental concern. Why? Although in theory this industry should be a profitable one, filmmaking [in China] is still a risky business. But the current system, specifically the censorship system, is making this risky business even riskier. Investors are not so stupid: Since I don't even know whether your project will pass the censors, why should I put my money into it? So, the whole industry is short of money. Few people in China invest in film. Someone who throws money into filmmaking must be out of his mind. Yes, from a purely business point of view, such a person is certainly crazy. No one in his/her right mind would invest in Chinese films. Of course I am now referring only to the situation in China's domestic film market. This does not include the scenario where some investors might be willing to throw money into filmmaking because the film is aimed at the overseas market. This is also the reason that a lot of money for filmmaking comes from outside of China. Although small, there is a healthy market in some foreign countries for Chinese cinema. Only when there is such a market in China will there be investment. Since we don't have either investors or a market, it is absolutely futile to talk about what kind of films, artistic or commercial, we ought to make. It is simply premature.

To become a cinematic power like Hollywood is an extremely remote issue, far from what we need to deal with today. It requires a comprehensive effort and extremely conducive conditions. The most likely scenario is that Chinese cinema will not need to "go global", because the Chinese market is already big enough to feed cinema. So, we must take one step at a time, solving our own problems first. [South] Korea is a case in point. It first solved the problem of film censorship. Then, the market issue emerged. It immediately realized that its own market was not big enough, which prompted it to turn to its neighbors in Asia. [South] Korea's strategy, therefore, has been to extend its influence throughout Asia. Only after Asia is "occupied" will it turn toward Europe or the United States. It is a healthy development. Indeed, Chinese cinema is far behind that of [South] Korea. There is a great distance for the whole Chinese industry to overcome. China is not short of good filmmakers, but the system is severely flawed. Maybe in several years, these talented directors will run off to [South] Korea to make films. It is a highly possible scenario, because [South] Korea is relatively short of filmmaking talent. Although there are frequent hits, [South] Korea's production power as a whole is not strong enough. It has money, but is relatively weak in directing power. So, Korean producers will waste no time in searching for talented directors outside of Korea, or will simply invest in foreign productions. There is nothing strange about this. Business speaks the language of profit.

Lu Chuan

I think Chinese cinema will no doubt survive the wave of globalization. Relying on its financial power and worldwide network of distribution, Hollywood may succeed in occupying a substantial market share in China. But there is still much room for Chinese cinema to maneuver. On the production side, the fact that two or three Chinese directors are hired by Hollywood to make Hollywood-style blockbusters won't seriously affect the nature of Chinese cinema. Besides, it is highly possible that although my money may come from Hollywood or other outside sources I will still make a distinctively Chinese film. An obvious example of this is He Ping's *Warriors of Heaven and Earth*. In my view, capital is not the only factor that determines the nature of a film. Like a seasonal wind, capital has no color and boundary. If this wind blows across China, it would only enable more Chinese directors to get their films made. This is absolutely a good thing for Chinese cinema, because most of them would still make Chinese films, not Hollywood products. To me, therefore, foreign money is a positive boost for Chinese cinema. Money alone can't destroy Chinese cinema.

Can Chinese cinema one day rival Hollywood? I don't see such a possibility, at least in the foreseeable future. As a matter of fact, it's already a daunting task for Chinese cinema to play a dominant role in Asia, let alone in the world. Why? Many people would probably point at the film censorship system in China. I don't deny the fact that the censorship system is a serious obstacle that hampers the growth of Chinese cinema. I always dream the dream that, like what happened in Korea years ago, censorship in China will suddenly disappear overnight, filmmakers will be allowed to make whatever

Chapter Eight

they wanted to make, and the Film Bureau will only handle the matters that concern market management, cinema chains, computer ticketing, and anti-piracy. However, I think the Chinese film system is only a secondary factor that affects the development of Chinese cinema. Most crucial is creativity or lack of creativity. There may be two or three world-class filmmakers in China, and occasionally they are capable of achieving breakthroughs. But a few exceptional directors or films cannot change the whole picture. Creatively, Chinese cinema as a whole is no match for the visual, cultural, and ideological power of Hollywood. What do we have to offer the world? So far we've only been able to export the image of a lamenting woman. How can you rely on a crying woman to conquer the world? You may be able to win a few sympathetic tears with such an image. To compete with the power of Hollywood, however, you also need powerful ideas and abundant financial resources. This is why I don't see Chinese cinema being a dominant player in the foreseeable future.

Lu Xuechang

I don't think there is a direct link between the lackluster performance of Chinese cinema and Hollywood's penetration. Before Hollywood blockbusters entered the Chinese market, Chinese cinema was not doing well, either. It's certainly not a bad thing at all for the Chinese to see more foreign films. When I was in Paris in 2002, what struck me most was the French enthusiasm for foreign films. I remember it was on a rainy day that I decided to go see Edward Yang's *A One and A Two*. When I arrived at the cinema, to my great surprise, there was a very long line of people waiting outside the box-office. All of them were there to see *A One and A Two*. The film was more than three hours long, but I noted that not a single audience member left the fully-packed theater in the middle of the screening. The audience was apparently drawn to the film, and some of them wept. To be frank, I was overwhelmed by this respect and enthusiasm for cinema and culture. I am quite envious of such an audience. It will take a long time to cultivate the Chinese audience to reach that level. I think the best way to raise Chinese people's level of film appreciation is to allow them the opportunity to be exposed to a variety of film cultures. Allowing more foreign films, not necessarily Hollywood blockbusters, into China will help to cultivate Chinese audiences' sensibility of cinema, which will in turn benefit Chinese cinema as a whole. I believe there is definitely a connection between cinema and the overall cultural attainments of a people. If a nation's educational and cultural levels remain low, its cinema will reflect that. Certainly this does not mean it's impossible for a few great filmmakers to emerge from such a cinema, such as Tran Anh Hung from Vietnamese cinema. But overall, the levels of education and culture and of cinema are correspondent. There may be a few cinematic masters in China, but mediocrity is the word that best describes Chinese cinema overall.

Despite the fact that the current trend of globalization, which is dominated by the global expansion of the Hollywood empire, will in the long run affect national cinema, I have to say that I am cautiously optimistic about the fate of national cinema. I remember, in 2001, the Cannes Committee sent me a questionnaire, on which all the questions asked were somewhat related to the issue of national cinema and its opposition to Hollywood. My feeling is that although Hollywood will probably continue to dominate the world commercial market, many films, such as those by cinematic masters, won't be overshadowed by the Hollywood-centered globalization. I can't see too far ahead, but I do believe that national cinema is not going to die in the near future. France, for instance, still produces some great works each year, including one of my favorites, *Rosetta*. These kinds of films will have a long life. Most commercial theaters in Europe will surely continue to play Hollywood blockbusters. There's nothing to be done about it. Although American pop culture is a target of resentment, Hollywood blockbusters are still the favorites of European commercial theaters. However, there are also many art cinemas in Europe. It is in these theaters that some amazing works find their home, including China's *Suzhou River*, *Xiao Wu*, and the classical works by [Jean-Luc] Godard. There is definitely a niche market for this kind of film. If one day the whole cinematic landscape were completely taken over by the Hollywood-style globalization, then I would quit filmmaking and make a fortune in the business of film distribution.

I guess what I want to convey is that you can't simply blame globalization for the internal problems of Chinese cinema. First and foremost, the overall system is of vital importance in determining the direction of Chinese cinema. I remember it was immediately after Deng Xiaoping's policy speech in the south that China began to unleash a series of earthshaking changes. I suspect if there were a film-friendly policy in place, Chinese cinema would probably undergo dramatic changes overnight. There are a lot of geniuses and intelligent people among the population of 1.3 billion. You can't imagine how many of them would emerge if such an environment existed. Certainly, some directors would still make equally bad films within an improved system, but many new ideas and talents would no doubt emerge. Besides the system, as I mentioned before, there is also something quite hopeless about the Chinese audience, which makes me feel that it is probably easier for Chinese cinema to establish its image abroad than home. I remember when *A Lingering Face* was shown in Nanning, a city in Guangxi Province, I was invited there to introduce the film. My original

Chapter Eight

excitement was soon replaced by bewilderment after the film started. I still vividly remember that the whole theater felt just like a market on that day. There were young lovers talking cheerfully to each other, and the sound of people cracking dried melon seeds permeated in the air. I suspect some people would have knit sweaters if the theater were a little brighter. After that experience, for a long time, I was not so sure about why I wanted to be a filmmaker in the first place.

As for the possibility that Chinese cinema could one day rival Hollywood on the world stage, I think this is too remote and idealistic. When Hollywood produced its first group of commercial movies, what was the situation of cinema in China? I've always wondered whether it is worthwhile for China to invest a large amount of money in the area of commercial filmmaking. If the money spent on a commercial movie only resulted in another worthless work destined to be stored away in warehouse without even minimum exhibition, why don't you just let Hollywood do it and label it as a Beijing Film Studio production? As a matter of fact, in the area of the art film, China has already established its reputation in the world, but China's commercial cinema is almost nonexistent in the global market. What I mean by "commercial cinema" includes not only production, but marketing, distribution, and exhibition as well. As a business operation, Chinese cinema is in no way a qualified competitor with Hollywood. That's why I always say that if we can't play soccer well, why not just concentrate on perfecting our Ping-Pong? In other words, why don't we just make full use of our advantages and concentrate on the lives that Hollywood is incapable of depicting? Personally, I find Hollywood blockbusters quite boring and full of clichés. From my childhood to my formal film education at BFA, small films from Europe have always been objects of my admiration.

Ma Liwen

I think national cinema will continue to grow despite globalization. Global financing doesn't necessarily mean all films will be stripped of their national character. *Crouching Tiger and Hidden Dragon* is one successful example of this. Although financed by foreign money, it's still a Chinese film. Some small films, such as *Xiao Wu* and *Old Men*, are even more exemplary. Despite the fact that money came mainly from outside sources, all these films are concerned about the ordinary people of China and their lives.

To me, therefore, it's more meaningful to focus our attention on improving Chinese cinema itself. Many people would blame the censorship system for the sluggish development of Chinese cinema. But my take is different. I think some Chinese filmmakers are simply too opportunistic. They view filmmaking more as a quick way to money and fame. Once this goal is obstructed, they find it easy to turn away from filmmaking and rush to something more profitable. In today's society, there are so many temptations and opportunities. Many people have simply lost their spirit of perseverance. Some of my former classmates have either "jumped into the sea of business" or married rich men. I think the whole Chinese film industry is being reshuffled.

Meng Qi

Chinese cinema has a long way to go to compete with Hollywood. First of all, I think there are few smart people working in today's Chinese film industry. My definition of "smart people" refers to those who are both thoughtful and creative. The lack of creative talents is probably the reason why I decided to jump into filmmaking in the first place. We should feel shamed of the fact that filmmakers like Zhang Yimou and Chen Kaige are still at center stage in Chinese cinema after two decades of domination. Why are there so few people who can take over the lead from Zhang and Chen? Don't you agree it is pitiful?

You might think I sound a little arrogant, but I view it as an expression of self-confidence. Although I've only made one film so far, I am confident that I will eventually earn myself a place in Chinese cinema. If I were an American, I would probably give up the idea of becoming a filmmaker, simply because there are too many smart people working in the film industry. As the old Chinese idiom says, I would rather be a chicken head than a phoenix tail. I don't know how the insiders really think of me, but I feel I am more experienced in life than those of my age who were formally educated in film. If given the opportunity, I think I could do better.

Of course the competitiveness of Chinese cinema also depends on a favorable environment. If current state controls are eased, I think people of talent will have more opportunities to explore a broader range of subjects, such as gangsters, prostitutes, and slums. Without censorship, the prospects for Chinese cinema would be very promising. It is always been my belief that to win other people's respect you must first be confident about yourself. When we are self-confident as a nation, why do we have to worry about the future of national cinema? Today's youngsters are living in an age of instant communication. They can approach the outside world through different means, the Internet, satellite dishes, pirated DVDs, you name it. As a result, they tend to blindly follow the trendy things of the West, and view their own tradition as nothing but outdated. If we as filmmakers felt the same way, then national cinema would be in real danger.

To enhance the competitiveness of Chinese cinema in the global market, therefore, it is imperative for us to first build confidence in our own culture.

Chapter Eight

Our ancestors left us a great tradition, within which many elements are timeless. If we can somehow utilize these rich resources and embed them in our filmic representations, I think we will pave the way for Chinese cinema to go global. To be frank, I don't see there is any culture in the world that can possibly match the richness and sophistication of Chinese culture, because it used to be at the peak of human civilization. Although not living in the glorious days of Tang China, we are still a privileged group of people with a rich tradition other people can only envy. As long as the spirit of this tradition runs through our cinema, I think Chinese cinema will for sure survive the global expansion of Hollywood.

Shi Runjiu

The issue of globalization concerns me to a certain degree, but I don't consider it a decisive factor that affects the development of Chinese cinema. It seems to me that the fate of Chinese cinema is ultimately determined by Chinese filmmakers themselves. Every one has his/her own view about what has gone wrong with Chinese cinema, but I always feel that Chinese filmmakers also need to do some soul-searching as to whether they are fully devoted to their profession. A devoted filmmaker sets high demands on himself/herself and fulfills his/her professional duty with honesty and wholeheartedness. If every filmmaker were following these professional standards, Chinese cinema wouldn't be as lackluster as it is today. If filmmakers are easily lured by money and fame, as well as the mentality of "get rich quick and instant benefits", then Chinese cinema would remain mediocre even if the general environment were conducive to creative filmmaking.

    I am not saying that Hollywood's presence doesn't constitute pressure for Chinese cinema, but compared to what I've mentioned above, this pressure is not of vital importance. To most Chinese audiences, watching Hollywood blockbusters is only a matter of occasional change of flavors. These films are light-hearted, eye-pleasing, and perfect for relaxation. But just as one is not going to eat every meal at McDonalds, Chinese audiences won't spend all their film time on Hollywood blockbusters. For this reason, I think there is no need to worry about the presence of Hollywood in China.

    It is certainly another matter if we are talking about the possibility of Chinese cinema becoming as influential as Hollywood in the global context. The success of the global penetration of Hollywood is a result of that country's youthful energy and unmatchable wealth. Hollywood is the place where film-related capital and talents are concentrated. Its creative energy and financial power attract almost all filmmakers around the world. To rival Hollywood on a global scale, China must first revitalize itself in creativity and imagination. But this is not an easy task for a country with such a heavy burden of a long history and tradition. If you've been to the vast Chinese countryside, you would agree with me that it is the reality of China: poor and underdeveloped. To China, therefore, rivaling Hollywood or the United States in general is neither possible today nor realistic for the generations to come.

Tang Danian

There is nothing one can do with regard to the global expansion of Hollywood. To a funny way today's Hollywood filmmaking very much resembles a transnational terrorist organization because it operates on an increasingly borderless level. To talk about Chinese cinema rivaling Hollywood, therefore, is absolutely illusionary. A few films from China might be able to cross borders and reach commercial theaters worldwide, but very likely these are the ones backed by international financing and distribution. One such example is Zhang Yimou's *Hero*. Being part of the global operation of the Hollywood empire, the film seems to be more a Hollywood production than a Chinese film. It appears that Asian cinema is also following this trend. Many pan-Asian productions consist of a mixed crew and cast, with people from Hong Kong, Korea, Japan, China, and other parts of Asia. In other words, Hollywood or Hollywood-style practices seem to have triumphed over national cinema. If this trend continues, I suspect that except for a few high-minded intellectuals few people will stand up to Hollywood's hegemony.

However, Hollywood only exemplifies one kind of cinema, the kind of cinema that is built on the logic of entertainment and money. There is another kind of film, the kind of film that is for the purpose of self-expression and human life. As long as human beings continue to exist, the urge for self-expression will never subside, and film is a powerful medium for this purpose. The main difference between the two cinemas does not lie in how an individual film is made and where the film originates, but in the conception of cinema: is cinema essentially a cultural industry or a medium for human expression? If the answer is the latter, then, in face of the global expansion of the former, the state needs to step in. To maintain a vibrant cinema that is either nationally distinctive or artistically expressive, it is not enough to rely only on the market forces. Just look at French cinema. It is exactly because of state support that French cinema remains an active force on the world stage in both quality and quantity. If the state relinquishes its power completely to the market, then the space for national cinema or art film would increasingly diminish. Consequently, most filmmakers in the world would be probably lured by the power of money and start to help Hollywood further expand its territory and domination.

Chapter Eight

Wang Chao

I think we need to make a distinction between the art film and the commercial film. Globalization means different things for different forms of cinema. As far as the art film is concerned, it is not so important to consider who the financier is or whether the market share is threatened by the global expansion of Hollywood. What matters most for the art film is the director or film *auteur*. For example, the most likely questions people would ask regarding *The Orphan of Anyang* are: Who is the director? Where does the director come from? This is because an art film has a strong individual style and cultural traits. No matter how an art film is financed, these features are unlikely to be sacrificed. As for market share, there is always a worldwide niche market for the art film, which tends to be independent of a globalization-sensitive commercial film market.

Speaking of globalization and its impact on a nation's commercial cinema, I always believe that if the life force of a given national cinema is not strong enough to withstand the "invasion" of a foreign force, namely Hollywood, why don't we just withdraw? I am not promoting capitulation here, but this is an issue that cannot be solved without strategic intervention and active support from the government. If the government is really sincere in backing up the Chinese film industry, it would be relatively easy to achieve the goal of curbing the dominant influence of Hollywood by issuing some policies that are favorable to its national cinema. For example, why couldn't we just stick to the quota of ten imported films? When increase this number to twenty, doesn't this increase also decrease the market share of Chinese cinema? This is a simple issue of mathematics. When this number reaches forty or fifty, I think we have no one to blame but ourselves if Chinese cinema is no longer a force in the domestic market.

From an unrealistic and overly optimistic point of view, I certainly hope and think Chinese cinema will have a brighter future, even without excluding the possibility of Chinese cinema becoming a dominant force worldwide. Realistically, however, I think these possibilities, especially the latter, represent nothing but the mentality of "slap one's own face so as to pose as a fat man". My minimum expectation is that, just like the division of East and West in civilization, there ought to be a place for Eastern cinema as opposed to Western cinema/Hollywood. To me, it would be satisfactory enough if this goal were achieved. Regrettably, I don't see the possibility of such a scenario today. Instead, we are still living in a world in which Western cinema greatly overpowers Eastern cinema, and Western civilization overwhelmingly dominates Eastern civilization. This is what I hate to see and what I want to firmly resist. I don't know how other cultures feel about this Western dominance, but at least in Chinese culture, it is naturally assumed that the world is divided into yin and yang: where there is the West, there is the East; where there is male, there is female. That is supposed to be the normal state of the world. What would the world become if there was only one force or one perspective left? I think the result is not hard to imagine.

It seems to me that Chinese culture in general and Chinese cinema in particular is what can truly represent Eastern culture and Eastern cinema. In other words, Chinese culture and cinema ought to be the vanguard in the noble effort to counterbalance the dominance of Western culture and cinema. However, we must match this status with hard work. As matters stand, I think Chinese cinema is far behind Japanese cinema in artistic achievement. In terms of commercial success, Chinese cinema is also far behind Korean, even Thai, cinema. Therefore, I think the urgent task for us today is not to fantasize about the possibility of rivaling Western cinema/Hollywood, but to restore the vanguard position of Chinese culture and cinema in the East, which to me is already a daunting task.

Wang Guangli

I don't think national cinema will die because of the global expansion of Hollywood. As a consumer product, I think film is very similar to food. You can find McDonalds everywhere in the world, but did Chinese noodles disappear? No. Maybe some people will add Western ingredients or French basil when eating Chinese noodles, but I don't think they will disappear from our menu in my lifetime. Not even local Chinese operas, let alone national cinema, will cease to exist.

I suspect that Chinese films and Hollywood blockbusters will co-exist in the market for a long time, and neither will replace the other. On the one hand, it is impossible to imagine that American audiences will get used to the screen images of black eyes and yellow skin. These images only possess decoration values for them. On the other hand, I don't think the Chinese audience will tirelessly admire the screen images of blond hair and blue eyes. I always contend that we should stop debating such grand issues as globalization and Hollywood domination. Instead, let's focus our attention on the tangible issue of creating a favorable condition for both established and would-be Chinese filmmakers. There are two dimensions to this issue: a creative environment and creative talent. There is an old Chinese saying: even a clever housewife cannot cook a meal without rice. Without both a clever housewife (i.e. creative talents) and rice (i.e. creative environment), where does the meal (i.e. films) come from?

Good crops result from both fertile land and skilled farmers. If our land is of low quality, but if there is no shortage of skilled farmers, we can at least produce something valuable; on the other hand, if we don't have enough skilled farmers, but if the land is fertile, then even a few bird droppings will help crops grow naturally. What I mean by this is that, first and foremost, we need to establish a good system that is conducive to filmmaking. A good system is just like a piece of rich land. If the land is fertile, just planting some seeds will produce satisfying results. Take Korea, for example. Without a good system in place, how could Korean cinema achieve such an amazing result in such a short period of time? The same logic also applies to Hong Kong. The fact that Hong Kong can produce so many good works is exactly due to the richness of this small piece of land. As for Hollywood, it has both rich land and skilled farmers. This is exactly the reason why Hollywood can produce a variety of good crops: rice, corn, wheat, you name it. People always say Hollywood blockbusters threaten the very life of national or art cinema, but it is in Los Angles, Hollywood's headquarters, that you find so many small or independent theaters that play art films non-stop. What I am suggesting is that Chinese cinema needs to be nourished by a favorable system. Only after the current censorship system is loosened can we expect the full-fledged growth of Chinese cinema as well as the realization of the potential of the Chinese film market.

Wang Quanan

When speaking of Chinese cinema, many people, particularly young filmmakers, claim that the current system, including censorship, is the major obstacle to a healthier industry. I don't deny that there is something wrong with the system. For one thing, as Chinese cinema rapidly transforms itself from political propaganda to entertainment, as the whole society is going through a period of commercialization, the film authorities run the risk of losing economic opportunities by not loosening their tight grip on individual creativity. But I wouldn't go so far as to say that this is the only problem. The toughest challenge facing Chinese cinema, in my humble view, is the lack of creative power. This is not an overstatement. It is true that, after so many years of destruction, our economy was on the verge of collapse. But the real loss for the nation lies more in the spiritual world. A fast growing economy cannot compensate for that. Skyscrapers can be quickly erected, and highways can be quickly built, but it takes a long time for people to recover from their spiritual and psychological wounds. Our ancestors left us a rich culture and a great tradition, but this wealth was almost exhausted owing to our destructive actions. In the realm of art, seldom do we see a work rich in creativity and imagination. Instead, it seems to me that Chinese "artists" are always tied to the swing of the pendulum. When the pendulum swung to politics in the past, they followed suit. But as it swings to the opposite, i.e., material gains, they once again follow suit. What is really lacking here is an artist's spirit of independence, which is of vital importance in nurturing creativity and imagination.

Based on the above reasoning, therefore, I don't think globalization, or more specifically, the Hollywood "invasion", constitutes a grave threat to Chinese cinema. Hollywood's dominance is a matter of concern, but it can also stimulate Chinese artists' creative power. In addition, I always feel that the Chinese mentality of either conquering the other or being conquered by the other is somewhat simplistic. It is quite similar to the idea of protecting the so-called national automobile industry. It is ridiculous to protect an industry that stands no chance to compete with its international rivals. I look at the issue more from a consumer's point of view. As a consumer, I generally don't care whether a car is made in China or elsewhere. As long as it is affordable and good in quality, I would call it a great buy. The same logic applies to Chinese cinema vis-à-vis Hollywood. Whether against it or not, Hollywood represents the most successful film industry in the world. Besides its balanced combination of art and commerce, what Hollywood brings to us is its successful business model and operation. Instead of shouting empty slogans like "Resisting Hollywood, Protecting National Cinema", I think we should first learn how to collaborate with Hollywood and work together toward the goal of mutual benefit. After all, we still have some cards in our hands, which cannot be easily replicated or replaced. So, I see the Hollywood "invasion" as more an opportunity than a threat to the Chinese film industry, which can enable a commercial film market of our own to reach its maturity. It seems to me the recent renascence of French cinema is partly due to the fact that it has successfully integrated certain Hollywood elements into its filmmaking. Traditionally, it isn't unusual for a French film to feature only a smoking woman chatting with her male companion while drinking coffee. But this is not the case for Luc Besson. By introducing Hollywood-style filmmaking into French cinema, Luc Besson has succeeded in creating a cinema that looks both French and international. I think this is also the direction Chinese cinema should take in the future.

When outside forces "invade" your territory, relying only on protectionism won't solve the whole problem. Instead, you must also break the constraint of self-protection and learn how to sail the ocean. Chinese filmmakers ought to realize that, although they are only relatively small fish, no one can prevent them from swimming to other parts of the ocean. With this boldness of vision, it is absolutely not a bad thing for Chinese filmmakers to collaborate with Hollywood or even directly work for Hollywood. You can either incorporate Hollywood experience into Chinese cinema, thus stimulating the whole industry, or enrich Hollywood with your style and vision. There is no such thing as a "pure" national cinema. Take Hollywood, for example. Is Hollywood purely "American"? I don't think so. For one thing, many studios are now owned by Japanese or other foreign entities. This being the case, why do I seldom hear the warning from Hollywood that the "wolf is at the door?" To Hollywood, this is not an issue of conquering or being conquered, but one that concerns quality and money. As long as you produce good works and make money, I don't care who owns the studio. This attitude resembles that of the Tang dynasty in China. That is to say, I want to absorb you and integrate you into my system. If you do things well, you become part of me; but if you don't, I'll kick you out.

Certainly it would be completely unrealistic to even fantasize about the possibility that Chinese cinema might one day "conquer" Hollywood and eventually replace it in the whole world film market. No single "national cinema" can match the power and influence of Hollywood. Can you blow up so many cars and airplanes in a film? This must be backed by money as well as the confidence that the money spent on spectacular effects will lead to more profits. To claim that Chinese cinema will one day replace Hollywood in the world, therefore, is at best a hallucination. Instead of fantasizing about a worldwide dominance of Chinese cinema, I think we must first concentrate on cleaning our own house. This is to say that we ought to create a favorable environment in which an entertainment-oriented cinema can steadily grow. Such a cinema will in turn boost the formation of a healthier film industry, an industry that is built on the production of a large number of commercial films and a smaller number of art films. Until now, what Chinese cinema has provided to the world audience is only an exotic spectacle. Our job is to demystify this spectacle and return Chinese cinema its normalcy.

Chinese cinema enjoys unparalleled advantages in Asia, however. A number of factors, including that of culture, history, geography, and population size, contribute to the possibility that Chinese cinema may one day occupy the largest market share in Asia. Most importantly, the rapid growth of Chinese economy has paved the way for the pan-Asia expansion of Chinese cinema. I hope this expansion will mostly rely on the growth of commercial cinema in China, not merely limited to art film. Although I may not be good at making commercial films, I know they are the ones that can really penetrate into the hearts of mass audiences. The art film is only a sign of honor and a bright star or a diamond in the vast universe. It is commercial cinema that determines the market share.

Wang Xiaoshuai

First of all, we have to acknowledge that Chinese cinema is not on the same level or even at the starting line to compete with strong cinemas in the world, including Hollywood. There is a huge gap between the two. Due to the fact that both classical and contemporary masterpieces from the West are readily available on pirated DVDs, which give the Chinese a glimpse of filmmaking practices elsewhere, some critics and scholars tend to horizontally compare Chinese films with those of the West. But in doing so, they neglect the fact that the two differ greatly in context. For critics or theorists, it is quite convenient to single out two films, one from China and the other from Europe or Hollywood, and compare them in purely aesthetic or textual terms. But it's unfair if you don't give each film's context equal consideration. I have no problem with the comments that are critical of the works of the "Sixth Generation" filmmakers. As a matter of fact, I am quite self-reflective about and self-critical of my own works, too. I am open to all kinds of criticism. At the same time, however, we also need to critically examine the hidden context behind filmmaking. We can't forget the fact that filmmakers in China must confront an unfair environment their Western counterparts don't have to.

Needless to say, everybody knows what I am referring to, which is the existing censorship system. I believe it is the system that determines everything. Although it would be irresponsible to say that we've already got a deep talent pool, at least it wouldn't be too difficult to find several thousand talented filmmakers in a population of 1.3 billion. There is also plenty of idle capital that can potentially be used for filmmaking. The most unpredictable element affecting the outlook of Chinese cinema, therefore, is the system. Most of us would agree that it's as easy as turning one's hand over in terms of building film-related hardware. Just look at all these skyscrapers in Shanghai. Isn't it a small task to build a few multiplexes or even megaplexes? In terms of production, I also don't see any difficulty in reaching the goal of 200 or more feature films each year. But money alone can't get at the core of the matter. If the current system remains intact, what's the use of having a high number of annual productions as well as more multiplexes?

Despite Chinese cinema's disadvantage in today's competitive environment, I think it's absolutely groundless to be fearful that globalization will destroy our nation's cinema. If a country as small as Korea can even lift up its cinema from the hostile presence of Hollywood, why can't we achieve the same thing as a country that is supposed to have the biggest market in the world? It is certainly another matter if you simply give up without a fight when the enemy comes. Threatened by the overwhelming presence of Hollywood, Korean filmmakers dared to shave their heads to appeal to the government to support the local film industry. In response, the government implemented a series of policies friendly to local talent. As a result, Korean cinema soon emerged as a formidable force in Asia. All of us have witnessed the miraculous recovery of Korean economy after the 1990s' crisis. In Korea, you seldom see BMWs or other foreign cars on the streets. Instead,

Chapter Eight

what greet one's eyes are Daewoos and Hyundais. This passion for things "local" is not merely a reflection of Koreans' well-known sense of national pride. It is also built on the strength of Korea's competitiveness. Daewoo or Hyundai cars are built to be as comfortable as Hondas, but they are much cheaper. Here patriotism and pragmatism complement each other.

    Cinema is a universal language, and globalization ought to be part of its nature. As a matter of fact, globalization is not a new phenomenon at all. In some respects, it's an archaic topic. In cinema, French and Italian filmmakers have fought Hollywood's global expansion for years, but did you see French or Italian cinemas being destroyed? Historically, China had tended to view itself as the center of human civilization, and the rest of the world as "barbarians". Because of this lingering conception of self/other, there has been a strong sense of boundary in China, based on which the dichotomy of "within/without" was formulated. It seems to me that this kind of thinking is at least self-centered. Since the earth is round, how can you possibly distinguish "within" and "without?" Europe is at the beginning stage of dismantling its national boundaries, and I think when humans' IQs reach a higher level, what Europeans are doing today will become tomorrow's trend. Looking at from this perspective, globalization is indeed a natural development of human history. Why are we afraid of it?

Xu Jinglei

I don't think foreign imports will have a negative impact on domestic films. On the contrary, I feel we need more American blockbusters. Why? It's because more crowd-drawing films can at least help to cultivate a larger audience for the cinema. When I was little, movie-going was a habitual act. Most people around me viewed it an important part of their life. Today, however, people seem to have lost that habit. They'd rather play games in the Internet bar, watch TV at home, or simply go to karaoke parlors. If there are more foreign imports, at least more people would be attracted to movie theaters.

    What I mean by "foreign imports" includes not only Hollywood products, but also films from France, Japan, Korea, and other parts of the world. We are desperately in need of variety and diversity. Take Huaxing Multiplex as an example. It is a state-of-the-art multiplex in Beijing. But I went there the other day and was quite disappointed, because almost the whole multiplex was playing *Star Wars*. This is to say that Chinese moviegoers have very limited choices. Theaters in some foreign countries often play a variety of films, sometimes about twenty different titles on a single day. But in China, movie theaters are often dominated by only one title for several weeks. Only when the Chinese audience is exposed to more film cultures will they become more sophisticated in film appreciation. I don't know how other people feel, but I'd rather go to theater to watch the film if it's available both in theater and on DVD. When I am abroad, besides doing what I went there to do, the first thing I'd do is to watch as many films as possible. I remember one time I watched three films in a single day. This is almost impossible in China, because our theaters offer few choices.

I don't think globalization is necessarily a threat to the growth of Chinese cinema. I tend to view Chinese cinema as an integral part of world cinema, and it shares more common attributes with its global counterparts. I often have the feeling that the stress on "national flavor" provides an excuse for the excessive use of folk elements in Chinese cinema, as if doing so would give it a distinctive "Chinese look". To me, this is as strange as adding a glazed tile roof on a modernist skyscraper. My feeling is that film shouldn't be bound by national "distinctiveness". As an art form, film is about the human race, and human beings share many commonalities. Of course national or regional differences do exist, but they can't overshadow the fact that we as human beings have more common things to share. Besides, what are the elements that constitute "national flavor" or "national characteristics"? Oftentimes the answers tend to be quite elusive. For example, my conception of Beijing is quite different from that of Jiang Wen. He grew up in a government compound, and I grew up in an entirely different time and environment. We see Beijing differently. Can you say that his Beijing is more "national", mine not? Or maybe Zhang Yimou's China is more "national", Jiang Wen's not? It would be more meaningful, therefore, to stress the importance of individuality in filmmaking and see how this individuality is translated into common concerns of human beings.

The major challenge to Chinese cinema is not globalization or foreign imports, but the slow development of a sustainable film market in China. Today, commercial films do not always have commercial success, and art films are oftentimes driven by the hidden desire for commercial success. A few years ago, as lead actor in *Spring Subway*, I was invited to Singapore to attend the screening of the film. Singapore has only 4 million people, but its annual film box-office totaled more than 500 million RMB. I always hear people saying that China is the largest market in the world, and its potential is enormous. But just look at the total box-office figures: in the same year of my Singapore trip, China's annual film box-office was only around 600 million RMB. Isn't there a deep hole in the so-called Chinese film market?

Chapter Eight

Zhang Ming

Based on the current situation, I can't guarantee that Chinese cinema will survive the global domination of Hollywood. What do I mean by "the current situation?" It means that a few bureaucrats can determine the fate of a film. These bureaucrats' conception of film is entirely different from that of filmmakers. They view film not from a creative or artistic angle, but from a perspective that aims to control anything deemed sensitive to the government. What concerns them most is how to use economic or ideological means to contain creative arts at a manageable point. Their logic is quite simple: I don't care about whether your film is popular or profitable, but you can't transgress what has been set before you.

Because our creative energy is contained by bureaucratic forces, I don't think we should bear the responsibility if it happens that Hollywood eventually manages to take over the whole film market of China. What I mean by this is that since the state is not willing to give up its tight grip on filmmaking it should also take care of the terrible mess caused by its ideology-driven film policies. Compared to state power, individuals are simply powerless to fend off the Hollywood invasion.

Zhang Yang

I think the major obstacle to the development of Chinese cinema is the censorship system. If there are no fundamental changes in the system, it is useless to indulge in the talks about Chinese cinema competing in the globe. Audiences always desire a cinema that is rich and diverse. You must have a list of interesting films available to lure the audience into theaters. But in China, we are unable to deliver what the audience asks for, largely because of the constraints imposed by state censors. On the one hand, within the system, it's impossible for us to make the kind of films that are critical or provocative. But to be critical or provocative is one of the most effective strategies for attracting an audience. If a film tackles issues that deeply concern the audience, such as the one that touches the thorny history of modern China, I suspect people would flock to theaters. Unfortunately, because of the current system, this kind of film won't be able to achieve theatrical releases. On the other hand, with regard to commercial cinema, because there is no rating system in place, every film we make has to meet the viewing standard of a seven-year old, which inevitably limits the creative freedom of filmmaking, particularly of genre films. For instances, it is a tacit rule that a horror film can't be too scary, because it is believed that children would be terrified; crime film can't be too bloody, because this would arguably have a negative impact on adolescents. But if filmmakers can't maximize genre potentials, how can you expect the audience to come to the box-office? Hong Kong martial-arts films are known worldwide because the martial-arts genre is exploited to the full there. This is also true for Hollywood genre films. In China, however, none of the genres can be fully exploited. To me, genre films are the basis of commercial cinema. If the potential of each genre cannot be adequately explored, how can we even talk about the film market?

The fundamental obstacle to the healthy development of Chinese cinema, therefore, is the current censorship system. The reason why Korean cinema has made great progress in recent years is largely due to filmmakers' decade-long struggle with the government. With the liberalization of cultural policies, Korea's creativity suddenly exploded. This creative energy is the key force that animates the film market in Korea and drives audiences' passion for cinema.

I've always rejected the notion that American-style culture or Hollywood would play a dominant role in China as a result of globalization. I think none of the existing cultures in the world can possibly replace China's own culture, simply because some deeply rooted customs and ways of thinking are almost impossible to change despite globalization. This cultural tenacity provides fertile soil and a basis for national cinema to grow. Even Hollywood studios are aware of this. Their policy is not to knock you down completely with their products, but instead to enter the Chinese market in a more culturally sensitive way, sometimes financing Chinese directors to make Chinese films. More than a decade's history of Hollywood's entry into the Chinese market has also taught us that although some Hollywood blockbusters did quite well in the market, the Chinese audience has gradually grown tired of Hollywood's formulaic ways of filmmaking. In general, Chinese audiences are quite picky when it comes to movie-going.

I guess what I want to say is that the fact that Hollywood or American culture will continue to "invade" China is almost unstoppable, Chinese cinema and Chinese culture in general are well positioned to rival the presence of Hollywood in the domestic market as long as there is a cultural environment conducive to the emergence and growth of Chinese talent. As a matter of fact, I see the relationship between Hollywood and Chinese cinema more as a mutually beneficial relationship. In Korea, for example, domestic films co-exist with Hollywood blockbusters, and the two complement each other. Both are doing well in the box-office.

Opening the Chinese market to foreign films will also benefit the Chinese film industry in terms of distribution and exhibition. In less than two decades, China's economic reform has produced remarkable results in almost all sectors, but reforms in the film industry didn't gain momentum

Chapter Eight

until quite recently. I think absorbing foreign funds and opening up to foreign films will greatly benefit the ongoing reforms of the Chinese film industry. This has been the case in other sectors of Chinese economy, as well. With the opening-up of markets, we first saw the emergence of joint-ventures, then of foreign-funded enterprises. Taught by their foreign counterparts, Chinese companies started to emerge and were eventually capable of competing with their teachers. This is the general process of China's economic reform. I feel reforms in the film industry should and will also take this path. In the past, we were scared to death that the in-pouring of foreign capital and movies would destroy China's own cinema. It seems to me that people have gradually come to realize the positive effects of this trend. We can see that in recent years China's film exhibition and distribution has slowly opened up to foreign investment. I think we will be able to see the concrete results of this opening-up in a few years—the improvement of the cinema chain system and the establishment of a well-managed distribution system among them. These two will result in a healthy and normal film market that will encourage competition and diversity. I am cautiously optimistic that, ten years from now, Chinese cinema will be at least as thriving as today's Korean cinema and its market return will make the industry self-sustaining.

Despite my optimism, I still think it would be quite difficult for Chinese cinema to achieve Hollywood-like global influence, unless we are speaking of a remote future or of China becoming the most powerful nation in the world. We can talk about this possibility only when China grows a great appetite for cultural "invasion", and when Chinese cinema is being supported by a strong industry base. Right now, what China is able to contribute to the global film market is only art film.

One way of making Chinese cinema more vibrant is to set up more film schools or departments to train filmmakers in a variety of skills, particularly the ability to make commercial movies. It is very strange that many of our film academy-trained directors can't even make an eye-pleasing, entertaining movie. They might have studied film for years, but when it comes to commercial filmmaking, they are in no way close to those Hong Kong filmmakers who, despite little formal training, learned their filmmaking techniques from working as apprentices on the set. The key issue here is China's conception of filmmaking. Out of ten trained filmmakers, eight of them aspire to become cinematic *auteurs*. The remaining two are deemed incapable of making films with "real" value. To me, this conception takes the branch for the root. Throughout the world, with no exception, a nation's film industry is chiefly based on its commercial filmmaking. Art film is only a branch, not the base or the root, which caters to the taste of intellectuals. I think we need to set right our view of filmmaking, with the majority making entertaining movies of all sorts. Only those who have accumulated rich life experience and have a genius for film art are capable of making quality art films and subsequently leave their mark in film history. In China, however, everybody seems to be confident that he/she would become a cinematic *auteur*. Many of them simply disdain commercial movies.

I think in the near future Chinese cinema will surely become an influential force in Asia, simply because cinema is connected with the general strength of a nation, particularly with its economy. Just look at Korean cinema. Ten years ago, did you hear people talking about Korean cinema? Yet, as Korea emerged as a force to be reckoned with in Asia, its cinema, along with other sectors, including sports, also began to attract more and more international attention. This is what we call "as water rises, the boat floats higher". I think Chinese cinema will follow a similar path. If hosting the Olympic Games is a hallmark that symbolizes international recognition of the hosting nation's status, then Korea achieved this goal in 1988, and China will arrive there in 2008. Between now and 2008, I think the Chinese economy will continue to develop at a healthy speed. As a result, Chinese cinema will also gradually build and expand its audience base in Asia. It's by no means remote to talk about such a day when Chinese cinema exerts its dominant influence throughout Asia, including Japan and Korea.

Zhang Yuan

I always wonder why we still stubbornly cling to the notion of "Chinese cinema" or "national cinema". What I mean by this is that this notion in China is often associated with the films made specifically for political purpose or Party propaganda. For example, my film *Sister Jiang* is quite "national" in its characteristics, but it was made to pay tribute to the Party. In contrast, my underground films are not "national" at all, because they are quite "international" in both subject matter and style.

I don't see anything wrong with globalization. I frequently work with an international cast and crew, and oftentimes my money comes from outside China. By so doing I can at least get my films shown overseas. Frankly, I am quite pessimistic about the film market in China. Here you can easily buy a cheap pirated DVD. What's the use for the theatrical release of your films?

CHAPTER NINE

FILMMAKING IN THE NEW MILLENNIUM: POST-CINEMA, POSTMODERNISM, AND THE CRISIS OF ORIGINALITY

Since the birth of new digital media, including computer-based new media, the Internet, and DV technology, the fate of the theatrically exhibited motion pictures shot on celluloid film has never been more uncertain. Some say the rapid development of new digital technology will eventually make production, distribution, and, most importantly, "traditional" ways of exhibition of celluloid films obsolete. On the other hand, the advent of new digital technology has also coincided with the so-called "postmodern" turn of cinema in the late 1980s and 1990s. Although cinema has a history of only just over 100 years, the wealth of artistic works has already made it very hard for today's filmmakers to avoid borrowing or quoting past cinematic styles and content. With the emergence of directors such as Quentin Tarantino and P.T. Anderson, parody, pastiche, repackaging, and recycling have shed new light on Walter Benjamin's "The Work of Art in the Age of Mechanical Reproduction" and [Jean] Baudrillard's conception of "Simulacra". As a result, one has to wonder if originality in its classical sense is still possible in the vast majority of artistic works. Do the Chinese filmmakers also feel the threat, perceived or not, of new digital technology? In a time when more and more of us have access to similar data and experiences, and when global icons and language are becoming increasingly omnipresent, are Chinese filmmakers, or filmmakers elsewhere for that matter, capable of creating something completely "new" and "original?"

* * *

Guan Hu

My view may be biased, because I've been involved in filmmaking for so many years. I am emotionally attached to celluloid film. Sitting in a dark theater makes me feel I am in a different world, totally detached from the mundane of everyday life. Cinema is the only venue that makes me feel that way. Watching a DVD at home does not give me that feeling. I think the real attraction of cinema lies neither in image nor in sound or light, but in the isolated and somewhat mysterious space that the theater provides. The impact the theater brings you is simply enormous. I think every human being needs such a space. The space of reality is one thing, and the space of the inner self, which is beyond the reality principle, is another thing.

It is true that I've spent much of my time making TV dramas, but it is not because I've lost my hope in cinema. Making TV series brings me economic benefits, certainly. But there is another reason, which is the opportunity television brings me. China produces thousands of TV episodes each year, which opens up a space filmmaking can seldom provide. Things that are impossible to incorporate into or not allowed in filmmaking can be experimented with in television productions. Despite this, I won't give up on cinema. That's also certain.

Jia Zhangke

I don't necessarily agree that being original is no longer possible in the so-called "postmodern" age, because what determines the relevance of a given film is not how we tell a story, but the historical context based on which the story is told. Narration and discourse gain importance through their relevance to the times. Being original, therefore, means offering something new to the time from which the film emerges. Take *Xiao Wu* as an example. I don't think there is anything particularly original if seen from the angle of film history. It is quite "conservative" in its storytelling. But if we look at the film in relation to the Chinese society in 1997, or even in relation to the problems people around the world faced in 1997, I think it offered something original, something that speaks to the symptoms of that particular historical moment. This being the case, I've never been bothered by the so-called "anxiety of creativity", because real life can always supply fresh inspirations.

I am less confident about the fate of cinema, however. I think one day cinema will eventually become obsolete. As a medium, cinema has already lost its original vigor. Increasingly, its position in society resembles that of Peking Opera. If you raised this question two years ago, I would vehemently defend the vitality of cinema. But I am now more sympathetic with the view that cinema will die out. For example, today's kids are natural born computer whizzes. As they grow up with the ubiquity of the computer, their interest in visual consumption and taste for entertainment differ greatly from that of previous generations. This is simply unavoidable. It is very similar to the declining status of the shadow play. How many young folks would spend money on a shadow play? There is a great danger that cinema will become tomorrow's shadow play.

Of course I am not saying that cinema will immediately disappear from the horizon. This may take a while, maybe thirty years or half a century from now. Since I also make documentaries, I have the opportunity to really get close to kids. Many of them actually spend their whole night in Internet cafes. They'd rather spend RMB20 to play online games or talk to their virtual friends than attend an all-night film screening. To them, the interactive, role-

Chapter Nine

playing games such as the *Romance of the Three Kingdoms* are far more interesting than their "passive" and "dull" film versions. It is very empowering for some kids to play the roles of ancient generals like Guan Yu and Zhao Zilong.

Watching films collectively in a dark room certainly has its ritualistic appeal, but the real issue is whether the young audience cares about this kind of ritual. Today, public discourse is seldom centered on or generated by a film. I remember when Wu Tianming's *Life* became the talk of the nation after it was released. It brought about a series of public debates and therefore contributed to the formation of a Chinese-style public sphere. Since then, however, film has disappeared from the public discourse, and the increasingly diversified society has also rendered that kind of public debate impossible. Unless film as a medium transforms itself, I don't see that there is much hope.

Film also faces challenges from the Internet. Besides the fact that people are spending more and more time browsing the Internet, there is also a proliferation of authorship on the Internet. The sudden resurgence of the "I-novel", for instance, has to do with the fact that a lot of people, particularly the young, like to post their personal stories online. Naturalistic in style, these Internet stories are oftentimes modified or even collectively authored through the interactive function of the Internet. It is another kind of narrative, the one that snowballs. Compared to the Internet, I think film is quite slow in responding to this narrative change.

In recent years, we've also witnessed the diminished importance of theatrical films in comparison to films on DVD. In Japan, for instance, screening art films in theaters is predominantly regarded as a marketing strategy. The real goal of putting these films on big screens is to promote their soon-to-be-released DVD versions. In other words, a film's theatrical release may well become the bargaining chip for it to be sold at a higher price for DVD and VHS rights. In France, the situation isn't much better. In the past, many French audiences refused to watch a film on DVD or VHS, but nowadays the situation is reversed. Isn't this a sign that cinema is in danger?

Jiang Wen

The relationship between cinema and audience has changed. For a long time, cinema has always been associated with dark theaters. The lights had to be turned off in order for films to be appreciated. But nowadays theater is no longer the only exhibition venue for films. People can watch films on DVD or on the Internet, and the popularity of home theater is also on the rise. I think this development is quite natural. As technology evolves, our relationship with cinema is also going to change. There is nothing new about this. On the other hand, however, we should also realize that traditional film-watching still exists. In other words, we should ask ourselves this question: even though it's more convenient to watch films online, on DVD, or at home, why do we still flock to traditional theaters? I guess the attraction of a bunch of strangers sharing the same dream collectively in a dark room is not so easy to ignore. Just look at the situation in more developed countries. Isn't it true that cinema-going is still a live activity? So, I don't think film theaters will disappear. If theaters are well equipped, particularly in sound and screen, I think people will not abandon them. There is something unique in the theater environment that you simply can't recreate at home. It's a communal act.

As to the issue of originality, I think it's logically unsound to dismiss the possibility of being original in contemporary society. Human beings have lived in this world for thousands of years. Would you claim we've exhausted all possible ways of life and it's time to end humanity once and for all? People have written so many books and articles since the invention of written language. Can you claim there is no longer a need or thirst for great writers and authors? At the time when some people are tolling the knell of originality, great works keep emerging on the horizon. By instinct, therefore, I think it's totally groundless to deny the possibility of being original.

Jin Chen

The age of the Internet and DV has already arrived. In the future, I think the boundary between "professional" and "amateur" will become more blurry because of the popularity of the Internet and DV. This is a positive trend. However, I don't think this means the death of cinema. A lot of people thought opera would become obsolete after cinema was born. But isn't opera still alive? Compared to opera, which is often considered "ancient", cinema is quite young, with a history of just over 100 years. Despite the fact that the distance between "professional" and "amateur" is shrinking, therefore, I suspect one thing will remain unchanged: that is, the irreplaceable role of the author. At the core of a great film lie the rich life experience and intellectual acuity of an exceptional director. This cannot be duplicated no matter how "new" the technology becomes. Even without a trained eye, one can easily distinguish between good and bad films. Why? It is because every film bears the individual mark of the author. Recently we've seen fiction writing on the Internet becoming more and more popular. In spite of this, "traditional" publications haven't lost their growth momentum. I suspect the author is the key behind this. In other words, the difference between a renowned or successful writer and an ordinary Internet "writer" won't disappear because of the thriving development in technology.

In addition, movie-going also has its ritualistic dimension. It seems to me that this cinema-related sense of ritual won't vanish at least for a long period of time. We all agree that the experience of watching a film in theaters is quite different from that of watching at home. Many films must be watched in theaters so that the emotional and visual pleasures cinema brings us can be fully enjoyed. DV or DVD can enrich cinema in many ways, but it can't replace the leading role of cinema in entertainment and art.

It is hard to create something completely original in today's environment because the language of cinema seems to have developed to its full extent. The birth of DV led to the emergence of such films as *Dancers in the Dark*. To certain extent, this film did bring us something fresh. But when it comes to film language, I don't think it has created anything "new". As the old saying goes, "all articles under heaven are created out of the act of plagiarism". My understanding of "plagiarism" in this context is that we can't escape from the shadows of our predecessors. But by drawing upon all the intellectual resources from the past and incorporating them into our own thinking, we can at least create something fresh and possibly have a style of our own. Although I haven't achieved this goal, I hope I'll arrive there in the future as the number of my works increases one by one.

Li Xin

I don't think cinema will disappear one day, even though high-tech is pushing cinema in that direction. I don't know how you feel about the films that rely heavily on special effects and computer generated images or CGI, but I can't quite understand why there are so many people obsessed with this kind of film. I need some slow-paced or quieter art films to fill in the blank space between two special-effect and CGI-driven blockbusters. Story and the character, not high-tech, hold the key to a film's success. To me, the use of virtual characters is only meaningful in some special cases. In no way can virtual characters replace actual actors. By the same token, images captured by the traditional camera lens will be never wiped out by CGI. The relationship between cinema-going and DVD-watching at home is the one that resembles sleeping. Humans usually sleep on a bed. They sometimes sleep on couch or sofa, but eventually they will return to the bed.

The issue of originality can be viewed from two perspectives. On the one hand, in today's society, throughout the world, it becomes more and more evident that the age of great sages or masters has gone. This is not only the case in cinema, but also in music, poetry, painting, and other forms of creative art. A sage or master must be universally acknowledged. You can't simply attach that symbol to yourself. On the other hand, cinema or any other form of creative art have always striven to break boundaries, rewrite conventions, and explore frontiers. This spirit of exploring the unknown is the very factor that keeps creativity and originality alive in cinema and art. What I was taught not to do at BFA, for instance, is being widely used in today's filmmaking.

Liu Bingjian

There has been talk about the "death" of cinema for quite a while, but the issue has never been a concern to me. Nobody can predict what the future will look like. I am neither optimistic nor pessimistic about the fate of cinema. For the time being, the thing that can replace celluloid film hasn't emerged. As technology advances, one day celluloid may well be replaced by something else. Who knows? Ten years ago, talking about the extinction of film theaters might sound unfounded, but what about now? It may well be the case that ten years from now no one will bother to sit in a dark theater. Or, maybe cinema-going will be as rare as going to an opera or concert today. This is at least what the Chinese situation tells us. In Europe and North America, the situation is not as bad as that in China. There are still a lot of cinema audiences in those places.

I also don't worry about DV posing a challenge to cinema. DV is mainly an individual medium, good for two or three people's collaboration. Strictly speaking, there are still some hurdles to cross before digital cinema matures. How many industry-standard digital films are there? Only a few, I think. DV for the time being, at least in China, works more or less as a pre-exercise for would-be filmmakers. Go ask those so-called DV filmmakers yourself. You will learn that most of them are not really serious about exploring the aesthetic potential of the technology. Instead, they use DV as a stepping stone to 35-mm films. The cost of real digital film, at least for the time being, is just as expensive as that of celluloid film. Did those self-proclaimed DV filmmakers realize this?

Lou Ye

I don't feel the threat of new technology, because I don't see filmmaking as my lifelong career. I will probably quit directing after a few features. It certainly serves me well to continue my career as a director, but I am perfectly fine if I don't have filmmaking opportunities in the future. I have plenty things to do if I stop making feature films. Shanghai Animation Studio would surely hire me as a director, for example. Besides, there has been talk about the "death" of cinema since the 1980s, but cinema is still alive today, isn't it?

To look at the issue from another angle, however, the whole film industry has in fact shrunk dramatically worldwide in recent years. It will definitely shrink even further. Even a giant like Kodak is getting nervous.

Chapter Nine

This trend is probably irreversible. In the remote future, it is highly possible that film will become an art form catering only to the tastes of a small minority. But there will forever be a few people insisting on watching films shot on celluloid and projected in a movie theater. On the bright side, going to the cinema is also a lifestyle. Over the weekend, you dine out with your friends, go to see a movie, and then have a few drinks at a bar. This is no longer simply a matter of watching a film. It will gradually become that way in the future. The audience size may decrease, but there will always be a loyal audience. To the audience, all kinds of entertainment forms co-exist on the same level. It is up to them to choose which form they enjoy, whether a DVD at home or a movie out, or something else. So, cinema as an art form is not going to completely die out.

To be truly original requires one to see every single film that has been previously produced, which apparently is an impossible task. Indulging in empty talk about originality, therefore, is meaningless. In other words, how can you guarantee that your film is truly original? It is impossible. If you claim that your film is both unprecedented and unique, then you must be out of your mind. This claim only proves that you haven't seen many films. How many films are being made and released every year worldwide? How many films have been made since the birth of cinema? Besides this huge number, there are also a great number of excellent scenes in the films that have never been released theatrically or simply are locked inside producers' or distributors' safes. So, how can you guarantee that what you are doing is original and unprecedented? As far as I am concerned, I can't guarantee the true originality of my work.

What I can guarantee is something more limited. I can say I am doing something "original" only based on my limited scope of knowledge. Beyond this scope, there might be some works I am unaware of that have already experimented what is in my eyes "original". Generally speaking, therefore, I don't think anyone today can achieve true originality. What we can do better is to start with ourselves, because I can at least guarantee that there is only one Lou Ye in this world, who is un duplicatable. This again directs us to the importance of narcissism. As an artist, if you look at the world truly from your own point of view, then this distilled world itself is original. It is the only thing *I* can get hold of. You may say that there have been many stories about two girls who resemble each other, but there is only one that is told from my point of view. My subjective view makes this story "original". It is quite coincidental that *Suzhou River* is actually trying to address this issue of the relationship between the author and the story. On the surface, it seems there is nothing new about *Suzhou River*: "A love story is always the same". If the whole film was only about love, then it at best would be a smart duplication. But love is beside the point. What I really intend to do is discuss the author's view of this beautiful story as well as the relationship between the author and the story. I believe there is some originality in that.

Lu Chuan

Originality in creative art is relative. I remember after Meng Jinghui made *Chicken Poet* he published an article titled "I am at the Vantage Point of Cinema", claiming that he has invented a brand new language to make his film. How can he be so new? Anyone with a little knowledge of film history would know that such a bold claim is far off the beam. Being original or new is only relative. *The Missing Gun*, for instance, is "new" only in the context of Chinese cinema. If you compare the film with that of Europe, it is quite "old" and conventional in style. However, originality is possible when your works are faithful to the times and true to the unique features of your characters' lives. Form and language cannot be separated from content. To me, state of mind is the most important. Only by following this can you find the most suitable way to express yourself. Perhaps you will be able to come up with something really original in this process.

To me, cinema is first and foremost an art form. The technical and commercial aspects of cinema, such as editing, printing, and distribution, are secondary. As an art form, cinema will be always with us. At least in the next 100 years, cinema as an art of storytelling won't die out. Worrying about cinema's death at the current moment is quite ridiculous. Digital cinema is by its nature a form of cinema. Shooting a film in a remote location and then transmitting it through cable to a server or directly to consumer households does not alter the nature of cinema. As a film director, I don't believe or worry about the claim that "cinema is dead". Like the art of sculpture, which has endured thousands of years, film will have a long life. It is true that in China the old generation seldom watches films now, but there are quite a number of young film fans. I remember when I went see *Star Wars* in Beijing, I noticed the whole theater was packed. I am not saying that *Star Wars* is a good film, but we must be aware that the demand for cinema is still very much alive. It is our obligation to meet this demand from the audience. We have to remember film is not supposed to be elitist or intellectual-oriented. It must appeal to the popular masses.

Lu Xuechang

Regarding the issue of originality, I can only speak for myself. Frankly speaking, I have never worried about this issue, because filmmaking to me depends very much on whether you really have something important to say. If you are overly concerned about creating something new, I am quite doubtful that you would be able to make a good film. With the exception of montage and other technical means that may help storytelling, I think filmmaking is mainly an art of self-expression. Only when you really feel the urgency in your inner world should you get involved in filmmaking. To me, one of the criteria to judge the quality of a film is too see whether the film is honest. In other words, a good film must at least show me the honest attitude of the filmmaker toward filmmaking itself. If you don't have a sense of urgency to express something important, then you should just refrain from filmmaking.

As technology develops, I think the traditional way of watching films in a dark theater will also change. It won't be too long before many people will watch films online. To me, this change does not affect the creative process. People's fascination with stories won't fade. Materials, technologies, and ways of viewing may change along the time, but we as filmmakers must still create good stories to meet the demand of the audience. This is what the Chinese call "the central theme remains the same despite kaleidoscopic changes". Of course that's only my understanding. Who knows what will happen in the remote future? Nothing is impossible. Because the future is hard to grasp, I think I should just concentrate on what I am doing now.

Ma Liwen

I think the key issue here is that the film market is increasingly diversified. New technology won't completely wipe out "old" habits. It will only further diversify the market. Maybe it is the case that many people will no longer go to cinemas as technology develops, but this does not mean that all of us will lose interest in cinema-going. Use the Internet as an example. I started web serving in 2001, but I still don't like reading books and news on the Internet. There is something irreplaceable about skimming through a real book or a real newspaper. That taste and smell is just irresistible.

Meng Qi

I don't think cinema will be replaced no matter how technology advances. The big screen, lights, and sound effects of cinema are what make cinema a unique form of entertainment. Subjects that are deeply concerned with human psyche can be most effectively communicated through the means of cinema. DV cannot be put on a par with cinema. A good film can be watched time and again, and there are many layered meanings in it. A DV work, on the other hand, usually does not carry such an intellectual weight.

A good film also evokes our memories of the past. *Cinema Paradiso*, for instance, reminds me of my cinema-going experience during childhood. I spent my childhood in a government compound. The auditorium adjacent to the compound was the place where many restricted films were shown. Whenever there was a screening, the whole compound was suddenly filled with a holiday spirit. Much like a pop music concert today, the auditorium was packed with people from every corner of the compound. Children were running around, and cheerful greetings could be heard miles away. I usually liked to sit on the opposite side of the screen to see what other people were not able to see. It was film that brought us together. Even today, that particular scene still comes into my dream quite often. This is the power of cinema. Can DV bring you this magic?

Shi Runjiu

I think films on celluloid will definitely die out. Celluloid film will gradually fade in people's memory. It is just natural that humans will explore new areas and pursue new things. Middle-aged people may not fully understand the significance of digital technology, but young people are the ones who are not only aware of this change but also are an active force for leading the wave of change. Old things or old ways of doing things might be good, and they can also give us a sense of stability, but the changing times requires us to change, too. I don't see that there is anything wrong with DV as a future form of cinema. The success of a film lies not in what technology we've used, but in how human spirit is portrayed in the film.

I hope people will still watch films, whether celluloid or digital, in a dark theater. I also strongly believe that cinema-going will stay with us in the future. It is because both intellectually and emotionally, human beings need communication and interaction. Modern civilization has made us more and more isolated from each other, and theaters and cinemas are the possible channels to overcome this isolation and remoteness. Besides exhibition, I think cinema also plays another role, which is to function as a gathering place for peoples of all walks of life, making human interaction and social communication possible. Sometimes this kind of communication or interaction is more important than film exhibition itself. It would be more rewarding if there were after-film chats and discussions in cinema. When in Amsterdam attending a film festival, for instance, I went to a midnight show in a local cinema. When I walked into the cinema, I was shocked to see the whole place was packed with nearly two thousand people! This is why I say cinema-going won't fade in the future, since these people came to the theater not only to watch a film, but also to have the opportunity to interact with other members of the audience.

Speaking of the issue of originality, there is an ancient proverb in China, claiming that "plagiarism is universal for all the existing essays, and the key is how to smartly plagiarize". Although this is somewhat an exaggeration, it also

Chapter Nine

says a lot about the dilemma creative writers and artists are facing. It goes without saying that imitation is part of the learning process, particularly in the age of digital revolution. But I think one has to go beyond the phase of imitation in order to be creative and "original". We might be drawn into the works of our predecessors and be unable to resist the temptation of imitating their successes when we are young, but we must also get past that and create our own stories, the stories that are solely based on our lives and experience. Seen from this perspective, I think it is always possible for latecomers to filmmaking to be "original", albeit difficult.

Tang Danian

As Internet technology becomes more mature, there will be drastic changes in people's viewing habits. You can order films online, which means that the theater is no longer the only option for film buffs. I think the size of theater audiences will decline steadily and the audience base for theatrical films shrink significantly. Maybe in the future the scale of the theater audience will resemble that of the audience for stage plays. Home theaters will also play a role in this decline. If your home is equipped with a large screen as well as a sound system that rivals that of a theater, why would you even bother to go to a cinema? Some people claim that the communal experience of watching films in a dark theater with a bunch of strangers cannot be replaced, but I think there are new ways in which people as a group can experience that kind of catharsis. A rave party, for instance, takes one on a fanatic ride with thousands of strangers. People still need group gatherings, but how people engage in collective activities may change dramatically. Gathering inside a quiet theater to dream the same dream has been a favorite pastime of many people. But new ways of collective dreaming are challenging this old habit. I've been to rave party several times, and I found this indeed to be a new form of entertainment. Loud music, rapid images, and hundreds of shaking bodies: this is really some kind of collective catharsis.

The impact of DV on filmmaking lies not only in technology. It also has its aesthetic implication. Before DV, filmmakers tended to pay a lot of attention to picture quality, lighting nuances, and *mise-en-scene* subtleties. But DV brings us another kind of aesthetics. Unstable images, rough cuttings, and un-scripted storylines: all these have contributed to the rise of a different style of filmmaking. Also, with new technology come virtual characters. Maybe in the future real human actors will become obsolete, and a new kind of art form will come into being. If cinema is the "seventh art", then this could be called the "eighth art".

As for the issue of originality, I think it's really difficult to be "original" in the true sense. We grow up reading novels, watching films and television, and playing games. We've been exposed to so many influences that we tend to forget where these influences come from. Sometimes we think what we come up with is quite "original", but in fact many people have already tried that. In most cases, we are imitating the works of our predecessors in a creative way. What I mean by this is that there is a difference between plagiarism and creative imitation. If you are careful enough, you will see many imitations are actually meant to challenge our conventional thinking or deconstruct the existing logic of thinking. As a matter of fact, parody and ironic use of conventional tropes are themselves creative. I don't know if parody can be considered "original", but for me Stephen Chow's parody is no less creative than Shakespeare's plays.

Wang Chao

I hope cinema won't die out, at least for the next 100 years. On the other hand, it's somewhat meaningless to speak of the unknown future. Why do you even care about the unpredictable future? Can you live so long to witness the arrival of that judgment day? At least I don't expect that day to come, because cinema after all plays an important role in bringing people together, making people feel they are somehow connected. For this reason, I don't want to see that day coming, and we should also work hard not to let it happen.

New technologies may bring some changes to people's film-watching habits, but its direct impact on cinema is minimal, at least from my perspective. To me, film is film, and DV is DV. If my project is originally planned as a film, I won't even consider using DV. It's ridiculous to switch to DV just because of financial constraint. I will use DV only in the case that the subject can be more effectively represented on DV.

Wang Guangli

Although it's quite hard to predict the future, I think there is something especially charming in the cinema-going experience that cannot be replaced by new technology. For example, hand gestures are still vital on the trading floor of the New York Stock Exchange. Old teahouses in Sichuan won't disappear despite the popularity of the Internet café. What can't be replaced, I think, is a sense of ritual or the way in which humans interact with each other. Technology can deliver convenience to us. In filmmaking, technology has made it much easier for amateurs to get into the business. However, technology alone can't determine the future fate of cinema.

Of course I don't deny the possibility that theater attendance will steadily decline as more and more people watch films online or on DVDs. You can sense this trend right here in Beijing. But the most important reason for this decline, I think, is the poor quality of the exhibited films as well as the shabby condition of Beijing cinemas. How can you expect audiences to come to a theater still equipped with 1970s' facilities? Quality films and a comfortable environment will bring back the audience.

As for the issue of originality, I don't think we have exhausted all the possible themes. To be original is to see if you are able to approach some fundamental issues from today's point of view. Despite great achievements in history, so far we haven't solved all the problems that concern human existence. For example, fundamental issues such as "who we are", "where we come from", and "where we are heading" have been explored time and again since ancient times. However, it is still possible for us to shed new light on these age-old questions, because our thinking and our environment are quite different. Today we are living in the age of the Internet. What does the issue of life and death mean to us as the Internet continues to alter our thinking? How do we choose love and the way in which love is developed? I bet the answers to these questions are quite different from what they were in the 1960s and 70s. Many things in human society remain unchanged. For instance, I don't think literary works of today can escape the prototypical models of Greek mythology and Chinese classics. Love, friendship, loyalty, betrayal, all of these will remain the same. However, the ways in which we live our lives and communicate with each other are destined to change. Many previously taken-for-granted ideas, particularly those related to marriage, sex, love, and sexuality, will be challenged as times change. AIDS is an issue humans didn't have to deal with in the past. Five or six years ago, homosexuality was considered "disgusting" to a lot of Chinese. What about now? There are bars catering to gays and lesbians, and quite a number of people even want to be transvestites. Therefore, I don't think we are living through a "crisis of creativity". On the contrary, there are plenty of explosive subjects and uncharted territories for us to explore.

Wang Quanan

Speaking of new technology and its possible impact on cinema, I think I am slow in reaction and afraid I can't offer any meaningful comments. Although I don't have an obsession with celluloid film, technically I am very doubtful that DV could ever match the quality of film in both texture and resolution. So far I haven't seen on the big screen digitally filmed and projected works surpassing those shot on celluloid film in terms of technical qualities. To me, DV and film are two different media, each with its own characteristics. DV can probably help us explore the previously neglected or hard-to-represent subjects, but it is not something that can be taken for granted in creative filmmaking. Unless filming a subject that is hard to capture on film, I'll never shoot my film on DV. At the 2002 Cannes Film Festival, I saw Wayne Wang's sex-themed film *The Center of the World*. Most scenes of the film are interior. To be frank, I was quite puzzled by Wayne Wang's choice: why did he choose DV instead of film? Such a subject would have been better represented if film was used. If money was not the main reason for his choice of DV, I think this director was somewhat confused.

I might be a little "traditional" in the sense that I believe film will always be film. As a medium for artistic expression, its unique charm won't be overshadowed by the so-called "new" technology. In China, DV is being celebrated almost as much as a politically charged student movement. To me, it's ridiculous. In the past, a few political elites scrambled for power, and they were regarded as China's future. Today, it seems that DV has replaced them to become the weapon for political gain, as if DV could pave the way to power. Isn't it ironic? In my view, those who attribute so much value to DV are not the people who really understand or respect cinema. If you have a passion for cinema and truly understand the artistic nature of cinema, you would agree that using a DV camera to record something in life does not qualify you as an artist. A real work of art requires both skill and depth.

Viewed from a consumer's point of view, changes in movie-going habits are nowhere more evident than in China. Since bootleg DVDs are so rampant in China, almost every fan can build his/her own film library. The result is the steady decline in theater attendance. But does this mean the death of the movie theater? I don't think so. To many audiences, going to the movies has a double function: enjoying a film and participating in a social event. In other words, movie theaters provide a venue for social communication. As people become less worried about their basic needs in life, such as food and clothing, their demand for entertainment and social activities increases. Movie-going can fulfill these two functions at the same time. Despite the availability of a variety of entertainment forms, people in the United States and France still go to the movies. Why? I figure it is partly a result of urbanization and its byproduct: sense of rootlessness and alienation. Going to the movies can be viewed as a communal act. Although audiences seldom talk to each other, watching a film in the dark with a group of people is itself an act of social communication. You can watch a soccer game on TV, but the experience is entirely different from that of watching it in the stadium with thousands of people. The same contrast is also true for watching DVDs at home and watching films in theaters. You can't expect real emotional exchanges with other people if watching the game at home. Viewed from this perspective, therefore, I think cinema won't become obsolete because of the popularity of the Internet or the talk of virtual

Chapter Nine

reality. In addition, I always feel that some day people will awake to the fact that technology is not the solution to all human problems. It can't play the role of God.

As for the issue of originality, I think we need to understand that originality today carries different meanings from that of yesterday. In the age of instant communication and global village, it's almost impossible to claim that your work is free from any source of influence and therefore is completely original. In other words, the time when somebody could seclude oneself from society and single-handedly invent a brand new school of Kung-fu has already gone. But this doesn't mean that we are no longer entitled to new understandings of life and the world in an ever-changing context. Just use Quentin Tarantino as an example. It is not hard to tell that traces of many films in history are clearly discernible in Tarantino's works. But as susceptible to outside influences as Tarantino is, he showed indisputable originality in his masterpiece, *Pulp Fiction*. What makes this film original, I think, is its view of the human world. Take a look at that black killer. He lives under the illusion that he is a clergyman even when he is executing people. He just feels it's cool to be that way. It is through the characters like this that we get a glimpse of the uniqueness of Tarantino's understanding of the world. This is the most important thing that makes the film original. Because of this, it no longer matters whether *Pulp Fiction* is a pastiche. It is just like weaving a piece of cotton cloth. While you have to use reels of thread to make the cloth, the final product is uniquely your own work.

What concerns me most, therefore, is whether I can succeed in presenting my own understandings of life and the world through my films. This is the key. Back in old days, people didn't have sufficient means to communicate with each other. Mozart and Bach could end up with composing their own music without knowing each other's presence. But today, when you hum a tune here, people on the other side of the globe may hear it instantly. However, this does not mean that we can no longer create something original. The tune you hear could well become an integral part of your own vocabulary. In other words, despite all the influences out there, I can still rely on my own sensibility to experience purity. I often feel that American films can from time to time sharpen one's sensibilities with new ideas and twists. Despite a lot of rotten movies, occasionally, Hollywood is able to create fresh flowers out of the muddy pond. Sometimes you can even find poetic meanings in some films. In *American Beauty*, for instance, that flying plastic bag adds a transcendent layer to the film. It is pure and poetic. What amazes us most is the fact that the filmmaker was able to find poetic meanings in the most un-poetic object. Furthermore, the flying plastic bag can also be read as an abstract object that symbolizes the aimlessness and rootlessness of the human soul. This is originality in its pure sense.

Wang Xiaoshuai

Some people think cinema will die out, but I disagree. It is more likely that the number of people watching film in a cinema will decrease. In other words, the way in which films are consumed will probably change, not film itself. It is beyond my capacity to imagine how people will live their lives in the remote future, but I assume they will still need food to fill their stomachs, although how this process will be conducted is another question. Instead of debating about the fate of film, therefore, I think we should really worry about the future of film theaters and celluloid. It is already a reality that films are consumed more frequently on the Internet or DVDs than in traditional theaters. Will film theaters become more and more like today's museums in both rarity and elitism? I think it is quite likely.

Being original and creative is always an issue independent filmmakers are most concerned with. Imitation and repetition are no concern of commercial films. Audiences of commercial films usually don't care who the director is and how formulaic the film looks. What they care about most are the stars of the film. But for independent filmmakers, creativity stands at the core of their works. That being said, it is a daunting task for them to always maintain a creative edge. Cinema has had a history of more than a century. It seems there is nothing in film language that has not been explored and experimented with. Therefore, it is almost impossible for today's films to be entirely "new" and "original". On the other hand, however, one can always find something new and original in great works of today. This is the wonder of cinema. Quentin Tarantino's *Pulp Fiction*, for instance, is a perfect reification of this wonder.

Xu Jinglei

I don't think cinema will die out. Some people claim that high-tech based entertainment will eventually replace cinema, but I disagree. High-tech is only one of the means to help people convey what they want to explain. It cannot determine the quality of the content, such as the literary virtue of a film. As for the newly arrived medium of DV, although I find it more capable of delivering liberating effects, not only in terms of ideology but also in terms of the means of expression, I still have an undying passion for celluloid film. I've heard there is a digital version of *Star Wars* with painting-like bright colors. If this is the case, I doubt that I would be particularly enthusiastic about it. When I was in Singapore, I saw *Minority Report*. I don't know whether it's intentional, but the film has a rough look. For no reason, I think this is exactly how the film defines itself. If every film were made to

Chapter Nine

resemble Disney animations in color and texture, I suspect it would be a disaster for cinema. To me, therefore, the texture of celluloid film is as important as the content of a film. I would be very upset if film gave way to DV or other forms of high-tech based media.

As for originality, I think it's determined by nothing but content. Technically, filmmaking is not a big deal at all. Even my lighting engineer knows such phrases as "long shot", "medium shot", and "close-up". In other words, there are many fixed patterns in film technique, just like those in mathematics. But it is the contents that either elevate or drag down your work. Originality comes from your perception and understanding of the world in which you live.

Zhang Ming

I don't worry about the future of cinema, because it will definitely survive the test of time. What will change is how films are going to be exhibited and appreciated. Despite the fact that digital videos may replace films on celluloid, and more and more people will watch films online or on DVDs, film production and film as a medium of storytelling will remain the same. It is just like the tradition of tea drinking in China. The look and feel of the tea cup may change over time, but tea drinking as an everyday habit won't change. Technology will alter people's life, but the essence of human nature will remain the same. It is only a wishful thinking if someone attempts to change human nature.

In the long run, it makes no difference which material you use in filmmaking, as long as digital tape matches the quality of celluloid. On the other hand, DV is probably more flexible and convenient than celluloid, which gives the filmmaker more freedom to capture the scenes that are not easy to grasp with celluloid. DV is especially good for documentary filmmaking, since a lot of valuable scenes are impossible to capture if you wait until the film camera is ready. That being said, the arrival of DV does not mean all of a sudden everybody is now equally talented. It's just the same as the invention of automatic camera didn't turn everybody into a photographer. Similarly, everybody can now post his/her fictional writings on the Internet, but most of the posted writings turn out to be garbage. Technology can't turn a mediocre *poseur* into an artist.

As to the issue of originality, surely it becomes harder and harder to maintain the edge of originality and creativity. Living in the age of instant communication, people are more aware of each other's presence and of things that are happening in other parts of the world. In the past, because of difficulties in communication, there was more potential for peoples of different cultures to come up with something completely original. But nowadays the globe is increasingly shrinking due to the rapid advancement of communication technology. Consequently, the space for originality and creativity is also shrinking. We have little room left to create something completely new and refreshing. Fortunately, however, human society is constantly changing and evolving, and new social phenomena continue to emerge. In response to these new phenomena, our thinking and viewpoint will also change. This is to say that there will be always a renewed sense of originality and creativity. Otherwise, life would lose its meaning.

Zhang Yang

If based on the Chinese situation, I would say that cinema-going as a form of entertainment may become obsolete in the future. It is definitely not the case if you look beyond China. In both the United States and Europe, cinema-going has become an integral part of the lifestyle, a cultural event. It is hard to imagine that such an important part of their life would disappear. Actually, to many Westerners, cinema only serves as a venue through which people manage to gather together ritualistically and engage in some kind of communication. By nature, human beings need collective activities, and cinema-going can partially fulfill this need. Strangely, it seems China is an exception. I am more pessimistic about cinema's fate in China because there is no indication that cinema will become part the cultural environment and lifestyle of the Chinese. I've observed many theaters and noticed that there is only one kind of film audiences in China: couples. With the exception of premieres and special engagements, which are usually attended by organized groups, 90 percent of the audiences are young couples, few over forty years old. The situation is quite different in other countries. In art cinemas of the Unites States and Europe, the main audiences are older people. In China, piracy and the Internet seem to be the main reasons for cinema's declining attendance. In Western countries, however, I don't see the advancement of technology having a negative impact on cinema-going.

I don't know what "originality" means, but I know I am not a filmmaker who believes that technique or film form determines the quality of a film. Perhaps because I was not trained in a film school I think the subject matter is of vital importance in filmmaking. To me, what matters most is the story, probably also including the characters and the performance. Creativity and originality come from these, not from techniques or dazzling images. I believe what touches me emotionally will also have an impact on the audience. That's my understanding of being "original".

Zhang Yuan

I think cinema, like many ancient art forms, will become obsolete and eventually die out. At least this will be the case for art cinema. There are two reasons for this: first, cinema-going as a leisure activity will become increasingly *passé*, since it is inconvenient, time-consuming, and passive; second, as technology develops, people will find they can achieve the same satisfaction through a variety of entertainment forms other than watching films. Many people are shooting their own DV films and making their voices heard through the Internet. As the computer screen merges with the TV screen, I guess in the future film theaters will very much resemble today's museums in both number of people there and in the aura of antiquity.

THE INTERVIEWERS

Sun Shaoyi
Li Xun

Shaoyi Sun is Professor of Film and Media Studies at Shanghai University's School of Film & TV Art and Technology and Associate Director of Shanghai University's Center for Media Policy Studies. He is also Visiting Professor at the University of Southern California and the University of California, Irvine, where he is teaching courses on Chinese cinema, literature, and culture. He was the NETPAC (Network for the Promotion of Asian Cinema) juror of the 2007 Brisbane and 2001 Hawaii international film festivals and a jury member of the 2000 Dhaka International Film Festival.

Born and raised in Shanghai, Sun received his Ph.D. in Asian literature and film from the University of Southern California in 1999. He is the author/editor/translator of *Global Media Policies: New Perspectives* (Shanghai Joint Press, 2005), Rey Chow's *Primitive Passions: Visuality, Sexuality, Ethnography and Contemporary Chinese Cinema* (Taipei: Yuan-Liou Publishing Co., 2001), *Urban Landscape and Cultural Imagination: Literature, Film, and Visuality in Semi-Colonial Shanghai* (forthcoming in Chinese), as well as more than fifty articles on Chinese film, literature, and cultural studies.

Li Xun is Professor and Director of the Graduate Department of the China Film Art Research Center and the China Film Archive in Beijing. Widely regarded as one of the pioneers introducing Western film theories into China in the mid-1980s, Li is the translator of Robert Allen and Douglas Gomery's *Film History: Theory and Practice* (China Film Press, 1997 & 2004) and author of more than twenty articles on Chinese and foreign films. Li is Deputy Secretary-General of the Chinese University Association for Film & TV Studies and a member of the China Film Association and of the Editorial Board of *Contemporary Cinema*, a leading journal in Chinese cinema studies.

Index

A

A Beautiful New World (Mei li xin shi jie), xli, 20, 79, 104
A Beijinger in New York (TV drama), xxii
A Lady Left Behind, 56
A Lingering Face (Fei chang xia ri), xxxv, 77, 138, 189
A One and A Two, 178, 188
A Passage to India, 162
A Room for Two People (Liang ge ren de fang jian), xxxv
A World without Thieves, xv
Akira Kurosawa, 173
All the Way (Zou dao di), xli, 20, 104, 145
Almodovar [Pedro], 106, 164
Amelie, 51
American Beauty, 220
Anderson [P.T.], xi, 206
Ang Lee, 89
animated film, 119
Antonioni [Michelangelo], lv, 13, 37, 159, 165, 168, 170, 173, 175
Aranda [Vicente], 126
Archives of Chinese Avant-Garde Plays, 20
Asian New Talent Awards, 65
auteur, xxxi, li, 58, 194, 205
autobiography, 97
avant-garde, xxvi, li, 94, 113, 159, 164, 237

B

Baudrillard [Jean], 206
Bazin [André], 23
Bei Dao, 23, 237
Beijing Bastards (Bei jing za zhong), xiv, xliii, lviii, lix, 65, 90, 133
Beijing Bicycle (Shi qi sui de dan che), ix, xiv, xliii, li, 22, 94, 98, 106, 126, 177
Beijing Broadcasting Institute (now named Communication University of China), 28
Beijing Film Academy (BFA), v, vii, x, xi, xii, xv, xviii, xxi, xxvi, xxviii, xxx, xxxii, xxxiv, xxxix, xl, xlii, xliv, xlvi, xlviii, li, lii, lv, lvi, lviii, 3, 4, 5, 6, 7, 9, 10, 11, 12, 13, 14, 19, 21, 23, 24, 25, 26, 28, 29, 31, 32, 33, 34, 35, 37, 38, 39, 40, 41, 42, 43, 44, 45, 46, 48, 50, 52, 54, 55, 56, 63, 64, 130, 137, 146, 149, 159, 160, 164, 165, 168, 169, 170, 171, 172, 173, 175, 190, 211, 237
Beijing Film Studio, xiv, xviii, xxxiii, xxxiv, lvii, 12, 14, 38, 68, 76, 155, 190
Beijing Yinian Cultural Development Company, vii
Bengbu Municipal Government, 10
Benjamin [Walter], 206
Bergman [Ingmar], lv, 37, 159, 167, 170
Berlin International Film Festival, xxxiii, li, 151
Bertolucci [Bernardo], 159
Besson [Luc], 197
Best Asian Film award, xxxiii
Best First-Time Director award, liii
Best New Director Award, liii
Big Shot's Funeral, 71
Bitter Moon, 168
Black Hole (TV series), xix
Blow Up, 173
Braveheart, 169
Bresson [Robert], 170
Bunuel [Luis], 37
Buñuel [Luis], lv

C

Cai Chusheng, 169
Cala, My Dog! (Ka la shi tiao gou), xxxv
Cameron [James], 153
cankao pian, 6
Cannes Film Festival, xxii, li, 177, 219
Cao Xueqin, 135
cartoon, 24
Cassavetes [John], 165
Celebration of the Founding of the People's Republic of China, 8
Cello in a Cab, xix, 65
celluloid, xxxix, 67, 206, 211, 212, 215, 218, 221, 222
censorship, ix, xii, xiii, xiv, xv, xlvii, lv, 18, 19, 32, 65, 66, 69, 70, 71, 73, 74, 75, 76, 78, 79, 81, 82, 83, 85, 86, 87, 88,

Index

90, 103, 146, 176, 177, 182, 184, 186, 187, 190, 191, 196, 199, 202, 203
Central Academy of Fine Arts, xxx, xxxiv, l, 13, 33, 123
Central Academy of Theater Art (CATA), v, xxii, xxiv, xxv, xxxvi, xxxvii, xxxix, xl, lvi, lvii, 3, 6, 7, 13, 14, 19, 38, 39, 45, 51, 53, 137, 144, 169
Central Television Station (CCTV), 13
Central University of the Communist Youth League, xlvii, 27
CGI, 210
Changchun Film Festival, xxxvii
Chen Kaige, x, xlv, 11, 25, 40, 50, 53, 55, 61, 64, 148, 160, 166, 168, 170, 172, 175, 191
Chen Kaige Film Workshop, xlv, 25, 55
Chen Liting, 169
Chicken Poet, 213
China Film Archive, vi, 34, 159, 169, 227
China Film Art Research Center, vi, 227
China Film Association, 227
China Film Group, viii, 143
Chinese opera, 174, 195
Christianity, 26, 107
Chrysanthemum Tea (Ju hua cha), xxv, 70, 118, 119, 138
Cinema Paradiso, 69, 214
City Paradise (Du shi tian tang), xiv, xliii, 23, 65, 79, 105, 126
Class of 1978, x, 41, 50, 52
Class of 1985 (*bawuji*), x, xv, xxx, xxxiv, xlii, xlvi, 22, 23, 41, 44, 50, 53, 146
Closer Cultural Partnership Arrangement (CCPA), ix
College Entrance Exam, xlvi, 31, 34
Columbia Pictures Film Production Asia, xxxiii
commercial, xv, 34, 54, 63, 102, 105, 135, 138, 139, 142, 144, 147, 148, 149, 150, 151, 153, 154, 155, 156, 157, 158, 160, 162, 169, 178, 182, 183, 186, 189, 190, 193, 194, 195, 197, 198, 201, 202, 204, 213, 221
Communication University of China (formerly Beijing Broadcasting Institute), 28
Contemporary Cinema (journal), 227, 237
Coppola [Francis Ford], 99, 140, 165
Crazy English (Feng kuang ying yu), lix, 158
Cries and Whispers, 167

critics, x, xi, xii, xxix, xlix, 31, 41, 57, 67, 72, 91, 103, 106, 108, 138, 153, 161, 164, 171, 176, 199
Crossing Over (Feng huang), xxv
Crouching Tiger and Hidden Dragon, 190
Crows and Sparrows, 171, 173
Cry Woman (Ku qi de nu ren), xxix, 140
Cui Zien, 120
Cultural Revolution, xxiii, l, 12, 48, 54, 59, 60, 85, 95, 96, 129, 150, 161, 237

D

Dangerous Game (Bang zi lao hu ji), xlvii
Day and Night (Ri ri ye ye), xlv
Dazzling (Hua yan), vii, xxvi, xxvii, liii, 46, 72, 99, 139, 164
De Sica [Vittorio], 168
Deng Xiaoping, 28, 86, 189
Devils on the Doorstep (Gui zi lai le), xxii, xxiii, 65, 161
Dhaka International Film Festival, 226
Ding Zhanhong, xxxix
Dirt, xviii, xix
Dream of the Red Chamber, 135, 136
Dreams May Come (Meng xiang zhao jin xian shi), liii
Drifters (Er di), li
Duel, 24
DV, xxvii, 78, 80, 206, 209, 210, 211, 214, 215, 216, 217, 218, 219, 221, 222, 224
DVD, 11, 14, 51, 58, 155, 159, 201, 205, 206, 208, 210, 212

E

Early Spring in February, 167
East Normal University, xii, xlvi, 27
East Palace West Palace (Dong gong xi gong), lix, 65, 90
Eat, Drink, Men, Women, 89
Edison [Thomas Alva], 176
Edward Yang, 168, 170, 175, 178, 188
Eight Model Operas, 4
Eisenstein [Sergei], lv, 37
Eyes of a Beauty, xix, 113, 114

F

Fan Zhongyan, 53
Far Away Love, 169
Farewell 1948, xix

230

Index

Farewell My Concubine, 52, 163, 168, 175
Fassbinder [Ranier Werner], xxxi, 24
Fassbinder Prize for Best Director, xxxi
Fast Runner or Nowhere to Hide, 20
Fei Mu, 159, 160, 166, 169
Fellini [Federico], 117, 159, 165, 167, 175, 178
Feng Xiaogang, xxxv, 178
Fifth Generation, vi, ix, x, xi, xv, l, li, 11, 22, 41, 43, 44, 45, 47, 48, 49, 50, 51, 52, 53, 54, 55, 56, 57, 58, 59, 60, 61, 62, 63, 64, 93, 108, 117, 118, 134, 148, 159, 160, 161, 162, 163, 164, 166, 170, 172, 174, 175, 182
Film Translation Series, 24
Flying High with You, 8, 118
Forbidden City Company, 143
Foreign Moon, 160
Fourth Generation, 50, 52, 54, 166, 174
Fribourg Award, lv
Frozen (Ji du han leng), li, 22, 35, 65
Fu Yanxin, vi
Fujian Film Studio, li, 34

G

Ge Fei, 27
Ge You, xxxv
genre films, xli, 202
Getting Home (Luo ye gui gen), lvii
Gibson [Mel], 169
globalization, 176, 177, 182, 183, 184, 185, 187, 189, 190, 192, 194, 195, 197, 199, 200, 201, 203, 205
Go for Broke (Heng shu heng), xii, xlvii, 81, 82
Godard [Jean-Luc], 49, 159, 171, 189
Golden Bear prize, xlix
Golden Horse award, xxii
Golden Lion Award, xxi
Golden Rooster Awards, xxv, liii
Gone Is the One Who Held Me the Dearest in the World (Shi jie shang zui teng wo de na ge ren qu le), xxxvii, 14, 16
Good Morning, Beijing, xlii, xlix, 33
Goodfellas, 161
Grand Cinema Circuit in Shanghai, viii
Grand Prix award, xxii
Great Expectations, 162
Green Tea (Lu cha), xliii, lix, 92

Guan Hu, xvii, xviii, xix, 3, 22, 41, 65, 93, 113, 134, 159, 176, 206
Guan Yu, 208
Guerrilla Forces on the Flatland, 161
Guo Xiaolu, 117

H

Han Sanping, 155
Harvard University, 151
Hawaii International Film Festival, xix
HBO, 143
He Ping, 187
He Youzhi, 13
Hero, xv, 158, 193
Heroic Sons and Daughters, 161
Hibiscus Town, xxii, 166
Hitchcock [Alfred], 10, 164, 165
Hollywood, vii, ix, xi, 31, 34, 57, 75, 86, 102, 127, 149, 150, 153, 154, 159, 165, 168, 174, 176, 177, 179, 180, 181, 183, 184, 185, 186, 187, 188, 189, 190, 191, 192, 193, 194, 195, 196, 197, 198, 199, 200, 202, 203, 220
Homicide in the Black & White Apartment, 118
homosexuals, 100, 103, 109, 126
Hong Kong Film Awards, xxxiii
Hong Kong Independent Short Film & Video Award, xxi
horror film, 88, 119, 202
Hou Hsiao-Hsien, 160, 170, 175
House of Flying Daggers, xv
How the Steel Was Tempered, 12
Hu Jintao, 151
Hu Xueyang, 47, 56
Huang Jianxin, 54, 103
Huayi Brothers Company, 142

I

I Love You (Wo ai ni), vii, liii, lix
IFFS/FICC Prize, lv
Imar Film, xli, 20
In Love We Trust (Zuo you), li
In the Heat of the Sun (Yang guang can lan de ri zi), xxii, xxiii, 65, 96, 97, 161, 173
International Confederation of Art Cinemas prize, lix
Iran, 84, 86, 171, 185
iron rice bowl, 134

Index

J

Jasmine Women, xxii
Jia Hongsheng, 112, 133
Jia Zhangke, xii, xiv, xv, xvii, xx, xxi, 4, 35, 42, 43, 46, 51, 60, 65, 66, 94, 100, 114, 135, 160, 177, 207, 237
Jiang Wen, xvii, xxii, xxiii, 6, 43, 65, 68, 95, 117, 135, 154, 161, 173, 179, 201, 208
Jiang Wu, 145
Jiang Zemin, 109, 151
Jin Chen, xvii, xxiv, xxv, 7, 44, 69, 98, 117, 136, 162, 182, 209
Jin Fang, 21
June Fourth student movement., 53
Jury Prize, li

K

Karmic Mahjong (Xue zhan dao di), xii, xlvii
Kekexili Mountain Patrol (Ke ke xi li), xxxiii
Ken Takakura, ix
Kieslowski [Krzysztof], 164
Kim Hee Sun, ix
King of Children, 59, 134, 148
Kong Fansen, 95
Korean cinema, xiv, 79, 151, 177, 182, 196, 199, 203, 204, 205

L

Last Love First Love, liii
Lawrence of Arabia, 162
Lean [David], 162
Lenin in 1918, 161
Lenin in October, 161
Letter from an Unknown Woman (Yi ge mo sheng nu ren de lai xin), xxii, liii
Li Hong, 9, 118
Li Jie, 27
Li Xin, vii, xvii, xxvi, xxvii, 8, 45, 46, 71, 99, 119, 138, 163, 183, 210
Liang Xiaosheng, xxxix, 18, 19, 237
Lili Marleen, 24
Lin Biao, 96
Lincoln Center, 153
lingdao, xiv, 68
Little Red Flowers (Kan shang qu hen mei), lix
Liu Binjian, xvii, 100, 120, 139, 184
Liu Fengdou, 21
Liu Xiaofeng, 26, 237
Lock, Stock, and Two Smoking Barrels, 145
Loehr [Peter], 20, 145
Lou Ye, vi, x, xii, xiv, xvii, xxx, xxxi, 10, 22, 43, 46, 53, 65, 73, 100, 104, 107, 120, 137, 140, 164, 185, 211, 212, 237
Love in the Internet Age (Wang luo shi dai de ai qing), xxv, 70, 117, 136, 137, 138
Love Spicy Soup (Ai qing ma la tang), liii, lvii, 132, 157
Lovers, 126
Lu Chuan, xvii, xxxii, xxxiii, 11, 41, 49, 75, 102, 121, 142, 167, 178, 187, 213
Lu Xuechang, x, xvii, xxxiv, xxxv, 12, 47, 50, 77, 102, 122, 138, 142, 168, 188, 213
Lumiere Brothers [Auguste and Louis], 76
Lunar Eclipse (Yue shi), xlix, 56, 84, 109, 113, 129, 130, 151, 153
Luxury Car (Jiang cheng xia ri), xlv
Lynch [David], 164

M

Ma Liwen, xvii, xxxvi, xxxvii, 14, 51, 77, 103, 113, 124, 143, 168, 190, 214
Ma Xiaojun, 96, 97
Ma Xiaoying, xxxvi
Madam Jiang, 167
Maiden Work (Chu nu zuo), xii, xlvii, 30, 31, 108, 128
male chauvinist, 128, 130
Mama (Ma ma), lviii, lix, 39, 40, 90, 133
Mandarin Duck Apartment (Yuanyang lou), 166
Mannheim-Heidelberg Film Festival, xxxi
Mao Zedong, 85, 95, 96, 135, 136
Marco Polo, 38
marginal, 50, 60, 63, 87, 93, 94, 95, 96, 98, 99, 100, 102, 103, 104, 105, 106, 107, 108, 109, 110, 111, 112, 137, 138, 172
Marquis de Sade, 106
martial-arts films, 38, 203
Master of Everything (Zi yu zi le), xxvii
masturbation, 108
Me and My Dad (Wo he ba ba), vii, xxii, liii, 87, 111, 131, 154
Mean Streets, 175
Méliès [Georges], 76

Index

Men and Women (Nan nan nu nu), xxix, 10, 65, 73, 120, 139, 140
Meng Fan, 23
Meng Jinghui, 20, 213, 237
Meng Qi, xi, xvii, xxxviii, xxxix, 16, 52, 78, 103, 124, 144, 169, 191, 214
Mephisto, 24
Michael Haneke, 168
Mine Warfare, 168
Ministry of Public Security, 75
Minority Report, 221
Moscow International Film Festival, xlix, 138
Mozart, 149, 150, 220
MTV, 20, 35
Murdoch [Rupert], viii
My Sassy Girl, 168

N

narcissistic, 26, 93, 94, 97, 98, 99, 101, 102, 104, 106, 108, 110, 111, 112, 138
national cinema, 42, 179, 180, 181, 183, 184, 185, 189, 190, 191, 193, 194, 195, 197, 198, 205
National Film Bureau, vii
NBC Universal, viii
neican pian, 3
Neo-Confucianism, 119
Network for the Promotion of Asian Cinema (NETPAC), xix, 226
New Currents Award, lv
New Director award, xxv
New Hollywood, xi, 140, 165
New Wave
  French, 13, 49, 58, 164, 168, 173
  Japanese, 164
New Woman, 169
New Year's Sacrifice, 124, 167
News Corporation, viii
Ni Zhen, 50
nostalgia, 97

O

Ohio University, 23
Old Men, 51, 190
One and Eight, 11, 50, 134, 161, 164, 166, 170, 172
Orphan Rescues Grandfather, 174
Oscar Wilde, 106
Out of Xibaipo, 8

P

Paris, Texas, 24
Pasolini [Pier Paolo], 167
Phoenix TV Station, 29
PLA International Relations University, xxxii
Plastic Flowers (Chun hua kai), xxix, 10
Platform (Zhan tai), xiv, xxi, 65, 67, 68, 94, 114, 115, 135, 178
Polanski [Roman], 24, 168
popular, 63, 81, 82, 138, 139, 148, 149, 150, 155, 163, 181, 202, 209, 213, 237
primitive, 96
Production Code, xi
propaganda, ix, xiii, 76, 83, 85, 86, 96, 180, 196, 205, 237
Pulp Fiction, 145, 220, 221
Purple Butterfly (Zi hu die), xxxi, 75
Pusan International Film Festival, lv

Q

Quitting (Zuo tian), lvii, 71, 112, 133, 157

R

Rainclouds Over Wushan (Wu shan yun yu), lv, 37, 38
Red Sorghum, xxii, 11, 50, 52, 134, 164, 166, 175
Regulatory Rules of Film, vii
Renoir [Jean], 170
Resurrection (Fu huo, TV drama), xxv
Riding Alone for Thousands of Miles, ix
River Stone, vi
Romance of the Three Kingdoms, 208
Rosetta, 189
Rotterdam International Film Festival, xxxi
Run Lola Run, 51, 168
Russian Ark, 177, 185

S

Salinger [J. D.], 11
San Sebastian Film Festival, liii
Schwarzenegger [Arnold], 180
Scorsese [Martin], 6, 99, 161, 165, 168, 170, 175
Seven Gentlemen, 29

Index

Seventeen Years (Guo nian hui jia), xii, lix, 91, 94, 138, 158
Shanghai Academy of Theater Arts, 10
Shanghai Animation Studio, xxx, 10, 211
Shanghai College Student Film Festival, 28
Shanghai Dreams (Qing hong), xv, li, 87
Shanghai Film Studio, xxvi, 8, 9, 31, 65
Shanghai International Film Festival, xxvii, 65
Shanghai Media and Entertainment Group, viii
Shanghai United Cinema Circuit, viii
Shanghai University, vi, 139, 226
Shanxi University, 4
Shenzhen Baoan Investment Group, 10
Shi Chuan, vi
Shi Dongming, 68, 78
Shi Jian, 28
Shi Runjiu, xvii, xxv, xl, xli, 19, 52, 79, 104, 125, 144, 169, 192, 215
Shower (Xi zao), lvii, 132, 133
Silver Bear Award, li
Single Feature Permit, vii, viii, 87
Siqin Gaowa, 16, 143
So Close to Paradise (Bian dan, guniang), li, 138
Sokurov [Alexander], 177
Song Lin, 27
Sons (Er zi), lix, 90, 158
Sony Pictures Entertainment, xxxiii
Southwest Normal University, liv, 37
Spielberg [Steven], 24, 75, 153, 165, 169, 178
Spring Festival, 18
Spring in a Small Town, 159, 160, 169, 173
Spring River Flows East, 174
Spring Subway, vii, 201
Stage Sisters, 166
Stanislavski [Constantin], 169
Stanley Tong, ix
Star Wars, 200, 213, 221
State Administration of Radio, Film, and Television (SARFT), vii, viii, xv, xxi, 65
Stephen Chow, 217
Still Life (San xia hao ren), xxi
Street Angel, 160, 165, 171, 173, 174
Su Tong, 124
Suburban Dreams (Meng huan tian yuan), li
Suicides (Da you xi), li

Summer Palace (Yi he yuan), xxxi
Sun Jie, vi
Sun Zhou, 54
Sundance Film Festival, xliii, 79
Sunflower (Xiang ri kui), lvii
Suzhou River (Su zhou he), xiv, xxxi, 22, 65, 74, 75, 107, 141, 165, 183, 185, 189, 212
Swan Song, 160
Symposium on the New Generation of Chinese Filmmakers, vi
Symposium on Young Chinese Filmmakers, vi

T

Takeshi Kitano, 67
Tang Danian, xiv, xvii, xlii, xliii, 21, 53, 65, 79, 104, 126, 147, 169, 193, 216, 237
Tang Dynasty, xiv, xvii, xlii, xliii, 21, 53, 65, 79, 86, 104, 126, 147, 169, 192, 193, 198, 216, 237
Tarantino [Quentin], xi, 60, 206, 220, 221
Tarkovski [Andrei], lv, 37
Taxi Driver, 175
Temptress Moon, xlv, 25, 26
Teng Wenji, 178
Tess, 24
The Battle of Neretva, 3, 237
The Boys from Fengkuei, 161
The Catcher in the Rye, 11
The Center of the World, 219
The Child Soldier Named Zhang Ga, 161, 167, 175
The Color Purple, 169
The Contract (Zu qi), xxxv
The Days (Dong chun de ri zi), li, 34, 35, 65
The Dead Tired Man, xxxix
The Emperor and the Assassin, xlv, 26, 168
The Fugitive, 176
The Godfather, 6, 79, 169
The Horse Thief, 134
The Last Metro, 24
The Lion King, 95
The Making of Steel (Zhang de cheng ren), xxxv, 12, 14
The Missing Gun, xxii, xxxiii, 75, 76, 121, 142, 178, 213
The Mysterious Buddha, 38

The Myth, ix
The Orphan of Anyang (An yang yin er), xlv, 24, 26, 65, 80, 107, 108, 127, 147, 148, 170, 194
The Piano Teacher, 168, 170
The Promise, xv
The Road Home, 168
The Shang Gan Mountain, 161
The Son's Room, 170
The Square (Guang chang), lix, 90
The Stone Bed (Yan chuang), xxix, 10, 72, 73
The Story Circle, 24
The Story of Ermei (Jing zhe), xlix, 109, 129
The Story of Qiu Ju, 168, 175
The Sun also Rises (Tai yang zhao chang sheng qi), xxiii
The Sun Hung on the Crotch (story), xxi
The Underground, 172
The Winter Solstice (TV series), xix
The World (Shi jie), xv, xxi, 65
Three Doors (San chong men, TV drama), xxv, 70, 118
Three Gorges Dam, 37
Three Women, 169
Tian Zhuangzhuang, 29, 68
Tianjin Television Station, 28
Titanic, 135, 168
To Live, xli, 52, 173, 175
Tokyo International Film Festival, xxxiii
Tokyo Story, 173
tongzhi, 141
Toward the Truth on the Cross, 26
Tran Anh Hung, 188
Truffaut [Francois], 13, 24, 49, 159, 165
Tsai Ming-liang, 178
Tunnel Warfare, 168
two-camera shooting, 14
Two-Four System, 13, 22

U

underground, ix, xi, xii, xxi, xxix, xxxix, xli, xliii, xlv, li, 20, 29, 31, 61, 65, 66, 67, 68, 72, 73, 74, 75, 76, 78, 79, 80, 84, 86, 89, 90, 91, 92, 103, 154, 205
University of California, Irvine, 226
University of Southern California, 226
Unknown Pleasure (Ren xiao yao), xxi, 135, 177

V

Van Gogh, 149
Variety, 30, 48
Venice International Film Festival, xxi
VHS, 159, 208
video-tape generation, xi
VRPO Tiger Award, xxxi

W

Walt Disney Organization, 222
Wang Chao, xvii, xliv, xlv, 23, 54, 65, 80, 106, 127, 147, 170, 194, 217
Wang Guangli, xii, xvii, xlvi, xlvii, 26, 55, 65, 81, 108, 128, 148, 171, 195, 217, 237
Wang Lin, 23
Wang Quanan, xvii, xlviii, xlix, 32, 56, 82, 108, 128, 149, 171, 196, 218
Wang Shuo, xxii, 97, 161
Wang Xiang, 27
Wang Xiaobo, 22
Wang Xiaoshuai, ix, x, xii, xv, xvii, xliii, l, li, 11, 22, 33, 46, 47, 53, 55, 56, 65, 86, 94, 98, 104, 110, 130, 138, 153, 172, 198, 221
Wang Yao, 21
Wang Yu, 142
Warriors of Heaven and Earth, 187
Wayne Wang, 219
Weekend Lover (Zhou mo qing ren), xxxi, 65, 107, 137
Weekend Plot (Mi yu shi qi xiao shi), lv, 37, 88, 132
Wenders [Wim], 164
Western feminism, 128
What a Snowy Day (Wo zui zhong yi de xue tian), xi, xxxviii, xxxix, 18, 78, 104, 125
Wings of Desire, 164
Wong Kar-wai, 164, 165
World Cinema, v, 24, 159
World Trade Organization (WTO), vii, 89, 176
Wu Yujuan, 121
Wushan Teacher's College, lv

X

Xia Gang, 29
Xia Yu, xxii
Xia Zhongyi, 27

Index

Xiao Shan Going Home, xxi
Xiao Wu (Pickpocket), xxi, 52, 65, 67, 94, 100, 114, 135, 189, 190, 207
Xie Jin, xxii, xlvi, 27, 31, 166, 174
Xie Jin Model, 27
Xishi, 113
Xu Jinglei, vii, xvii, lii, liii, 35, 46, 60, 87, 111, 113, 131, 154, 173, 200, 221
Xu Xiaofeng, 25
Xu Zidong, 27

Y

Yao Fei, 27
Yasujiro Ozu, 170, 173
Years (Niandai, TV series), xlix, lix, 92
Yellow Earth, v, 4, 11, 34, 41, 50, 52, 134, 148, 161, 164, 166, 170, 172, 174, 175
You and Me (Wo men liang), xxxvii
Your Black Hair and My Hand (Tan qing shuo ai), xxvii, 9, 99
Youth Experimental Film Group of BFA, xxi, 5
Youth Political College, xlvii, 27
Youth Theater Art Academy, 3
Yuan Muzhi, 160
Yuan Zhiming, 27
Yue opera, 113

Z

Zhang Huaxun, 38
Zhang Jie, xxxvii, 14, 15, 124, 143, 237
Zhang Junzhao, 11
Zhang Ming, xvii, liv, lv, 36, 60, 87, 111, 131, 156, 173, 202, 222
Zhang Nuanxin, xlix, 33
Zhang Xiaobo, 27
Zhang Yang, xvii, xxv, lvi, lvii, lix, 38, 62, 71, 89, 111, 132, 156, 174, 202, 223
Zhang Yibai, vii
Zhang Yimou, ix, x, xxii, xli, 11, 15, 26, 40, 49, 50, 53, 61, 64, 131, 158, 168, 173, 175, 178, 191, 193, 201
Zhang Yuan, vii, xii, xvii, xliii, lviii, lix, 22, 39, 53, 55, 63, 65, 90, 94, 112, 133, 138, 158, 175, 205, 223, 237
Zhang Zeming, 160
Zhao Dan, 167
Zhao Jiyun, 25
Zhao Zilong, 208
Zhejiang TV Station, xxiv
Zheng Dongtian, 11, 50, 166, 237
Zhongshan University, lvi, lvii, 38
Zhou Xuan, 167
Zhou Xun, 142
Zhu Dake, xlvi, 27, 31
Zweig [Stephan], liii

ENDNOTES

[i] Interview with Xu Jinglei, conducted on July 21, 2002, Beijing.

[ii] In 1998, for example, China only made eighty-two feature films, whereas the number of films released in 2005 was an all time high of 260, an increase of 300 percent over 1998.

[iii] See http://xian.allnet.cn/Article/27178.html and http://sinoflicker.com/portal/content/view/74/36/. Visited on April 28, 2005.

[iv] The article was published in *Shanghai Artists Bimonthly* (Shanghai yishujia) 40 (April 1993).

[v] Shuqin Cui, "Working from the Margin: Urban Cinema and Independent Directors in Contemporary Cinema". *Post Script* 20, Nos. 2&3: 77-93.

[vi] Interview with Wang Guangli, conducted on July 26, 2002, Beijing.

[vii] Interview with Zhang Yuan, conducted on July 25, 2002, Beijing.

[viii] Broadly speaking, their group identity could be seen as focusing on the everyday reality of contemporary Chinese city life, as their works tackle a wide spectrum of social experiences and "gray" issues in contemporary China: unemployment, troubled sexuality, alcoholism, homosexuality, mental illness, prostitution, criminal activity, bohemian lifestyles, migrant workers, and the widening gap between the poor and the rich. Of course there are exceptions.

[ix] Interview with Jia Zhangke, conducted on July 24, 2003, Beijing.

[x] Interview with Tang Danian, conducted on July 19, 2003, Beijing.

[xi] Interview with Lou Ye, conducted on November 29, 2002, Shanghai.

[xii] *The Battle of Neretva* is a Yugoslav film made in 1968 and stars Orson Welles and Yul Brynner. It is often considered the best motion picture made in Communist Yugoslavia. It was nominated for an Academy Award for best foreign language picture.

[xiii] The term "Main Melody Film" refers to the works that are financed by the Chinese government as propaganda to promote the Party's agenda.

[xiv] *Twenty Four Eyes* (1954, b/w) was directed by Teinosuke Kinugasa.

[xv] Zheng Dongtian teaches film directing at the Beijing Film Academy. He is also a domestically well-known filmmaker and critic. Zheng's most recent film is *My Bittersweet Taiwan* (2002).

[xvi] Born in 1937, Zhang Jie in 1978 published her first work, "The Music of the Forests", which won the National Best Short Story Prize. Her works include "Love Must Not Be Forgotten", "Leaden Wings", and "Ark". She is now a full-time writer at the Beijing branch of the Chinese Writers' Association.

[xvii] Born in 1949, Liang Xiaosheng has consistently been among the most prolific and widely read writers in China. He is best known in China for the portrayals of the plight of educated youths sent to the countryside during the Cultural Revolution.

[xviii] Born in 1964, Meng Jinghui is one of the most active theater directors in Beijing. He is famed for his innovative and dashing style. To some extent, Meng's name has become synonymous with "avant-garde" and "alternative", but his plays have also been very popular in the small theaters in Beijing.

[xix] Bei Dao, whose original name is Zhao Zhenkai, was born in 1949. Mainly identified with the "misty" school of Chinese poetry, Bei Dao has been in exile since 1989. He lives in Davis, California.

[xx] Born in 1956, Liu Xiaofeng began his doctoral studies in systematic theology under Professor Heinrich Ott in Basel, Switzerland, and received his Doctor of Theology degree there in the 1990s. Liu is presently academic director of the Institute of Sino-Christian Studies in Hong Kong. He is considered the most visible and prolific "Cultural Christian" in China.

Endnotes

[xxi] Both Zhu Dake and Li Jie were young professors of Chinese teaching at the East Normal University of Shanghai in the 1980s. Zhu led the attack on the "Xie Jin Model" of filmmaking in the summer of 1986 by publishing an article calling for a profound reassessment of the socio-cultural foundations of Chinese mainstream cinema.

[xxii] A less known name internationally, Hu Xueyang studied film directing with Lou Ye, Wang Xiaoshuai, and Lu Xuechang from 1985 to 1989 at the Beijing Film Academy. His representative work is *A Lady Left Behind* (Liushou nushi, 1991).

[xxiii] "The Post-*Yellow Earth* Phenomenon in Chinese Cinema", signed by the "1985 Admitted Graduates of the Departments of Directing, Cinematography, Sound, Art Directing, and Literature of the Beijing Film Academy", was published in *Shanghai Artists Bimonthly* (Shanghai yishujia) 40 (April 1993).

[xxiv] Ni Zhen was a professor teaching at the Beijing Film Academy until the late 1990s. He has lived in Shanghai since retiring from BFA.

[xxv] *Purple Butterfly* was officially selected to compete at the 2003 Cannes International Film Festival, and Lou Ye, together with the star Zhang Ziyi, attended the festival.

[xxvi] *Kong Fansen* is a "main melody" film made in 1995.

[xxvii] According to Chinese legend, Xishi (506 BC- ?) was one of the renowned beauties of ancient China. She was said to have lived during the end of Spring and Autumn Period in Zhuji, the capital of the ancient State of Yue. King Gou Jian of Yue was once imprisoned after a defeat in a war with the State of Wu. Secretly planning his revenge, King Gou Jian trained Xishi and offered her to King Fu Chai of Wu as a tribute. Bewitched by the beauty of Xishi, Fu Chai forgot all about affairs of state and on Xishi's instigation killed his best adviser. As a result, the strength of Wu dwindled. In 473 BC Gou Jian launched his strike against Wu. King Fu Chai then committed suicide.

[xxviii] "Buick Sail" is an automobile model manufactured in Shanghai for the Chinese market. Priced at about 100,000 RMB, it was considered "cheap" and "shabby". It was replaced in 2005 by the Chevrolet Sail. Both models are variants of the Opel Corsa B.

[xxix] Here Jin refers to the "Symposium on Young Filmmakers" organized by the semi-official Association of Chinese Filmmakers, China Film Group, Beijing Film Studio, and *Film Art* Journal, and held on November 27-29, 1999. Twelve young filmmakers, including Jin Chen, Lu Xuechang, Wang Xiaoshuai, Guan Hu, Wang Quanan, attended the symposium. For details, see *Film Art* Editorial Board's article "Young Images in the New Millennium;" *Film Art*, No. 1, 8-11, 2000.

[xxx] Born in 1942, Xie Fei has held various administrative positions at the Beijing Film Academy and now teaches directing at BFA. Winner of both the Golden and Silver Bear Awards of the Berlin International Film Festival, Xie is also internationally known as one of the most prominent directors from China.

[xxxi] The interview was conducted on November 29, 2002, at a café across from the front door of the Shanghai Film Studio. During the interview, both Lou Ye and the interviewer smoked.

[xxxii] Teng Wenji (1944-) graduated in 1969 from the directing department of the Beijing Film Academy and has directed more than twenty films, including *Ballad of the Yellow River* (1995).

LIGHTS! CAMERA! KAI SHI!
INTERVIEWS WITH CHINA'S NEW GENERATION OF MOVIE DIRECTORS

Shaoyi Sun is Professor of Film and Media Studies at Shanghai University's School of Film & TV Art and Technology and Associate Director of Shanghai University's Center for Media Policy Studies. He is also Visiting Professor at the University of Southern California and the University of California, Irvine, where he is teaching courses on Chinese cinema, literature, and culture. Born and raised in Shanghai, Sun received his Ph.D. in Asian literature and film from the University of Southern California in 1999. He is widely published in the field of Chinese film, literature, and cultural studies.

Li Xun is Professor and Director of the Graduate Department of the China Film Art Research Center and the China Film Archive in Beijing. Regarded as one of the pioneers introducing Western film theories into China in the mid-1980s, Li is also the author of more than twenty articles on Chinese and foreign films. Li is Deputy Secretary-General of the Chinese University Association for Film & TV Studies and a member of the China Film Association and of the Editorial Board of *Contemporary Cinema*, a leading journal in Chinese cinema studies.

EastBridge
Signature Books
J.C. West, FRAS, Imprint Editor

The *Signature Books* imprint of EastBridge is dedicated to presenting a wide range of exceptional books in the field of Asian and related studies. The principal concentrations are texts and supplementary materials for academic courses, literature-in-English-translation, and writings of journalists, scholars, diplomats, and travelers.

See our entire list at
eastbridgebooks.org